Depraved New World

For Jill

Introduction

More than 18 months since the start of the first lockdown in March 2020, there was still no end to the Covid pandemic in sight. Indeed, there was no real agreement as to what an end might look like, barring some kind of miracle where the virus mutated into a more benign variant.

Some on the libertarian right called for an end to all lockdowns and to just let Covid rip through the population. The more widely backed approach – and one adopted by the government and supported by the opposition parties – was to continue locking down the country to try and reduce the number of infections.

Even so, the government had not covered itself in much glory, though it had received plaudits for its financial bailouts to business and the self-employed, and for the speed with which it introduced the vaccine programmes – something it continues to wrongly attribute to the UK having left the European Union.

In the early days of the pandemic, the prime minister, Boris Johnson, had failed to take the situation seriously. He had missed five COBRA meetings and had repeatedly been slow to heed the scientific advice of implementing lockdowns. He was late to introduce the first lockdown in March 2020. Late to introduce the second in November of that year. Late to try to stop the Delta variant reaching the UK from India in 2021. Just how many extra lives might have been saved, we can never know for certain.

By October 2021, the UK, like many other countries, was in a state of muddling through things, introducing ad hoc regulations and guidance in response to an ever-changing scenario. It was a surreal time, and something that we're still trying to process.

It wasn't just the population's physical health that was affected. Many people's mental health was badly damaged by the long periods of isolation at home. Businesses are also still feeling the long-term impact. Some people decided they rather liked working from home and have been reluctant to go back into the office. Others took Covid as an existential wake-up call and chose to retire early. Carpe diem and all that. The UK has changed in all sorts of ways we have yet to fully understand.

In the early days of the pandemic, we all got used to the daily 5 p.m. press conference, in which Boris Johnson, chancellor Rishi Sunak, health secretary Matt Hancock and scientists Chris Whitty, Patrick Vallance and Jonathan Van-Tam would release the latest Covid stats, offer advice on how we could protect ourselves better and explain government policy. Such as it was. Soon enough, though, everyone got a bit bored with the press conferences, so they began to take place only every now and again. When someone thought they might have something to say.

Besides, the country had long since been disabused of any thought that the government had a coherent plan. For a start, there had been Johnson's key adviser, Dominic Cummings, breaking the lockdown rules back in 2020 by taking himself off to Durham when his whole family had Covid. That had taught us that the rules were something only the little people had to obey. This was an attitude we would learn a great deal more about in the coming months.

Then there had been the sacking of Cummings some months later. Not because he had broken the rules, but just because of a general falling-out with Johnson and his then partner, and now wife, Carrie. After leaving Downing Street with his possessions in a cardboard box, Cummings dedicated himself to exposing the failures of Johnson's government in a series of rambling blog posts. He claimed that Boris thought Hancock was 'fucking hopeless'; that billions of pounds had been wasted on dodgy PPE; that Johnson couldn't make decisions, was unfit for office and hated confrontation.

It turned out that Johnson had been right about Hancock. In the summer of 2021, CCTV footage of Hancock kissing and groping his lover in his office emerged in the national press. This didn't just end Hancock's marriage; it ended his career in cabinet.

Snogging and groping someone who was not in your bubble was not in the government's Covid rules. Few were sorry to see him go. He had made few friends on his way up the ministerial ladder. He would make even fewer on the way down.

Believe it or not, the government was also trying to get on with its normal daily business, if there was such a thing in such strange days. What Johnson seemed most intent on was breaking as many election manifesto promises as possible. First he ditched his promise to maintain a triple lock on pensions, and then he rowed back on his commitment to not raise national insurance contributions.

Finally, he arbitrarily decided to cut back on his promise to spend 0.7% of gross national income on overseas aid. We could now afford only 0.5%. Having spent the best part of £450 billion on bailout packages – one of which, Sunak's 'Eat Out to Help Out' scheme, had actually increased Covid deaths – we could no longer find another £4 billion. The weird thing was that nobody thought any of this was that weird. Partly because we were living through such dislocating times, but mainly because most people had long since stopped expecting Johnson to tell the truth or keep his word. If they ever had in the first place.

As for Brexit, it was almost as if we were going backwards. Lord Frost, whom Johnson had appointed to negotiate the Northern Ireland protocol back in late 2019 and early 2020, now seemed to disown his own deal.

Frosty the No Man had had a rethink. It was outrageous of the EU to imagine the UK had negotiated in good faith, to believe that we'd seek to implement our deal in accordance to the law. It should have been obvious that it was just a fudge to allow us to say that we had got Brexit done. Seriously. This was the state of Brexit in late 2021. To Johnson, this was all perfectly normal. Go figure.

Then, to add to the chaos, in September 2021 Johnson chose to reshuffle his cabinet. Out went Dominic Raab as foreign secretary. No surprises there. Raab had been on holiday in Crete during the Taliban take-over of Afghanistan, failing to provide safe passage for Afghans who had helped the UK. Psycho Dom had been rather more concerned that the 'sea had been closed' in Crete. It proved easier to get a plane-load of pets out of Afghanistan than an extra flight of refugees.

Gavin Williamson was another cabinet casualty. Though again, the main mystery was that he had survived as education secretary for so long, given his role in the exam fiasco of 2020. Not that this would stop Williamson becoming Sir Gavin within a matter of months. In this topsy-turvy world, failure gets rewarded. The beneficiaries of incompetence were equally disturbing. Priti Patel got to stay on as home secretary. Imagine having no one better to replace her with. Liz Truss got to be foreign secretary. Unthinkable. As should have been Nadine Dorries getting the culture secretary brief. A sick joke. Truly, a government of all the talentless.

Not that Labour weren't having difficulties of their own. Keir Starmer had made a good start on detoxifying the Labour brand after Jeremy Corbyn's leadership, but being in opposition during countless lockdowns was far from straightforward. Starmer's job much of the time was to endorse the government's actions in following the scientific advice – not the easiest way of making a mark.

In the polls, most people thought Starmer was a fairly decent guy, but they weren't sure exactly what he stood for. He even resorted to going on Piers Morgan's TV show to try and get his message across, but what we mostly learned was that he didn't much care for his middle name: Rodney. Still, baby steps and all that.

So far, so weird. Eighteen months into the looking-glass world of pandemic politics. What none of us could have guessed was that we would soon be looking back on this time as an oasis of calm.

Tory conference bubble rises to applaud PM's light entertainment

6 OCTOBER 2021

Not so much a conference speech, more an extended *Daily Telegraph* column. One knocked off in a hurry at the last minute. This was politics as light entertainment, with any collision with the real world entirely accidental. Plenty of jokes – one or two even moderately good ones – and soundbites for the TV, but nothing of any substance. Just another day like any other in the life of Boris Johnson.

The lights went out and Spandau Ballet played through the PA system. 'Gold' is the narcissist's theme tune. No wonder Boris loves it. He is the man who doesn't have to try too hard. Even when the country feels like it is falling apart around him, in his universe he can reconfigure it into his own image as a roaring success. All you need is to believe. If you don't like the world you're in – and 4 million households were waking up to a £20-a-week cut in universal credit – then it's probably your own fault.

Moments later, the cabinet trooped into the new hall – expanded to twice the size to both accommodate Boris's ego and remind his party he is its Supreme Leader – to polite applause. Still, it was more than many of them had received for their own 10-minute slots in the Tiny Tent earlier in the week. Then a short video of Boris being nice and interacting with grateful little people before the prime minister took the stage.

Johnson looked up and smiled. The conference centre was his kingdom. His bubble. He could say what he liked and no one would care. The audience just wanted to be embraced into his realm. To experience his vision of an England where there were no queues for petrol, no food and labour shortages, no inflation and no tax rises. Those things were all constructs of a media and Labour Party obsessed with talking the country down.

And what a world it was. First off, Johnson all but declared that Covid was over. It had been a difficult 18 months – made trickier for everyone by Labour's insistence on treating it as a major public health issue – but now it was pretty much business as usual. Thanks to the vaccine that he personally had developed, the UK was way ahead of other countries in getting back to normal.

Then there was the problem of social care, which he had solved merely by saying he had a plan for dealing with it. Yes, it might involve higher taxes – almost all of which would go to the NHS rather than on social care – but he was hopeful things could be sorted just by eliminating some red tape. It was that easy.

The gags came thick and fast. Funny stories in funny

voices, with even some Franglais thrown in. The old ones are the old ones. Diversionary tactics as Boris jumped from subject to subject, never allowing himself to get side-tracked into detail in case anyone noticed the total lack of any substance or policy. He could impose his reality merely through the force of will. Because his narrative was more attractive, more comedic and, above all, less painful than anyone else's.

He was creating a high-wage, low-tax economy. Like many of his colleagues, he is oblivious to the fact that many people have taken a wage cut after inflation and that his government has raised taxation to its highest level since the 1940s. And he was going to get levelling-up done. Whatever that was. It has had so many meaningless definitions over the past few days at the Tory conference that it's been hard to keep up. Today, it meant that people in Stoke Poges could relax about any outsiders trying to move in to their village, because there would be plenty of houses and jobs for them in the north.

Above all, Boris was keen to make sure that reality should not intrude on his world vision. Labour was cast as the party of Islington, when it was he who actually used to live there, before he got kicked out of the family home. Selling beef to the US was the crème de la crème of trade deals. Build back burger. Groan. The Kabul airlift had been a magnificent triumph.

Weirdly, he fancies himself as a historian, but seems totally unaware that one of the purposes of history is to re-interrogate the past. So there was the obligatory clickbait of a war on woke. We can't have people editing Wikipedia entries, he said. Conveniently forgetting he had failed to acknowledge that he has six children until recently.

The longer he went on, the more rambling and lazy the speech became. It lasted a thankfully brief 45 minutes, but it wasn't even immediately clear that he had actually ended, as he seemed to finish mid-sentence. No one cared. The audience cheered, no one more so than the cabinet – each of whom was desperate not to be seen as the first one to stop clapping.

It had been classic, complacent Boris. He hadn't really tried because he hadn't needed to. He feels impregnable. The Tories had loved him because they always do. He makes them feel good about themselves. Comfort binge-eating on a diet of nostalgia and wishful thinking. And besides, if nothing else, the conference had been a stark reminder that they weren't exactly spoiled for choice in the search for alternative prime ministers.

But it had also been a speech that had ignored the lived experience of most people in the country. Queues, shortages, feeling broke. A Brexit that wasn't really turning out as promised. The faithful might have knelt down to worship, but actually his speech had been an act of contempt. Both to them and everyone else. The speech may have bought Boris a bit of breathing space but not much else. Sooner or later something's got to give. And then the shit will hit the fan.

Boris Johnson drags Tories ever deeper into sleaze bath

10 NOVEMBER 2021

If only it were that simple. In BorisWorld, all Boris Johnson has to do is turn up to sprinkle the stardust of mindless optimism and things fall into place. It worked for Brexit and it worked for his 2019 general election campaign. Bertie Booster ruled OK. But climate change is a rather tougher nut to crack. Other countries aren't quite so susceptible to his charms, and the Cop26 summit in Glasgow is in danger of ending in disappointment.

Quite what Johnson expected to achieve by turning up to Cop26 for a few hours on Wednesday afternoon was anyone's guess. Still, at least he travelled by train this time. Maybe he just couldn't accept his powerlessness and that his presence was a total waste of time. That talk of banging negotiators' heads together really wouldn't cut it after all. Whatever it was, there was no Bertie Booster tub-thumping in the 25-minute press conference he gave shortly before he scuttled back to London. It was about as close as you'll ever get to Johnson admitting defeat. He did go through the motions of saying, '1.5 was still alive,' but his body language rather suggested the opposite. His shoulders were stooped and his opening speech was delivered with little enthusiasm.

We were into the hard yards, he said. Stuck in a rolling maul in the final furlong. Our children and grandchildren would not forgive us if we didn't agree a deal. And right now he would settle for one that he could sell as significant, even if it was effectively worthless. Just to save face. What was required was more ambition and implementation. It wasn't clear who he expected to supply them. 'When are leaders going to lead?' he asked. It's a question some of us have been asking about him for a while now.

There were a few token questions about the conference, but most of the media seemed to have already made up their minds that Cop26 wasn't going to be the game-changer the government had tried to build it up as before it started. Rather, they used the time to encourage the prime minister to break his *omertà* on Tory sleaze. For the last week or so, Bertie Booster has been uncharacteristically quiet.

It soon became clear why. Because Johnson was about to rewrite history to suit himself. Even for such an accomplished liar, this was quite something. A deception on the grandest of scales. A self-deception on the most tawdry of scales. Here was Johnson, a man incapable of honesty and bereft of self-esteem, pulling out all the stops to distance himself from the scene of the crime. This is his special talent. Because he doesn't just always betray his family, friends and colleagues, he also always betrays himself. The self-loathing must be intense.

Boris began by saying that any MP who was found to have broken the rules must be punished. Er . . . yes. Only he appeared to have totally forgotten that Owen Paterson had been found guilty of multiple egregious cases of paid advocacy. And that Johnson had imposed a three-line whip on his own MPs to get his suspension put on hold until the case had been re-examined by a new committee with a majority of well-disposed Tory members, who would now come to the right conclusion. It was about as sleazy as it gets.

Yet here was Bertie Booster, admittedly on worn-out Duracell batteries, trying to portray himself as a champion of natural justice. Boris Johnson is going to be very angry when he catches up with the Boris Johnson who fucked up so badly. He could scarcely bring himself to mention Geoffrey Cox. There again, he must be sick with envy at the amount Geoff has raked in since becoming an MP.

From there on in, it was something of a pile-on. Johnson was entirely unrepentant. Three times he was asked to apologise, and three times he said nothing. Not even an insincere expression of regret for impressions that might have been given. The Tory MPs whose second jobs have come under the microscope as a direct result of his own misjudgement might at least be hoping for a 'sorry' in private. Despite all evidence to the contrary, he also declared that the UK was about as uncorrupt a country as you could find – £3 million for a peerage, anyone?

There again, he is a prime minister who once declared the £250,000 a year for his *Telegraph* column to be 'chicken feed', so no wonder he can't see what all the fuss is about.

Still, Boris wasn't finished. He then said there was nothing wrong with second jobs, provided MPs put their constituents first. Something he had failed to do when he had carried on as London mayor despite being elected to Westminster in 2015. And he insisted his own behaviour was beyond reproach. It was nobody's business who paid for the redecoration of his Downing Street flat. Or if he accepted a free holiday from someone he put in the House of Lords. Wrongdoing must be punished, he said repeatedly. Perhaps he has a subconscious desire to be found out. One for his therapist.

None of this would have gone down well with Tories hoping to draw a line under the corruption scandal. Far from killing the story, Johnson had taken politics a step further into the sleaze bath by refusing to accept any responsibility. Par for the course for a self-destructive narcissist. He was asked why didn't he stay in Glasgow, even if the chances of a meaningful deal were minute? Just to show he cared. But then he doesn't really. The only thing he really cares about is himself.

Empty benches at PMQs amid fury at Johnson's inability to do one job

17 NOVEMBER 2021

It was yet again the gaps on the Tory benches that most caught the eye. During the good times, it's standing room only for prime minister's questions, but these days the three rows behind the government front bench are barely half full. And it's almost certainly not because dozens of Tory MPs are preoccupied with their second jobs: it's because they are profoundly pissed off with the way Boris Johnson is doing his first one.

Mind you, the ones who did show up as a token gesture of support for their hapless leader may well have made a mental note to give PMQs a swerve in future weeks. For what we got was Boris at his absolute worst. Not the 'everything's great, Bertie Booster' Boris. Not even the nauseating, ersatz, absent-minded joker Boris. But the raw, childlike, unchannelled, psychotic Boris. Angry, out of control and out of his depth. Lashing out randomly while blaming others for his own shortcomings, the shallowness of his empty narcissism ruthlessly exposed. Not a pretty sight, and one normally seen only by women and friends he has betrayed.

To no one's surprise, Keir Starmer focused on matters of trust. Never Johnson's strongest suit, even on a good day. And especially not now. Could the prime minister guarantee not to go back on his promise to build both a new railway line between Manchester and Leeds and the eastern leg of HS2? 'Pifflepafflewifflewaffle,' said Boris. We can almost certainly take that as a 'no' then.

The Labour leader then moved on to sleaze and Tory corruption. Other people had apologised. Would he? Again, Johnson made no pretence of answering, while Jacob Rees-Mogg, the homunculus in an oversized suit who is the unthinking person's idea of a thinking person, shook his head furiously. He definitely hadn't apologised. Oh, no. He had only expressed the mildest regret. Saying sorry was for the little people. It wasn't a great look.

'But what about the money you took from Mishcon de Reya?' Boris asked. 'The leader of the opposition is guilty of Mish-conduct.' He was so pleased with that schoolboy gag that he repeated it three times. For some reason, the Tories have got it into their heads that Starmer had been taking money to help Gina Miller stop Brexit. They don't appear to have noticed that the payment was received in 2016, well before Miller got involved in her legal fight. Details, details . . .

But Johnson went on and on, eventually getting called out by the Speaker for being generally unpleasant and obstructive. Keir normally plays it safe and passionless, but this time he went for the jugular. Johnson was a coward, not a leader. Someone who had been investigated by every organisation to which he had been elected. And most places that he's worked, for that matter. He can't say sorry; he believes the rules don't apply to him and he rows back on every promise. 'The joke isn't funny any more.' It hasn't been for a while.

Things didn't get any better for Boris when he appeared before the liaison committee, the supergroup of select committee chairs, later in the afternoon. Even the mild-mannered William Wragg, who is one of the more docile Tories, inadvertently managed to get the better of him by asking Boris a simple question about the ministerial code. Something in which Boris doesn't believe, having forced one independent adviser to resign by refusing to accept his findings on Priti Patel and replacing him with Lord Geidt – the Geidtadoodle – who could be relied on to not find anything compromising about Johnson's own financial arrangements.

Johnson smirked nervously, but somewhere in his subconscious was a growing realisation that the comedy was turning to personal tragedy. He was the chancer who had been found out by his peers. Even his own backbenchers had turned on him, sick of U-turn after U-turn and U-turns on U-turns. Taken for mugs and made to look not just stupid, but corrupt with it.

Labour's Chris Bryant quietly and methodically took advantage of the prime minister's discomfort to expose what everyone had long suspected. That Boris hadn't bothered to read the Owen Paterson report before whipping his MPs to ignore it. Just too much hassle. Too much work. Policy had been constructed on the hoof, reacting to whatever shitshow had been going on at the time. But he couldn't remember telling John Whittingdale that there was definitely cross-party consensus for his sham committee. Even if Whittingdale could.

It soon got worse. Yvette Cooper was having none of Johnson's usual prevarications. Did he think Paterson had broken the rules or not? Just saying he had fallen foul of the rules wasn't good enough. Boris looked horrified at being asked to tell the truth. But he ran out of road and had no option.

Cooper pressed on. People expected even higher standards of the prime minister – news to Johnson – so why hadn't he worn a mask at Hexham hospital? 'There was barely 30 seconds when I wasn't wearing a mask,' he whined. So that's all right then. It was just bad luck that that was the 30 seconds in which he was photographed. Perhaps there was a sign in that corridor saying, 'Please don't wear a mask here.'

If Boris thought his troubles were over once the questions moved away from sleaze, he was badly mistaken. Everyone went for him. Particularly his own MPs. Mel Stride, Philip Dunne, Julian Knight, Tobias Ellwood and Jeremy Hunt all took chunks out of an under-prepared and badly briefed Johnson. The prime minister's life was also falling apart thanks to an embarrassed Gillian Keegan, who was forced to explain how the government had managed to lose – presumably in the incinerator – the records of the phone calls between Paterson, Randox – who paid him more than £100,000 a year – and former health minister Lord Bethell.

It felt like a moment of no return. The government was in meltdown. Rules on second jobs were going to be kicked into the long grass. A minister had just guessed three separate figures of 10, 15 and 20 for the number of hours that MPs could freelance each week. Chaos. Johnson had never given much of a shit about his own MPs. But they had cared about him. Especially the red-wall MPs elected in 2019. They had believed he was a winner. Now, though, the last of his stardust had been brushed away. And all that was left was an emperor in all his pallid nakedness. From now on, it was every man and woman for themselves.

* * *

The country was now in the grip of the Omicron variant of the coronavirus. Sajid Javid, the health secretary, and other medical experts were urging caution. To wait and see how bad this strain of Covid really was. Boris Johnson, however, was in more boosterish form. Everything would probably be OK, as long as you kept your fingers crossed. You needed to wear a mask only if you were meeting people you didn't know. That kind of thing.

We had also been treated to one of Johnson's more eccentric speeches at the Confederation of British

Industry's annual conference. He came unprepared and could only mumble nonsense about Peppa Pig World. It was a performance that would have most CBI members voting Labour. It was as if Johnson was having a very public breakdown. Or as if he knew all hell was about to break loose with Partygate.

Master of the profane, maestro of the inane – this man has us as mugs

1 DECEMBER 2021

Call it the Quantity Theory of Inanity. It would be wrong to say that Boris Johnson doesn't still enjoy prime minister's questions. Like any sociopathic narcissist, he cannot resist being the centre of attention. The noise, the lights, the cameras. It's one of the few ways Boris can tell he's still alive.

It's just that the cracks are beginning to show. Even a few months ago, the cheers from the Tory backbenchers that greeted Johnson's appearances in the Commons sounded almost sincere. Now they seem forced. Pavlovian responses from a bygone era. The Fool is now the fool, a fading music-hall act reduced to babbling nonsense. A hollow man, bereft of redeeming qualities.

As Boris shrinks, so Keir Starmer grows. There was a time when the Labour leader looked awkward at PMQs.

He had all the right lines, but the delivery kept falling flat, his arrows mere paper darts that left Boris unharmed. He knew it, his MPs knew it, and the pretence that he was in his element was killing them both.

Now, though, Keir has found his range. There is a confidence, a swagger to him. He is beginning to look and sound like a leader. He's finally got the shadow cabinet he wanted, and he's not afraid to assert himself. Most of all, he is comfortable in the job, because he knows he's got Johnson's measure. Boris no longer holds any terrors or mysteries for him. He's just a third-rate chancer who always lets you down in the end. And, more often than not, in the beginning. He's someone who can be picked off at will.

For the last three PMQs, Starmer has effortlessly come out on top by attacking Boris on matters of trust, something that has never been the prime minister's strong point. And this week, the Labour leader was at it again.

He started with the story the *Daily Mirror* had broken overnight about Boris breaking his government's own lockdown rules by holding parties at No. 10 last year. Didn't this just show that he was not someone who kept his word?

Johnson did his best to look astonished. He didn't have the nerve to deny the party had taken place. Rather, he tried to make out that the party had never really been a party. It had just been a normal day's work that had morphed into someone opening a few cases of champagne.

Boris could make his own bubbles as he saw fit. A Westminster bubble.

And Boris knew it had not really been a Christmas party because, as far as he knew, no one had had sex with him. Which is his definition of a proper party. Keir was unimpressed. It had definitely been a party – there had been booze and games – yet Johnson was insisting it had taken place within the guidelines in force at the time. Both things could not be true.

'It's one rule for the prime minister and another for everyone else,' Starmer observed. Much like mask-wearing. Johnson had just about managed to strong-arm Jacob Rees-Mogg and Nadine Dorries, long-term mask refuseniks, into reluctantly wearing face coverings by telling them it would hide their lack of shame, but there were still at least 20 backbenchers boldly challenging the Omicron variant to do its worst. Though, in their minds, they were the untouchables. Covid was something only the little people got.

Having made plain there was little reason for the rest of the country to pay any attention to what the government said, as there was little chance it was listening to itself, Starmer moved on to a leaked report that showed that not only would most of the promised 40 new hospitals amount to little more than a paint job in A&E, but that the Treasury thought there was little chance of them ever happening.

Outrageous, Boris exclaimed. In his own world, every

time a new lock is fixed to a toilet door a new hospital is built. It won't be long before we find that the 40 hospitals are just the same hospital being built 40 times. 'He drivels on irrelevantly,' Johnson said of Starmer, bouncing up and down nervously and waving his arms sporadically.

Only it was Boris who was drivelling on irrelevantly. He had nothing to say. No defence. His MPs may have been willing to give him a bit of leeway, but two years on they expected some delivery. Two Tory backbenchers dared to ask when their constituencies might receive some levelling-up funds. Johnson laughed and all but admitted they wouldn't be getting a penny as long as there were Labour councils in charge of the local authorities.

The Tory benches went noticeably quiet. They can sense their leader is becoming a liability. The joke is no longer funny. Johnson has nothing left to offer but broken promises. The master of the profane, the maestro of the inane. A man incapable of leading by example. When the shit hits the fan, he's off partying with his mates, treating us as if we were mugs. And sooner or later the country will wise up and decide it's had enough.

It's my non-party and I'll lie if I want to: Boris Johnson is bang to rights

8 DECEMBER 2021

Some of the Tory backbenchers looked furious. The others just appeared bewildered at having been fooled for so long. Taken for mugs, like the rest of the country. But they needn't have been. After all, Boris Johnson was always going to be Boris Johnson. A liar is gonna lie. He speaks, he lies. He's a man without moral authority who degrades and poisons everything that he comes into contact with. A sociopath whose main pleasures are self-preservation and laughing at those to whom he has a duty of care.

There had been a few boos from the opposition benches and a silence from his own that Johnson tried to style out as he took his place for PMQs. But his eyes gave the game away. Bloodshot, furtive pinpricks. The telltale signs of the chancer who feels his world beginning to close in on him. Boris started with the non-apology.

'Let me get this straight,' he said. A sure sign he was about to start lying. Then again, breathing is also a sure sign Johnson is about to start lying. He was absolutely furious. But only that the video had been leaked. It would have been far better if its existence had never come to light. But now that it had, he was very, very angry with

Naughty Allegra Stratton and her mates for undermining lockdown guidelines by being caught practising their excuses for a hypothetical Christmas party.

Boris wasn't angry about the party itself, because that had never happened. It was just entirely coincidental that Stratton had joked about a party occurring on the same date as had been reported, had said she went home before the party that didn't happen started, and had appeared confused about how best to explain it. In the end, she had settled on a cheese and wine party that wasn't socially distanced. As a crap improviser, Allegra was up there with Boris himself.

Within seconds, we were on a mind-bending trip through the looking glass, as Johnson announced there would be an investigation, headed by the cabinet secretary, Simon Case, into the party No. 10 had spent a week saying hadn't happened. And if it was found that the party that hadn't happened had actually happened after all, then Boris would be sure to throw a few members at the bottom of the Downing Street heap under a bus.

Reality was soon distorted further. Boris could not confirm that Case had not been at the party that had never happened, so it was possible the cabinet secretary would end up having to interview himself. Before confirming the party had not been a party because no one had thought to bring him a 'secret Santa' present. That still hurt. Johnson also later made clear that Case's remit extended only to the one party on 18 December. All the other Downing Street lockdown parties that hadn't happened – including ones that Boris had definitely attended – would not be investigated. To save Johnson the effort of sacking himself.

Even by Boris's standards, this opening address was a shambles. It didn't fool anyone. Keir Starmer kept his questions sharp and focused. No one believed the prime minister, so could he at least show some self-respect by admitting the truth? Leadership started at the top, and the reason there had been so many illegal parties at No. 10 was because everyone working there knew Boris didn't give a toss about the rules.

The rules were for the little people. Like Tricia, who had not been able to say goodbye to her late mother in person, while staff at No. 10 were having a knees-up and rehearsing their lies. Like the Queen, who had sat alone during Prince Philip's funeral. Just not for Boris and his cronies. They could do what they wanted.

Johnson had no answer. He was bang to rights, but just lacked the self-respect to acknowledge it. So he debased himself further by repeating the same nonsense that not even he believed, before accusing Labour of playing party politics with Covid. Another lie, as Labour has consistently voted with the government on health measures. But once you've started lying, it's hard to break the habit.

There was no respite for Johnson when Starmer was done. The SNP leader, Ian Blackford, was, for once, not shouted down when he called on Boris to resign. Rishi

Sunak could even be seen nodding vigorously. It's an ill wind and all that. Labour's Rosena Allin-Khan wondered how Boris sleeps at night. The answer was simple. He sleeps on one side of the bed and his conscience sleeps on the other. God knows where Carrie sleeps.

The Tory William Wragg said he hoped Boris wasn't planning anything like a Covid press conference as a diversionary tactic later in the day. Though that's precisely what Johnson had in mind, because at 6 p.m. he appeared in the same room where Stratton had recorded her video, flanked by his two window-dressing stooges, Chris Whitty and Patrick Vallance, aka Bill and Ben the Flower Pot Men, to give a press conference. Hard new medical data had suddenly come to light, he said – it was the first time Downing Street parties had been classified as hard medical data – and he was going to have to move the UK to Covid plan B status at least 24 hours earlier than planned.

Inevitably, almost all the questions focused on Partygate. Where was the leadership? How come Stratton had been the only one to take responsibility for what took place in No. 10 by resigning? And she hadn't even been to the sodding party. Wasn't it about time the prime minister accepted that rules had been broken while he was in charge? Why not investigate all the parties? Boris hummed, hahed and dribbled. No fully formed, intelligible sentences emerged. Other than that, he thanked Allegra for whatever she had done. He couldn't quite remember what.

Still the questions came. It was now a matter of trust. Why should the public accept the new restrictions when there was every chance Boris wouldn't be following them himself? Boris cleared his throat. Because the public were better than him. They would suck it up, even though they knew he was lying through his teeth. For once, Johnson was probably telling the truth.

'Gathering' storm: ministers' party pieces fail to convince

9 DECEMBER 2021

The day off didn't seem to have done much to improve Sajid Javid's mood. The health secretary had cancelled his slots on the Wednesday-morning media round on the grounds that he was 'too upset' to appear.

Upset not so much by the Downing Street lie-rehearsal video, but more by Boris Johnson's enthusiasm for getting other people to cover up for him. Cowardice is one of Boris's more unreported qualities. For once the Saj had said no – the prime minister could do his own dirty work if he was so keen to have someone from the government on the airwaves – but he hadn't had the self-worth to tell Johnson to sod off two days running. And he hated himself for it.

So it was a decidedly grumpy and defensive Javid who tried not to make a fool of himself as he explained to

Radio 4's *Today* programme why it was fine to get pissed with your colleagues at a party but not work alongside them, all the while knowing that the really tricky questions were still to come. Sure enough, presenter Mishal Husain got there in the end. If there had been no party, as the prime minister and Javid clearly believed, how come Allegra Stratton had been allowed to resign? It just didn't make sense. Without a party, Stratton had merely been having harmless fun.

Now, the Saj got positively chippy. He had been given cast-iron assurances that no party had taken place, and he had believed them. Who had given these assurances? He couldn't say. Was it the same person who had been at the parties that hadn't happened and had reassured the prime minister? He would have to kill Mishal if he told her.

Husain acted confused. If Javid was so convinced, why didn't he just tell everyone the facts and save us the hassle of an investigation by the cabinet secretary? Because. Just because. Realising he had been backed into a corner, the Saj tried to distance himself from everything. His new line was that he didn't know anything about anything. He hadn't been in the room for any of these parties. In fact, he hadn't even been in government when these parties hadn't taken place. So Mishal could talk to the hand.

The health secretary retreated gracelessly. Not because he had been caught out in the interview, but because it had panned out just as he had expected. He had reached the end of time and no longer saw the world through a glass darkly. Like everyone else who had worked for Boris, he now realised, somewhat late in the day, that his main job was to be entirely expendable. To take the flak so that the greased piglet could escape unscathed. To be collateral damage.

There was more collateral damage on view in the Commons later on, when the oleaginous junior minister Mike Ellis – his boss Steve Barclay was mysteriously missing in action – was sent out to answer an urgent question from Labour's Fleur Anderson about the remit for the cabinet secretary's investigation. Ellis started by being ever so 'umble. Ever so apologetic.

He too had been horrified by the video footage that had emerged that made fun of a 'gathering' – Ellis couldn't bring himself to say 'party' for fear of incriminating himself and others – that definitely hadn't happened, because he too had been given assurances by the Somebody Whose Name Could Not Be Mentioned that no party had taken place and no rules had been broken. But even though nothing had happened, the investigation would now be extended to two further 'gatherings' that had also not taken place. We were all going to play a game of Let's Pretend.

It was like shooting fish in a barrel for Anderson. But she wasn't going to let that stop her. It's not every day that anyone can stand up to take free potshots at a minister in the Commons and they're obliged to suck it up. It all came down to a matter of trust, she said. And right now it was impossible to believe a word anything the prime minister or his lackeys said. A sentence that could have been written at almost any point in the last two years. Lying is what Boris does for a living. Being prime minister is his freelance second job.

Anderson continued. Would the cabinet secretary be investigating any further parties? The number of parties the Tories appeared to have had last year was now multiplying faster than Omicron. Almost every hour there was a new variant. And would the prime minister resign if he was found to have misled the house – yeah, right; was that a pig flying? – and could the cabinet secretary promise that he hadn't attended any of the parties that hadn't happened?

Ellis gave a solemn undertaking that Simon Case definitely hadn't been at the three 'gatherings' he was currently investigating, as they hadn't taken place, but couldn't offer guarantees about any other 'gatherings' that hadn't happened. Magical thinking for a magical realist.

The opposition benches piled on gleefully. Was it the cabinet secretary who had been going round giving all the assurances that nothing was amiss? Ellis couldn't say as he was sworn to secrecy. And if it came to that, how could we trust the police to investigate, given that the plods based in Downing Street seemed to have missed all the action?

But it was the Tory benches that made Ellis's life most difficult. Desmond Swayne observed that No. 10 was very large. It wasn't clear if he was defending Boris not knowing about a party or pointing out that there could have been two or more parties taking place at the same time. Boris could have been having a bash in his flat, while the apparatchiks raided the wine cellar downstairs.

Peter Bone, Philip Hollobone and Bob Blackman also contended that the government had to be held to higher standards if it wanted the public to obey Covid rules, and that Johnson had to obey the spirit as well as the letter of the law. Not Boris's strong point.

Tellingly, there were almost no Tories in the house, and none that would defend Boris. So it was left to Ellis to praise his boss. He had known Johnson for years and believed him to be a man of honour and integrity. Which said more about Ellis's judgement than anything else. Most of the house just wondered if there was a second Boris Johnson running around Westminster, one that nobody but Ellis had met.

The session ended with a question about the fine imposed on the Tory party by the Electoral Commission regarding the payments for doing up Johnson's flat. Ellis said nothing. This was above the paymaster's pay grade. It was an appropriate end to the Tories' crime week. They had certainly given the police plenty to do.

* * *

Partygate was already taking its toll. Though many of his MPs still supported him in public, in private the veil was starting to slip from their eyes. As it was from the public's. Johnson was no longer the golden boy, destined to be prime minister for as long as he wanted. Every comedian has their day, and people no longer found him funny. He was the Man Without Qualities. The lies were no longer believable and the jokes were far too tired to paper over the cracks. Johnson's japes about the parties not being parties and the rules being obeyed at all times – wink, wink – lay face down, dead in the water.

He had lost all trust, all credibility. Worst of all, he didn't even realise he was the author of his own downfall. Inspector Clueless. Johnson merely seemed bemused by his decline. Almost unable to govern. Unsure of what to do next in the fight against the coronavirus – so much so that he managed to alienate both the lockdown believers and the lockdown sceptics.

Go out, catch Covid, ignore the science. Or trust in Chris Whitty

16 DECEMBER 2021

You can tell who the country trusts. People no longer look at Boris Johnson on TV and ask themselves, 'Why is this liar lying to me?' They already know why. Boris lies because he knows no other way of interacting. Deceit is his default setting. It's not just the past that is a foreign

33

country; it's also the present. Truth and Boris have never been on speaking terms. So when Chris Whitty and the prime minister hold a press conference together, there's only one person to whom the country is listening.

In the earlier days of the pandemic, the chief medical officer appeared rather starstruck by the Johnson swagger and the Downing Street setting and would automatically tend to defer to anything Johnson said. Even the stuff he knew was bullshit. But, over the last nine months, the chief medical officer has wised up and is no longer fooled by the overbearing narcissist. Instead, he speaks his mind.

Wednesday evening was a case in point. Just as Johnson was talking drivel about people still needing to go out and about to parties – only don't turn up to your own – despite the Omicron variant being far more transmissible than the Delta, Whitty went freelance. In his view, the government advice didn't go nearly far enough and was just plain bonkers. If you wanted an even chance of making it through to Christmas without getting ill – never mind stopping the NHS from being overwhelmed – then it was time to start cancelling some engagements and reprioritising your social calendar.

The reaction was almost immediate. Though many people had already decided to cut back on social events on the basis that it's invariably safest to do the opposite of what the government suggests, given that its health policy is driven by what the boneheaded libertarians on the right of the Conservative Party will tolerate rather than the public good, a great deal more chose to follow Whitty's advice and cancel Christmas parties and outings.

It was no surprise, then, that Labour opted to table an urgent question, asking the Treasury to do more in terms of statutory sick pay for those off work and to offer financial assistance for the hospitality and entertainment industries. The shadow chancellor, Rachel Reeves, had a good excuse for not being in the Commons in person: she's at home self-isolating.

Rishi Sunak, not so much. He's on a chill-out tour of San Francisco, seeing friends in Sausalito, the Napa Valley and Haight-Ashbury. Oh, and obviously working extremely hard. Mainly at distancing himself from Boris. With the possibility of a leadership election sometime in the new year, he doesn't want to be seen as too close to the prime minister. Sunak and Johnson match one another in the self-serving disloyalty stakes.

In the absence of the chancellor, we got the hapless junior minister John Glen, who enjoyed a miserable 45 minutes of being harangued by MPs from all parties. 'It's going to be fine,' he said desperately. Could everyone just please wait for the afternoon? To give Rishi a chance to wake up, fit in a yoga session, followed by a tantric massage, and then make a 10-minute phone call with some unnecessarily stressed business dudes back in the UK? In the meantime, could everyone take some deep, Omicron-free breaths and realign their chi? Or kundalini? Or something.

None of which remotely reassured anyone. Glen tried again, repeating his comments about what the government had done and dropping heavy hints that something would happen in a day or so, once Rishi had completed his life-changing ayahuasca experience. So could people stop pestering the Treasury with their worries of going out of business? He was fed up with people always thinking primarily about themselves. That was the problem with society. Too much me, me, me. Om.

People should just knuckle down and follow the government advice of going out and catching Covid. That's what Boris wanted people to do, and that's what they ought to be doing. After all, that way no clubs and restaurants would be at risk. He would also like it on record that he would be taking his team out for lunch on Monday in Salisbury. And could someone please keep the receipt? I've got news for Glen. Someone in his team would probably be cancelling the reservation as he spoke, and he would be eating on his own. Not for the first time, I guess.

All of this was too much for the increasingly unstable Steve Baker, who is turning into a one-man vigilante unit, on guard against anything halfway sensible. He wanted to know why 'unelected' scientists, who actually know their subject, should be allowed to have a say in protecting the NHS. The people who should have the final say on public health were the politicians who were paid to make the wrong judgement calls. And if people died, they died. It was God's way of punishing a decadent society that no longer trusted its own prime minister. Glen and the rest of the chamber stared at the floor in embarrassment.

Brand Rishi – reassuringly expensive 'sliders' available at £99.99 from www.dishirishi.com – wasn't the only one to dodge a bullet in the Commons. Liz 'call me ma'am' Truss, Sunak's main rival for Boris's job, was working on her Britannia-themed Instagram account, and so was unable to answer Tom Tugendhat's urgent question on why Johnson had lied to him during prime minister's questions about the projected 10% cut to the Foreign Office's budget.

This time it was James Cleverly, who continues to be on a mission to disprove theories of nominative determinism, who had to clear up the mess. Read my lips, he said. There would not be a 10% cut to the Foreign Office's budget. There could be a 9.8% or a 10.2% cut. But definitely not a 10% cut. It was lame even by the normal standards of ministerial non-denials, and it fooled no one. We had a government that not even the Tories could trust and we'd given up on the Brexit lies of the UK as a global superpower. Happy Christmas, Little Britain.

* * *

The country had shambled its way through the Christmas break without another lockdown. More by luck than by judgement, Johnson had for once made the right call. People were able to go and see friends and family, and there was no spike in the death rate, the Omicron variant turning out to be less lethal than first feared.

Meanwhile, there had been further allegations of parties at No. 10, and a civil servant, Sue Gray, had been appointed to investigate them. It was a job that might once have gone to Simon Case, the cabinet secretary – only he might have known they were actually happening, or even been at a few of them himself.

Boris Johnson's best party excuse is that he's even dimmer than we feared

12 JANUARY 2022

Finally, we got some kind of explanation from the prime minister for his boozy parties at Downing Street. It turns out that Boris Johnson wants us to believe that Boris Johnson thinks that Boris Johnson is catatonically stupid. And that the British public are equally half-witted enough to believe any old lies he happens to come up with. There's just one problem with this: Boris may be dim, but he's not that dim. And the rest of us have long since learned to see through his mendacity.

This was the prime minister's questions at which Johnson finally ran out of road. An outright denial that he had been at the party on 20 May 2020 would no longer keep him out of trouble, as there was anecdotal evidence that he was there. So all that he had left was to come up with the best possible excuse and hope it would buy off a few of the more gullible Tory MPs. Only the best possible excuse turned out to be a crock of total shit.

Here's how it was, said Johnson, as he made a short statement to the Commons. He recognised the sacrifices the country had made, and he wanted to apologise for having got pissed with No. 10 staff in his own back garden. The thing was, he had just not realised the party was a party. When the email – which he definitely had not read – was sent, inviting everyone to enjoy the sunshine and bring their own booze, the last thing he had imagined was that a party was about to take place. Even though 60 staffers had made that assumption, realised it was against the law and decided to stay away.

So anyway, he and his then fiancée – Carrie always came along to work meetings – coincidentally turned up at the party that wasn't a party, even though they hadn't seen the invite, and stayed for 25 minutes just because it seemed rude not to. He discussed a few work matters before going back to his flat and remembered thinking how brilliant it was that so many people were staying late to work outdoors over a few bevvies.

And he hadn't even thought the party was a party when he saw the staff clearing up the empties from the flower bed the following morning. Indeed, it was only when Dominic Cummings mentioned last week that the party might actually have been a party that it occurred to him that the party could have been a party after all. He now bitterly regretted everything – most of all, getting caught – and all he was asking was that people gave him a bit of wriggle room before Sue Gray submitted the findings of her investigation. Hopefully, she would be as gullible as he imagined everyone else to be.

None of which cut any ice with Keir Starmer. This PMQs may have seemed like the most open of goals for the Labour leader, but he still needed to stick the ball in the net in front of a packed Commons' chamber. Which he did six times. Johnson was pathetic: after months of denial, was this the best he could come up with? The old dog-ate-my-homework excuse would be less insulting. The prime minister had attended the party. He had broken lockdown rules. He had misled parliament when he had said how sickened he was about the other No. 10 parties. The country thought he was a pathological liar. He needed to resign.

Boris visibly crumpled. Unlike Prince Andrew, he knew what it was like to sweat. Back in No. 10 he had managed to convince himself that his feeble explanation might be enough to get him off the hook. After all, he had a long history of getting out of tight situations by lying through his teeth. But now he could feel his optimism seeping away. He was fooling no one. Not even himself. He tugged at his toddler haircut in desperation. His eyes folded in on themselves to become bloodshot pinpricks.

The king of bullshitters was all out of ideas. Even he could see how abject his lies were. He willed himself not to exist. To be elsewhere. Somewhere he wouldn't be exposed to the starkness of his own self-hatred. His voice became strangely disconnected. Like an automaton. Without effect. He could only express his regret at the way events had panned out. A narcissist can't do empathy and can only feel sorry for himself. And this was ultimately his tragedy. His fall from grace. He had never felt so exposed. Just wait for Sue Gray. Hope that she dematerialises.

Rishi Sunak had made himself scarce in Devon. 'I'm right behind you, Prime Minister. Two hundred miles behind you.' The rest of the cabinet stared impassively at the floor, their expressions hidden behind their masks. They too would rather have been anywhere but the Commons. This was also their humiliation. They were the ones who had put a man transparently unfit to be prime minister into No. 10. They knew what Boris was like but hadn't cared. His incompetence and corruption was also theirs.

The Tory backbenchers were also out of sorts. No one could bring themselves to actually defend their leader, but neither did they dare attack him. His immorality cast a toxic pall over proceedings. Boris was the turd that would not flush and which no one dared to mention. So instead they asked him about irrelevant details of constituency business. A county motto. It was all somewhat surreal.

It was left to Labour's Chris Bryant to have the last word. How stupid did Johnson think we all were? Could he even imagine a 10-year-old getting away with lines like that? And would it yet again be people who had worked for Boris, like Allegra Stratton, that would end up losing their jobs? Johnson shrugged, still a semi-absentee observer of his own downfall. Needs must. If that's what it took for him to survive. It was a fight to the death. Whose exactly would soon become clear.

Hard-done-by Big Dog gets Patel and Dorries to dish out the catnip

17 JANUARY 2022

Big Dog was having a temper tantrum. He had been hiding out in Downing Street since Wednesday, and everyone was still talking about the number of parties he had held and how long he could get away with lying about them. It's just not fair, he had shouted at a member of staff. Why did the whole world blame him for every-one in No. 10 being pissed more often than not during lockdown, when he was merely the person who had been in charge and let it all happen? It wasn't his fault he was unable to see the difference between working and having a social event. Surely the person who warned him about the party on 20 May should have made a greater effort to get his message across?

'We need to move on,' he had said eventually. What was required was a secret plan. Or two secret plans: Operation

Save Big Dog and Operation Red Meat. Secret plans that were so secret he was going to make sure everyone knew what they were. First off, he was going to sack as many members of staff as were necessary for him to keep his job. Because that was the kind of threat that would be guaranteed to buy the loyalty of everyone in No. 10. And then he was going to offer up some policies that he hoped would be catnip to both the right-wing press and the far right of his party. With any luck, it would stop them writing letters of no confidence to Graham Brady. Big Dog might even get round to doing a bit of work after that. Then again, why break the habit of a lifetime?

Monday saw the plans go into action. At Home Office questions, Priti Patel declared she was going to set the navy on refugees who were trying to cross the Channel in inflatable boats. She didn't quite say what she expected the navy to do about them. But hopefully it would find a way of pushing them back to France. Failing that, it could just sink them. A warm glow of pleasure passed through Priti Vacant's veins as she thought of foreigners fighting for their lives in a gunmetal-grey sea. It was for moments like this that she lived. To be home secretary was very heaven.

Next up was Nadine Dorries, who, having already announced in the *Mail on Sunday* and on Twitter her plan to freeze the BBC licence fee for two years and then discontinue it from 2028, belatedly got round to informing parliament in a statement to the Commons. The BBC

43

had quite enough money to be going on with, people were broke, and the licence fee was an outdated business model.

Furthermore, it was about time the BBC learned to be a bit more impartial and stop reporting things that were damaging to the government. Stories about corruption and lying at the heart of government had no place in a national broadcaster's reporting. And while the Beeb was at it, it should get out of its London bubble and stop showing programmes for the metropolitan elite. Shows like *Strictly Come Dancing, Doctor Who,* David Attenborough and *Match of the Day.* It was an outrage that no one from the BBC had ever bothered to adapt one of her third-rate books for television.

Labour's Lucy Powell, the shadow culture secretary, wasn't having any of this. This wasn't a policy announcement so much as a minor distraction to prevent Red Meat from becoming Dead Meat. While there should be no blank cheques for the BBC, this really wasn't about the cost of living. If it was, then the government could have done more to help with energy price rises and tax increases. She could also have mentioned the £20 reduction in universal credit and the £4.3 billion the government had written off in fraudulent Covid schemes.

So what did Nad expect the BBC to do? Just show repeats or cut its local journalism and regional programming? Or it could just dump its offering for children and Bitesize education. And as for linking the licence fee to editorial content of which the government approved, that was the kind of thing you would expect of a tinpot dictatorship.

Nad merely shrugged dismissively. Nobody was thinking of getting rid of the BBC, she said. They were merely thinking of ways to make it more like how Big Dog wanted it to be. Even though Big Dog had been very supportive of the BBC before he went into politics. And no, she hadn't given a moment's thought to what funding model might replace the licence fee. All she wanted to do was whip up a distraction by starting a discussion about the BBC's future.

If Dorries had thought she was in for an easy ride from Tory backbenchers grateful for a chance to settle scores with the national broadcaster, she was in for a nasty surprise. Peter Bottomley, the father of the house, reckoned it was just petty to freeze the inflationary increases for the next two years. Damian Green suggested that the least the government could do was maintain the licence fee till 2038, but Nad wasn't having anything to do with it. As Tory after Tory got up to ask about the non-profitable parts of the BBC they admired, Nad became increasingly unhinged. It wasn't until an hour in that she got unequivocal support from Jonathan Gullis, who declared that the Beeb deserved to be dismantled because it hadn't supported Brexit unequivocally. That's more like it, Dorries cheered. Operation Red Meat was a success after all. Big Dog could relax. For one more day at least.

45

Even under the mask, Johnson looked like someone who knew the game was up

18 JANUARY 2022

Things fall apart. It had been intended as the comeback day. The day when Big Dog finally stopped barricading himself in his Downing Street kennel and came out to prove that there was life in the confidence trickster yet. That, by sheer force of personality and the odd gag, Boris Johnson could make the Tory party – and possibly even the country – fall back in love with him. And yet right from the start of his TV interview with Sky's Beth Rigby at Finchley Memorial Hospital in London, it was clear the prime minister was running on empty. All passion spent.

Things fall apart. This was Johnson as we've rarely seen him. Not contrite, exactly: he still doesn't really seem to believe he's the cause of his own fall from grace. But certainly Hang Dog rather than Big Dog. Someone who can tell that the game is up. Someone who has run out of last chances and has no more lies to tell. None that will be believed, anyway. A beaten man no longer in control of his own destiny who is waiting on a miracle to save him.

Things fall apart. Rigby went straight to the heart of the matter. Dominic Cummings says you are lying and that you were explicitly warned the party should not go ahead. This account has been confirmed by a second source. So, have you lied? she asked the prime minister. For once, Johnson was wearing a mask inside a hospital, but even so, there was no sign of the usual telltale smirk. His eyes were the giveaway, as they invariably are. Puffy, almost closed. Eyes that had stared into his soul and been surprised and alarmed to find that he had one. Albeit a primordial work in progress.

Things fall apart. 'I'm sorry for my misjudgements,' he said, before hastily correcting himself to speak in the passive voice. He was sorry for the misjudgements that had been made. That was better. It was his safe place, where he was not responsible for his own actions. Nobody had told him he was doing anything against the rules. When he had gone out to join the party – not that it was a party – he had thought he was attending a work event.

Things fall apart. This was either gaslighting of the highest order – after all, he had made the rules and told the country to obey them at numerous press conferences, so you would have thought he knew what they were – or we were witnessing the partial implosion of the Johnson psyche. Someone so detached from a painful reality that he could no longer take any responsibility for himself and could relate to himself only in the third person. A separate entity.

Things fall apart. What followed was a police interrogation as, slowly and forensically, Rigby destroyed every alibi. Was Johnson saying that Dom was a liar? Boris didn't dare do that. All he could do was repeat his assertion that no one had told him that the social event had been against the rules. Presumably because no one really thought they needed to spell it out that plainly, as they imagined the reasons for not having a party were blindingly obvious.

Things fall apart. Was Dominic Lawson a liar? He too had said he knew someone who had warned Johnson not to go ahead with the party. 'Um, er,' said Big Dog. 'All I can do is humbly apologise for what happened.' And repeat that no one told him it was a bad idea. Then again, no one had bothered to tell him to put on his shoes or wipe his bum that morning. Every time he said it, pulling nervously on his toddler haircut, he sounded a bit more feeble. A bit more pathetic. You could almost sense his grip on power growing looser by the minute.

Things fall apart. Rigby picked up the pace. Should Sue Gray interview Cummings? Should Cummings give testimony under oath? Would he resign if he was found to have misled parliament? How ashamed was he at having to apologise to the Queen? What did he think of the ministerial code? Presumably not very much, given he hadn't sacked Priti Patel when she was found to have broken it. Big Dog sighed sadly. How was it that everyone found it ludicrous that he could go into the garden, see trestle tables laden with food and booze and 40 people getting a bit pissed and imagine he was at a work seminar? Who hadn't done that?

Things fall apart. 'Will you still be prime minister beyond the end of this year?' asked Rigby. Johnson stared into eternity. He thought of how Dominic Raab had admitted the party had actually been a party to Sky's Kay Burley earlier that morning. And had then gone out of his way to distance himself from it by saying he definitely hadn't been invited and wouldn't have gone anyway. Thanks for nothing, Dom.

Things fall apart. Big Dog thought of how junior defence minister James Heappey had been laughed out of the Commons by all parties during an urgent question on bringing in the navy to control migrants in the Channel. The halfwit had been stupid enough to confess he hadn't a clue what the plan was. Operation Red Meat was dead on arrival. Big Dog thought of how that snake Rishi Sunak had yet again refused to offer him any support. Next year? He'd be lucky to make it through to the end of the week at this rate.

* * *

Johnson was learning a difficult lesson: that things can always get worse. First, the Tory MP for Bury South, Christian Wakeford, had crossed the floor of the Commons moments before prime minister's questions to join Labour – a sure sign the Tory grip on the red wall was weakening and that MPs were losing faith in Boris. Then came evidence of yet another party. This time Johnson's very own birthday bash.

Hard to argue he hadn't been at that one . . .

Big Dog was now the Suspect, but at least Gray's report would be delayed... Oh

25 JANUARY 2022

Big Dog was having a bad morning. Normally, he could rely on Grant Shapps to put up a spirited defence of any government lie, which is why he had been sent out to do the morning media round. But not even the transport secretary could be bothered to put a positive spin on the latest birthday party revelations. He had even made the schoolboy error of calling a party a party, when everyone knew that word was a no-no inside No. 10.

Nor had the usually reliable Nadine Dorries shown her face on Twitter, after being ridiculed for claiming the previous evening that a birthday celebration for the prime minister in the cabinet room, organised by his wife and attended by the interior designer Lulu Lytle, clearly constituted a high-level work meeting.

In fact, the only two MPs showing any public enthusiasm for him had been the always absurd Jacob Rees-Mogg and Michael Fabricant. Which was a mixed blessing, as he haemorrhaged support every time they opened their mouths.

Then had come the appearance of the Metropolitan Police commissioner, Cressida Dick, before a committee of the Greater London Assembly. There, she had announced that, after Sue Gray had forwarded some of the evidence she had gathered, a police investigation into some of the parties at No. 10 would be a good idea after all.

Dick had offered Boris Johnson some encouragement. For a start, she had said she would only be investigating parties for which there was already plenty of evidence. Far be it from the Met to actually go to the effort of digging up any new evidence for itself. That would be a waste of police time. And she had seemed reassuringly slow on the uptake about the failure of the police stationed inside Downing Street to wonder about what all the noise was and why so much booze had been smuggled into the building. It also appeared to have only just occurred to her that there might be CCTV footage of some of the parties. No, not parties. Work events.

Even so, a police investigation wasn't ideal. Big Dog sighed and poured himself a drink, even though it was only just past midday. On the plus side, it might delay things for a few weeks or even months. That was always good news, when your only game plan for the past few weeks had been to find ever more creative ways of trying to hang on to your job till the end of the day. The downside was that Sue Gray must have found clear evidence that he – and others – had broken the lockdown laws, and the shit was sure to hit the fan sooner or later.

His more immediate worry, though, was to find a Cabinet Office minister stupid enough to answer Labour's urgent question on the latest party allegations and the police investigation. 'Don't worry, Prime Minister,' said Steve Barclay, chancellor of the Duchy of Lancaster. 'I've got just the man. It's Mike Ellis, the paymaster general. He's already made himself look abject by doing two previous UQs on your parties . . .'

'Please don't call them parties,' said Big Dog. 'It makes me nervous.'

So it was that Oily Mike found himself up against Angela Rayner in the Commons for the third time in a matter of weeks. Labour's deputy leader went in studs up. What part of the prime minister stuffing his face with a Colin the Caterpillar cake, which his wife had just happened to bring down – along with darling Lulu – from the upstairs flat to the cabinet room, where 30 of his staff had just happened to gather to sing 'Happy Birthday', did everyone not understand was against the rules that the government had itself imposed on the rest of the country? You hardly needed a police investigation for that, but hell, now that there was one, we had better see it through. And in the meantime, why didn't Big Dog just resign?

Oily Mike was momentarily caught off guard. What should he call the prime minister? The Accused? The Perp? The Defendant? No, that was it: the Suspect. MPs shouldn't be so quick to pre-judge the Suspect. It was quite normal for the Suspect to drop in for a quick cup of tea with his wife.

And the 30 guests were all waiting to debrief him on an important, fraudulent Covid test-and-trace contract.

And they were only singing 'Happy Birthday' to wash their hands. And as it was a surprise party, there was no way you could expect the Suspect to remember having been there. Otherwise, it wouldn't have been a surprise. As for the cake, the Suspect had a long history of thinking he could both have it and eat it.

On previous occasions, very few Tories had come to the chamber to make idiots of themselves. But this time there was a hardcore of about 20 Boris loyalists. Edward Leigh raged that we were on the brink of war, and the PM was about to be brought down by a piece of cake. Theresa Villiers was adamant that the Suspect should have an exemption because he had helped to organise the vaccination programme.

Giles Watling moaned that investigating all the crimes committed by the Suspect was a vexatious waste of time, while Graham Stuart thought he could detect terror in the opposition benches. In the government benches maybe. Where do Tory selection panels find such idiots? Stuart Anderson reckoned the charges were destabilising the country and should be dropped, while Mark Jenkinson detected a media plot. To discover the truth. Richard Bacon thought the crimes were so minor they should just be forgotten and we should have a 10-day celebration of the life and works of St Suspect.

Back in Downing Street, the Suspect thought he had things nailed down for now. Maybe the Met would take so long to report back that everyone would forget he was a liar who had broken his own rules. That he could bring the country down to his level by implicating it in his nihilism and deception. That somehow we had got the government we deserved. People so disengaged they'd let anything go. Then came the unwelcome news that Sue Gray's report would be published this week. Now all hell might be let loose.

Even the Suspect thought it was touch and go whether he could talk his way out of this one.

Labour had Boris Johnson over a barrel, but he could still scrape the bottom of it

26 JANUARY 2022

That noise? The sound of the bottom of the barrel being scraped. Boris Johnson degrades not only himself, but the Tory backbenchers falling over themselves to defend him. Not so long ago, Conservative MPs could just about kid themselves that there were no parties in Downing Street and Big Dog's integrity was intact. Now the game is long since up, and no one even bothers to defend the lies. Apart from Chris Philp. He'll repeat any nonsense he's been told to say.

Instead, we get ever more improbable lines from Tory MPs, who seem to have forgotten that the Suspect made the laws, the Suspect broke the laws and the Suspect lied about it. Mostly stuff like 'It was only a small bit of cake,' 'It wasn't really a party,' 'It was a surprise, so he couldn't be expected to remember it,' and 'He's done such a brilliant job we shouldn't be too bothered if a little bit of law-breaking went on inside No. 10.'

The advocates of this last excuse have been excelling themselves. We've had Jacob Rees-Mogg as good as admitting that he couldn't think of anything Johnson might do that would cause him to reconsider his support. Conor Burns said the Suspect had been 'ambushed with a cake'. That Colin the Caterpillar can be a right bastard. Then there was Andrew Rosindell telling Sky's Kay Burley that 'it wasn't as if he had robbed a bank or anything'. Phew.

It can't be long before someone says, 'He hasn't killed anyone, as far as I know.' In the end, this kind of feeble moral relativism drags everyone down to the bottom.

But we are where we are. And come Wednesday lunchtime, MPs of all parties appeared to be in limbo as they waited for the Sue Gray report to land on No. 10's doorstep. So prime minister's questions had the feel of the Phoney War, with both leaders seeming to pull their punches, as if they were testing each other out for weaknesses before the real battle, when the two went head to head in the Commons statement in the coming hours or days.

Keir Starmer kept it simple at the start. Did the prime minister think the ministerial code, especially the section on knowingly misleading parliament, applied to him? The Suspect mumbled a quick, rather uncertain 'Yes', before going on to say that he couldn't possibly comment on matters that were the subject of a police investigation. Except he could if he wanted to. There was nothing stopping him giving a long and detailed explanation of how he was completely innocent of everything that had been alleged against him. Other than, of course, the fact that it would have been yet another lie. But then who was counting?

In which case, said the Labour leader, why didn't the Suspect do everyone – Sue Gray and the police in particular – a favour and just resign now? In December, he had said all guidance had been followed and that no parties had taken place. Now he wasn't even bothering to pretend there had been no parties, nor that he had attended them. So unless he was now pleading he had been in a fugue state for 18 months and had had no recollection of anything until Gray had reminded him, then clearly he had knowingly misled parliament. All that was missing as a *coup de grâce* was for Starmer to pass him a slice of cake.

The Suspect smirked and toyed with his toddler haircut, determined to appear upbeat. As much for himself as the MPs on his backbenches, on whom he was depending to prolong what was left of his career. He wanted to go down at least with a semblance of a fight. All hope of going with dignity had long since passed. If he had a conscience, he would have been up to his neck in shame. For him, it was still all a big joke that the police were conducting a criminal investigation into the prime minister of the UK.

What followed was a stream of unconsciousness. He rattled on about trying to stop Putin from invading Ukraine, while Labour just focused on his unfortunate habit of lying about everything. Why was everyone making such a fuss about something so trivial? I wouldn't be at all surprised if Big Dog believes he lies only because other people make him do it. It didn't seem to have occurred to the Suspect that it was him and his government that had spent virtually every waking hour for the past two months trying to protect his own job.

Nor was there any greater self-awareness when he went on to say he was cutting taxes – they were going up in April – and fixing the cost of living. Just as food and fuel prices were rising. He ended by declaring Starmer was 'a lawyer, not a leader'. In time he might come to realise that wasn't such a killer line as he'd imagined. Not least because he might be needing the services of a top lawyer in the coming weeks. It's also probable most voters would settle for a good lawyer running the country, rather than a pathological fraud. The only thing he can be trusted with is to be untrustworthy.

The Tory benches were rather louder in their support than they had been in the past two weeks. Though this was more for show than sincerity. Most would happily knife the Suspect in the front if they thought it would play to their advantage. Their loyalty is barely even skin deep. Only Sheryll Murray delivered a full-on love bomb to her leader. Which was as pathetic as it was touching. Johnson ended by claiming the difference between the Tories and Labour was that he had a vision. If he does, it's a drug-induced one. The main difference between the two parties is that the Tories are knee deep in their own shit. And still have no real idea how to get out of it.

Faced with the Gray report, Johnson was left without honesty and without honour

31 JANUARY 2022

Sometimes less is more. When the Metropolitan Police eventually got round to investigating the parties at No. 10, after being presented with the evidence by Sue Gray, and then insisted she doctor her final report, it was generally assumed to be a win for the Suspect. The Greased Piglet had escaped again after an establishment cover-up. Only Gray had other ideas. Rather than punting out a whitewash, she just said, 'Fuck you,' and downed tools. Gray wasn't going to play ball. She was going to make it clear that there was no way she could submit a meaningful report when 12 of the 16 parties were subject to a criminal investigation. At best, she could offer a partial update. Just 12 pages, two of which were blank, and all the others an indictment of the prime minister's operation.

It was no wonder everyone in No. 10 was shattered during the pandemic. Who wouldn't have been, with so many parties?

And it might be an idea to laminate Boris Johnson's briefing papers to save them getting ruined by wine spills. Gray concluded her brief update by noting that NHS staff were working under appreciably more stress than No. 10, and they weren't out breaking the rules and getting trashed every night.

So when he came to give his statement on the Gray report, it was a far trickier Commons appearance for the Suspect than he had hoped. He started by saying he was sorry. That was his first lie. He wasn't at all. He never is. Other than to be sorry for having been found out. And from that point, he just kept on lying. His main theme seemed to be: 'If only everyone else could read the redacted parts of the report relating to the 12 parties – one of which was in my own flat – that are the focus of a police investigation, then they too would see I was innocent.'

The Suspect blamed all those around him. There would be a wholesale restructuring of the entire No. 10 operation. How many people would be fired? Precisely as many as were required for the Greased Piglet to retain his own job. Besides, now that he had skim-read the update a second time, he had come to the conclusion that Gray was basically exonerating him of all wrongdoing. He was that mendacious. That delusional.

In reply, Keir Starmer was at his most damning. Often at prime minister's questions the Labour leader has used humour to expose the absurdity of the Suspect's lies. Now he chose outright contempt. Scorn for a leader who had brought shame on himself, his country and his ministerial colleagues, who, lacking the self-worth to stand up to him, had trashed what little integrity they might have had.

What part of a prime minister being investigated for an illegal party in his own flat did he think was OK? Johnson was left without honesty and without honour. A moral black hole that destroyed all those around him. When would the Tory party rediscover some decency? Hell, it wasn't as if much was needed. The government benches were eerily silent as the Labour leader spoke. Maybe the truth was slowly seeping into their consciousnesses.

Now the Suspect really began to lose it. First he accused Starmer of failing to prosecute Jimmy Savile when he was director of public prosecutions. Another outright lie. One that seemed too much even for his own front benches, as various ministers seemed to be having second thoughts about having come to the chamber to offer their support and were now looking to leave.

Then, Johnson claimed that he alone was propping up NATO against Russia's invasion of Ukraine. This when his first-ever phone call to Vladimir Putin was being cancelled because the Suspect was too busy saving his career. The reality is that he's seen as a joke around the world. The UK's own Berlusconi.

It was almost as if Boris was punch-drunk. Unable to connect with reality. Much more of it and he would have denied all knowledge of being prime minister, and it was up to the police to decide who was actually living in the Downing Street flat. Come to think of it, that shark had already been jumped. The Suspect lives in various multiverses in which there are any number of realities he might have lived. So when he says he stands by what he said, that phrase no longer has meaning as there are too many versions to pin down. He is the postmodern prime minister. A shambling exhibit of well-past-his-prime performance art. An embarrassment to everyone but himself.

A more considered, self-reflective Johnson might have at least pretended to be more apologetic. Instead, he just laughed and toyed with the toddler haircut, as opposition MPs made the error of asking him to tell the truth. The SNP leader, Ian Blackford, achieved his objective of getting red-carded from the chamber for calling Johnson a liar and saying he had deliberately misled parliament. This was a through-the-looking-glass moment. Blackford goes for telling the truth. Johnson stays for lying.

There were some unhappy Tories. Theresa May said the Suspect could have either failed to understand the rules or thought they didn't apply to him. Andrew Mitchell formally withdrew his support. Aaron Bell wondered if Johnson thought all those who obeyed the rules were fools. Mark Harper wanted Gray's final report published when the time came. Something to which Johnson would not commit. Though within minutes of the statement ending, a spokesperson said that he would, unless he could think of a way not to.

Otherwise, the few Conservatives who did have something to say – most kept quiet, and long before the end it was just opposition MPs doing the talking – could offer only nonsense. Voters were fed up with stories of cake and parties. What they were crying out for was a wholesale reform of the civil service in No. 10.

Yeah, right.

Natalie Elphicke was so moved by Johnson's contrition she begged him not to go easy on refugees. Keeping it classy.

* * *

As the evidence of rule-breaking on an industrial scale in No. 10 began to mount, so too did the number of Tory MPs sending in letters of no confidence in Boris Johnson. These were kept anonymous, so it was impossible to know who had and who hadn't submitted one – one MP was even thought to have submitted and withdrawn the same letter on numerous occasions – but it was hard to escape the feeling that a net was tightening.

Johnson was certainly feeling the pressure, going out of his way to ingratiate himself with his backbenchers, most of whom he usually preferred to ignore. With this in mind, he chose this moment to end all Covid restrictions. Sadly for him, this was somewhat overshadowed by the Daily Mirror *publishing a photograph of a party that Johnson had previously insisted had never happened. You lose some, you lose some.*

End to Covid rules wins over the MPs Johnson needs to help him survive Partygate

21 FEBRUARY 2022

You couldn't make it up. 'Now was the time for personal responsibility,' said the prime minister, with no sense of personal responsibility. His whole life has been conducted with a reckless disregard for other people. Boris Johnson is a man who has always done exactly what he wants, when he wants to do it, and he has a trail of broken marriages and promises to prove it. When the rest of us mugs were doing our best to follow the rules that he made to the letter, he was busy enjoying himself at one party after another. And when he was caught, he didn't have the decency to apologise. Instead, he chose to brazen it out, cheapening himself and his party still further.

No matter. Do as I say, not as I do, and all that. In any case, the changes to the Covid rules that the Suspect was announcing in his Commons statement had little to do with what was scientifically proven. Rather, it was to win over the libertarian right-wingers in the Tory party, who had always been against lockdown restrictions in any shape or form and on whom he was relying for support through his ongoing Partygate difficulties.

So here was how Covid was going to work from now on. Basically, we would be acting as if it was over. After all, it certainly was for the 175,000 people who had died from the virus over the last two years, and it was time for the rest of us to get with the programme. And if anyone was unlucky enough to get Covid, then they should just knuckle down and do the right thing. Whatever that was. Johnson tugged at the toddler haircut. We were in a world of moral relativism. It might be fine for some to carry on as normal. That would be people who couldn't afford tests and who would no longer have access to statutory sick pay from day one. They could work and infect vulnerable people. For others – that would be the better-off – not so much. It turns out you can put a price on personal responsibility.

Still, Omicron hadn't turned out to be as bad as all that, so it was time to end compulsory self-isolation, get rid of expensive test-and-trace programmes and see what happens. And if some of the elderly, vulnerable and unvaccinated died, then they died. They probably had it coming to them, and in any case they could all die happy, knowing that life for the rest of the country would be free of health restrictions.

There was one small caveat. Covid might not actually be over after all. It may return as a deadlier variant, in which case the decision to end all free testing could prove to be a huge advantage. Apparently. The Suspect hadn't quite thought this one through. So he ad-libbed. We'd just be relying on the Office for National Statistics' survey to detect future Covid strains – even though there would be far fewer tests to detect them. There again, on the plus side, the fewer tests that were done, the fewer infections would be registered. Put this way, you could eliminate Covid completely just by stopping all testing. Why hadn't he thought of that before?

Understandably, Keir Starmer was less than impressed. While not against the idea of loosening restrictions in principle, he just wasn't sure they didn't have more to do with party management than the nation's health. After all, they seemed to have been cobbled together at the last moment. So much so that the chancellor and the health secretary had been having a stand-up row over the cost of some of the changes that very morning. And judging by the frown on Sajid Javid's face, the health secretary still wasn't happy at having come off second best.

The Suspect merely laughed this off and went out of his way to deliberately misinterpret what had been said. Either that or he's dimmer than we thought. The Labour leader had grabbed the stick by the wrong end yet again, he said. Except he really hadn't. Only Johnson didn't care. No more than he did when other opposition MPs asked why it was that the World Health Organization and the British Medical Association weren't backing the changes. Or why there were no safeguards to protect the clinically vulnerable from being infected by their carers. Or countless other serious objections to plans that had been made on the hoof. Just rely on personal responsibility. Said the man without any.

Because this was all about him feeling the love from his own backbenchers. A national health policy designed only to please 250 or so Tory MPs. And in that respect, it appeared to be wholly successful. Because not a single one found fault with a word he had said. The intellectually challenged Graham Brady sought guarantees that there would be no more lockdowns. The equally intelligent Edward Leigh merely asked for a guarantee of no more lockdowns for 10 years – the length of time he expected the Suspect to remain prime minister. Really.

John Redwood wondered if the same ingenuity that Johnson had used on the pandemic could be applied to the cost-of-living crisis. That would be billions of pounds of state aid and several tax rises. So much for the free-marketeers. But the prize for maximum stupidity and toadying went to Matt Hancock. He declared it was entirely down to Johnson's self-restraint and personal responsibility that the UK was now the first country to have seen the back of the pandemic. To think he was health secretary once. How badly must he want to be loved by Boris?

The Suspect was rather more guarded in his later press conference – apart from insisting that the country should be proud of ending restrictions; as proud as he had been to break them, presumably – but then this time he was flanked by Chris Whitty and Patrick Vallance. Both men seemed to think that Covid was far from over and that the measures that had been lifted could easily be reinstated with just a couple of weeks' notice if a subsequent variant – and there would be variants, they were certain of that – proved to be more infectious and vaccine-unfriendly. As for self-isolating, it wasn't a matter of personal responsibility, it was a national necessity.

Johnson just stood there and sucked it up. He'd done what he set out to achieve by getting Tory MPs back on his side, and that was all that mattered. If he broke his promises and had to impose another lockdown in nine months' time because he'd screwed things up, then what the hell? He'd deal with that as and when. For now, as so often, he was just fighting for his life. And under those circumstances, anything goes. Especially when you've no sense of personal responsibility. Whoops.

* * *

The Russian invasion of Ukraine sent shockwaves through the West, even though it had been widely anticipated for some months. It was the biggest conflict in Europe since the Second World War.

To most people's surprise, Johnson rose to the occasion by uniting the country with his support for Ukraine. The war also offered Boris a temporary lifeline. While he was acting the global statesman, the opposition parties eased up on domestic matters. Every cloud and all that . . .

Putin's looming threat gives Johnson some breathing space

23 FEBRUARY 2022

Boris Johnson is in his happy place. The Russian invasion of Ukraine couldn't have come at a better time. At a stroke, people have stopped asking him awkward questions about the cost of living and the price of fuel. Better still, both Labour and – more importantly – Tory MPs have also suspended hostilities in terms of Partygate. At a time of imminent war in eastern Europe, a united front must be maintained at home. Just in case Vladimir Putin happens to be watching and starts taking our threats seriously. Not that there's much sign of that so far. But we can live in hope.

So, for the Suspect, the heat is off temporarily. He can swan around doing his Churchill tribute act – 'We shall fight them on the tennis courts. We shall fight them in the Tory party fundraising auctions. We shall never give up' – safe in the knowledge that right now it's hard for him to screw things up too badly. No one is coming after him and a vote of no confidence is not imminent. Because however many lies he happens to tell, they are nothing next to those being told by Putin. And his corruption is amateur hour when compared with the delusional venality of the Russian president. Though it's obviously something to which he can aspire.

All of which made prime minister's questions a curiously subdued affair, with both the Suspect and Keir Starmer on their best behaviour. Something that came far easier to the Labour leader, as he is by far the more serious politician. Even in an international crisis, Johnson can't totally conceal his inherent *levitas*. At heart, he still thinks the whole thing is a bit of a game.

Starmer began by making it clear that he was going to go easy on Boris. For the good of the country. The last thing people wanted to see at such a time was politicians squabbling and point-scoring. So he was thoroughly behind the efforts of the UK and other NATO countries to deter Putin. He was – as he had said the day before – just disappointed that the sanctions had been so feeble. The Russian president must have been delighted. That's if he had even noticed.

Steady on, old chap, the Suspect replied. While he was very grateful to have the support of the Labour Party in principle, he did want to point out that sanctioning five small banks and three individuals who had already been sanctioned by the US since 2018 was actually a massive deal. Not only had it caused Putin to rethink his invasion plans, but it had given other oligarchs time to liquidate their assets and get their cash out of the country. Which was a good thing, no? Johnson didn't really seem to have much of a grasp on how sanctions were supposed to work. In any case, it was important to remember that this was just the first phase of an internationally coordinated response. So our next sanctions would be marginally less pathetic. The UK's role was always to look like a soft touch compared with other countries.

The Labour leader then moved on to RT television. Surely it was time to have it banned? As it happened, Nadine Dorries had already written to Ofcom about this, the Suspect said. Though there had to be a place in the UK media for outlets that tolerated lies and made-up stories, otherwise Johnson would never have had a career at the *Telegraph*. As for donations from Russian oligarchs, he wasn't going to pay them back because he was sure the Tory party had never taken them. And just to be on the safe side, he definitely wasn't going to investigate, because who knew what you might find once you started.

Sensing that they might be on the verge of kicking lumps out of each other in their usual adversarial style, Starmer and the Suspect backed off. The Labour Party offers its full support, etc. The government appreciates the opposition's full support, etc. Only the Labour leader managed to sound halfway sincere.

In keeping with the mood, most Tory backbenchers went out of their way to avoid asking Johnson anything difficult about Ukraine, parties or the cost of living, and in return he congratulated them on doing whatever it was that they did. He still gives the impression of having no idea who any of them are.

Others weren't so docile. Caroline Lucas tried to ask about Russian involvement in UK elections. Her question went on a bit, and she got drowned out by Tory MPs shouting her down as they tried to protect their leader from all-too-believable truths. Lindsay Hoyle did himself no favours in his failure to allow Lucas to be heard.

The most telling intervention came from Margaret Hodge, who wanted to know if it was possible to sanction members of the Duma. 'It's quite a thing to sanction parliamentarians,' said the Suspect, inadvertently giving away far more than intended. Because few parliamentarians have more experience of getting away with things than Johnson. He knows he's lied to the police. To parliament. To everyone. And he still reckons he'll get away unscathed. People in power are untouchable. At heart, Boris is just another oligarch manqué. Only without the billions.

Rejoicing in his freedom, the Suspect went on to tell some lies. He'd forgotten how naturally it came to him. The UK was the first to appreciate the seriousness of Ukraine. Alex Salmond was a member of the SNP. He was on the point of telling the Labour Party Jeremy

Corbyn was still its leader when Hoyle called time. Labour's Chris Bryant made a point of order. For the first time ever, Johnson had apologised for lying to the house. About Roman Abramovich facing sanctions.

It had taken the fear of reprisals from a Russian oligarch to get him to do the decent thing. The sanctions were working. Just in the opposite way to what had been intended.

The new statesmanlike Boris quickly gives way to the old self-centred one at PMQs

2 MARCH 2022

The prime minister's parliamentary private secretaries were all decked out in blue and yellow. As were Theresa May and several SNP MPs. They could all have come straight from a Ryanair convention. Elsewhere in the chamber, MPs settled for rather more sober blue and yellow ribbons. But the sentiment was exactly the same.

This was a House of Commons united in its support for Ukraine. When the Speaker announced that the Ukrainian ambassador, Vadym Prystaiko, was in the gallery, the house rose as one to give him a prolonged and heartfelt standing ovation. It was as moving as it was unprecedented. Though NHS workers might point out that clapping sometimes comes cheap from politicians.

Over the last week or so, Boris Johnson has given tough speeches and gone on trips to the European mainland to express solidarity. All of which has played well with a home audience. The Russian invasion has not been a conflict on which it has been difficult to pick sides. Better still, all of his domestic problems seem to have melted away. For the time being at least. While people are dying in a cruel war, it seems almost too trivial to mention that the prime minister couldn't be bothered to follow his own Covid rules.

But at prime minister's questions the mask began to crack. The Suspect was no longer being asked to just Talk the Talk. He was also being asked to Walk the Walk. And he just couldn't do it. This isn't a leader likely to follow the Taiwanese president's example of giving one month of his salary to Ukrainian humanitarian causes. Well, not unless he could get Lord Brownlow to cough up again on his behalf. Dear, dear David. One more time, old chap.

Back came the bluster and the shiftiness. The tugging on his Toddlers R Us haircut. The childish outbursts of narcissistic rage that he can't control when challenged. Anything that is not on his terms cannot be tolerated. Come the end of PMQs, the new, not entirely convincing, statesmanlike Boris was beginning to look very much like the old self-centred Boris.

Keir Starmer began by reiterating that Labour was united with the government against Russian aggression. Just so there was no room for confusion. He didn't want Johnson to get the wrong end of the stick. What he really wanted to know was why the UK was lagging so far behind the US and the EU in imposing sanctions on Russian oligarchs. How about Roman Abramovich? He was on a Home Office list as a person of interest and is now in the process of trying to sell Chelsea. Why not go after him before he took the money and ran?

'It's not for me to comment on individual cases,' said the Suspect. Er . . . hello? Why the hell not? Surely it's precisely what a prime minister is there for, to talk truth to money. If he can't, then who can? There again, Johnson is on record as saying that he finds it 'inexplicable' that oligarchs aren't doing more – anything – to condemn the war. The rest of us merely find their silence to be entirely on-brand.

The Labour leader moved on. What about the two Westminster flats of Igor Shuvalov, Vladimir Putin's former deputy prime minister? We had only got to find out he owned the properties through a poisoned Russian dissident. Which brought him on to his next question. Why was the government kicking its heels over the economic crimes bill? It seemed to be going out of its way to make it easier for dirty money to be taken out of the country by giving every kleptocrat an 18-month head start.

Johnson had no answer other than to talk about cutting off the Swift payment system and banning Aeroflot. Which was beside the point as no one had any problem with him having done that. 'We're leading Europe,' he mumbled. Except we're not. At a time when we're looking for heroes – and who better fits the bill than Volodymyr Zelenskiy? – the UK government looks as if it is running scared.

If the Suspect wanted to prove many people's suspicions that the Tory party is in hock to Russian money, he couldn't have made a better job of it. At the very least, he made it look as if he wasn't that bothered about London's status as the world's laundromat. Or about the extent of Russian influence in British politics.

This was a point Labour's Bill Esterson made when he invited Johnson to donate the £2 million the Tories had received from Lubov Chernukhin, the wife of Russia's former deputy minister of finance, to the Ukrainian war effort. Just to clear the air and show that the Conservatives had nothing to hide. Now Boris lost his temper. Not all Russian money was dirty money, he shouted. Quite right. Though maybe Chernukhin's links to the Russian state might have raised some eyebrows. Then again, maybe the Suspect believes that every oligarch made their money through hard work or playing the lottery.

With all Tories, apart from Bob Seely, steering clear of difficult questions about oligarchs and sanctions, the session drifted to a close with John Penrose wondering what had happened to Brexit. Remember that? Johnson waved his arms and said we'd be seeing some benefits just as soon as Jacob Rees-Mogg got round to identifying any. Just don't hold your breath. Meanwhile, in the gallery, Prystaiko was anxiously checking his phone. Watching British politicians trade words had a limited appeal when his countrymen were fighting for Ukraine street by street.

Is Priti Patel vicious or stupid? It's a fine line for Ukrainian refugees

10 MARCH 2022

You can only imagine the *kompromat* that Priti Patel must have on the prime minister. As international development secretary in Theresa May's government, she had been sacked for going rogue with her own foreign policy. Her flight back to the UK from Kenya had been tracked every bit as closely as those made by Russian oligarchs today. That would have been the end of their career for most politicians. But not Priti Vacant. When Boris Johnson became prime minister, he promoted her to home secretary.

Then came the inquiry that found Patel guilty of breaking the ministerial code for bullying staff. Again, that should have been enough for instant dismissal. Instead, the Suspect ordered colleagues to protect 'the Prittster' at all costs. And so she survived to bumble on with her characteristic mix of incompetence and viciousness. Never more so than during the current war in Ukraine.

While most other government departments have upped their game over the past weeks, the Home Office has been a national embarrassment. While other European countries have opened their borders to welcome refugees, the UK went out of its way to make it almost impossible for any Ukrainians to reach this country: from not disclosing where most of the visa application centres were situated to making sure that those that were advertised were closed. Cue hundreds of refugees being sent on pointless journeys from Calais to Lille to Paris. And back.

None of this has gone down well with MPs on either side of the house. On Monday, Vacant had managed to give the Commons the wrong information about which visa application centres were open and where they were. One hesitates to say she lied, as she's genuinely stupid enough not to be across the finer details of what her department is up to.

The following day, she had gone AWOL during an urgent question about the Home Office's mishandling of the refugee crisis and let a junior immigration minister take the hit instead. Not that Kevin Foster seemed to mind. He went on Twitter to say that refugees could always take advantage of the Seasonal Agricultural Workers Scheme. Because picking fruit would help take their mind off the war.

On Thursday, Patel did bother to come to the Commons in person to answer yet another urgent question on refugees. Partly because she needed to reassure Tory MPs that she had at least some idea of what was going on; partly because this time she actually had something new to say. Though initially she did look a bit bewildered. She was under the impression – as most of us had been – that her sole role was to win favour with the Tory right by being beastly to foreigners, something at which she excels. Vacant couldn't quite get her head around the fact that all of a sudden every Tory backbencher – with the exception of Edward Leigh and Daniel Kawczynski – had gone soft on refugees.

But Patel gathered herself and ploughed on with the script. To make things easier, refugees with Ukrainian passports and family in the UK would now be allowed to apply for their visas online. Quite how this would work for refugees whose passports were lost or missing in the chaos of war, she didn't say. Nor how people without data roaming on their phones would manage to upload their visa applications. Even assuming they could still manage to charge their mobiles.

In any case, none of this could start until next Tuesday, as the Home Office needed to ensure all the necessary security measures were in place. Though given that the Russians had been planning the invasion for months, you'd have thought they had all the spies they wanted in place in the UK, without trying to pass a few off as Ukrainian refugees.

This was a start, said Yvette Cooper, the shadow home secretary. But why had it taken yet another urgent question to shame Patel into action at the dispatch box? And why was there still no clear humanitarian pathway for refugees without immediate family in the UK? For reasons best known to herself, Cooper went along with the security rhetoric. Almost as if Labour were terrified of being seen to be weak on immigration. Even though every other country in Europe was taking unlimited numbers of refugees without visas. And even though the majority of people in the UK are in favour of this country doing the same. Labour's response is to be a bit nicer than the Tories, but not too much.

Vacant, however, was a model of indignation. Contrary to appearances, she hadn't been dragged to the Commons. She had been gagging to be asked. It's just that she was a little shy and didn't want to appear too pushy. Patel: the model of modesty. And the Tories had a 'world-beating' record on refugees. This one again. No matter how often she and Boris repeat it, it doesn't make it true. The UK may score well in the narrow band of 'resettled refugees', but on refugees in general, we're hopeless. In proportion to population size, we barely make the top 20 of the most welcoming European countries.

Then came the moment that – temporarily at least – silenced the entire chamber. The visas and the bureaucracy were actually doing the refugees a favour, Patel continued. Because if we had an open border policy and let in as many as wanted to come, then we'd have a *Windrush* situation, where people couldn't prove they had leave to remain.

This was Vacant at either her most vicious or her most stupid. Because it wasn't the lack of paperwork that was the problem for the *Windrush* generation, it was the hostile environment that sought to deport people who were legally entitled to be here; the lack of full paperwork was just a means to that end. A hostile environment policy dreamed up by Theresa May in 2012 and slavishly pursued by Patel a decade later.

Most MPs were in a forgiving mood, though, ready to congratulate Patel on her baby steps towards humanity, rather than castigate her for the all-too-obvious shortcomings in her plans. There again, there was every chance that the home secretary would be back in the Commons to explain another policy disaster in the coming weeks. Time was on their side. If not on the side of those fleeing the war.

* * *

The pressure was well and truly back on Johnson with the revelation that the intelligence services had strongly advised him not to elevate Evgeny Lebedev – a Russian oligarch and son of KGB agent Alexander Lebedev – to the House of Lords. Despite the warnings, Johnson had done just this. A vanity peerage for a vain man. Lebedev never had any intention of taking part in British public life; he just fancied the title. And in return he would make sure that the newspapers of which he was the owner would give Boris an easy ride.

Soon, though, this scandal was subsumed by another. The Metropolitan Police had concluded the first round of its Partygate investigations and started issuing fixed penalty notices . . .

The Suspect becomes the Convict, but the 'Lion of Kyiv' is sure to keep lying

12 APRIL 2022

It had all been going so well. After his successful surprise weekend trip to Ukraine, Boris Johnson had been enjoying his newfound status as the 'Lion of Kyiv' during a few days off at Chequers. Then had come the news that the Metropolitan Police had now issued more than 50 fixed penalty notices (FPN). And that's before they had even got to work on the really serious parties. If only he had put the ruthless, forensic Christopher Geidt in charge of the investigation. Then no one would have been any the wiser about any of the parties.

Not that there had been any parties. The Suspect had always been very clear about this. In as much as he had ever been very clear about anything. First he had told parliament that he had been as furious as the rest of the country that staff at No. 10 could have been having parties that he knew nothing about. Then, when it emerged he had actually attended most of the parties he knew nothing about, he said that he hadn't been aware that the parties were parties. Because the presence of cakes, booze, trestle tables laden with food and empties littering the flower beds wasn't much of a clue.

Round about lunchtime, things got a whole lot worse, when Johnson discovered that he was one of the crims given an FPN. The Suspect was no longer the Suspect. He was the Convict. It was outrageous. Just because he had passed the law forbidding everyone from meeting up during lockdown, there was no reason to imagine that he was expected to obey the rules. Those had been for only the little people. The suckers. Narcissists like Johnson got to do as they chose. Theirs was a life governed by their own exceptionalism.

It hadn't helped that Carrie had also been given an FPN. Wilfred and Romy would just have to get used to the fact that both their parents were criminals. And he'd have to find out if Lulu Lytle had also been penalised, as she would be sure to add it to her bill. As it was, she deserved a £10,000 fine for crimes against interior design. Not that he would be paying hers or anybody else's, of course. Least of all his own. That's what David Brownlow was for.

The only upside was that Rishi Sunak had also been issued with an FPN. The chancellor had been in tears when he phoned. 'What shall I do?' he sobbed. 'Just pay it,' the Convict had replied. 'It's all right for you. You've got loads of dosh. You can afford it. And you'll probably find a way to offset it against tax in whatever country

– Mauritius, is it? – your family files their returns.'

Sunak had then gone on to have a meltdown about having lied to parliament about not having been to a party. What a baby. 'I was categoric about it,' he said. Whatevs. Personally, the Convict couldn't see what was so bad about having deliberately misled parliament. It was the sort of thing that he did the whole time, and none of the Tory MPs seemed that bothered about it. He'd always found that the best way of getting out of a lie was to double down with an even bigger lie. And if that didn't work, just keep lying until people got bored.

But if Rishi wanted to make a martyr of himself – imagine the absurdity of a cabinet minister being expected to have some principles! – then he could be his guest. The chancellor could learn the hard way that Johnson had the knack of invariably dragging anyone close to him down to his level in the end. As for the Convict, he wasn't going anywhere.

Instead, he would let some of his useful idiots fill the void. Thank God for Michael Fabricant and Nadine Dorries. While other Tory MPs and cabinet ministers were totally silent – it was as if the Conservative Party were totally paralysed with indecision: it's not every day your leader makes history by being the first prime minister to be found guilty of breaking his own laws – these two alone kept the faith.

Micky F managed to insult every doctor and nurse by suggesting they had spent most of lockdown pissed, while

Nad basically restated Boris's divine right to do what the fuck he liked. Nadine was a trooper. Even if Boris killed someone, she would find a way of making it the victim's fault.

But come 6 p.m. the Convict was ready to record a short television clip. He was deeply apologetic, he said. Though he didn't sound it. Rather, as he toyed with his toddler haircut, he seemed to blame the police for not having interpreted the law in his favour. In BorisWorld, ignorance of the law is a valid excuse, it seems. Johnson just wanted to move on. It would be wrong to resign now because of Ukraine. Though arguably the UK needs a leader with a strong moral compass more than ever these days. And it wasn't as if the UK didn't have a track record of replacing leaders during wartime. Not that we are at war.

Johnson was markedly less comfortable when facing questions. Could everyone just forget about the fact that he had lied so many times he had forgotten what he had lied about and had broken his own rules on multiple occasions? he begged. After all, he had lied in good faith because he had really, really believed his own lies. Honest. And if we could just ignore the fact that he is totally untrustworthy, he would get on with not dealing with the cost-of-living and energy crises.

I mean, he'd been at a party for only nine minutes – it's going down all the time; before too long he won't have been to it – so surely that didn't count. Well, fine.

Then what excuses would the Convict come up with in the future, when he was penalised for attending those parties that went on for hours and where everyone got thoroughly shitfaced? The other parties that Johnson insisted never took place? Boris shook his head. He would lie about that as and when the need arose.

* * *

With Johnson finding himself on the wrong end of newspaper headlines, he needed a distraction. And quick. So what better than a hastily contrived plan to send refugees to Rwanda, an idea that would be red meat to the right-wingers in the Tory party, who had been alarmed by the growing number of asylum-seekers and immigrants crossing the Channel in small boats . . .

Johnson the Criminal lays down the law for asylum-seekers

14 APRIL 2022

Humanity isn't the Home Office's strongest suit. But then neither is communication. Last week, Richard Harrington, the refugees minister, was asked by the broadcaster LBC if the government had any plans to offshore refugees to Rwanda. He replied with an unambiguous no. He had no clue where such an idea might have come from. No one in the Home Office had discussed anything like this with him. It was a non-story; scare tactics from paranoid liberals trying to discredit Priti Patel. Not that the home secretary needs any help. She never fails to discredit herself.

Cue 10 days later, and Boris Johnson was at a hangar in Lydd, Kent, to announce what he tried to convince a few bored service personnel and a handful of sceptical hacks was a new outpost of Butlin's in Kigali. A pleasure palace for refugees more than 5,000 miles away. In a country where the problem was well out of sight of British eyes. God forbid that any Brits might have to encounter desperate people fleeing war and persecution.

Some thought the timing was all a bit too convenient. After days of bad headlines about the prime minister's own criminality, a chance to move things on with a policy that would go down a storm with red-wall Tory voters before the May local elections and piss off just about everyone with a moral conscience. It was that cynical. All the more so because the Kigali hostel could well remain empty for years as civil rights lawyers take the government to court for acting illegally. The Potemkin Pleasuredome.

But the reality was that it was more like killing two birds with one stone. Sure, it was good to talk about something other than Partygate, but the Convict and Patel had genuinely been working on the deranged plan for months, despite the best efforts of civil servants to talk them out of it, and were finally ready to put their idiocy and cruelty on view. And still no one had thought to keep Lord Harrington in the loop.

Johnson started with the usual waffle. The stuff he needs to tell himself each morning so he can drag himself out of his bed and look in the mirror. Somehow he has to find a way of convincing himself he's a decent man, not some lying narcissist who will do and say anything to get him through the day relatively unscathed. So he mumbled something about Britain's fine history of openness and generosity to refugees.

Er, hello. We took just 9,000 children in the Kindertransport. And congratulated ourselves for that only because we hadn't taken any adult Jews who were fleeing Nazi persecution. And then we made almost no plans to take in any Afghan refugees last year after the US withdrawal and had to hastily scoop up a few thousand interpreters and other key workers at the last moment. And even then we seemed more interested in getting pets out of the country rather than people in fear for their lives. So, not so great. A quick reality check: the UK is the fifth- or sixth-largest economy on the planet and takes just 0.2% of the world's refugees.

Then the Convict got down to the nitty-gritty. He wanted to stop the trade in people-trafficking. But he didn't want to do it by making it easier for people to claim asylum in the country. At present, refugees are stuck in a catch-22. They can claim asylum only once they are in the UK, but the sole way to get here is illegally. Johnson didn't want to address that. What he proposed was that any asylum-seekers – including Ukrainians without a visa – who reached the UK without having been pushed back and drowned while crossing the Channel would be rounded up by the army and given a one-way ticket to Rwanda. Where they could rot while their applications were processed. And if they were cold, wet and frightened, then so much the better. That'll teach them not to come to the UK.

Then things just turned surreal. First the Convict tried to portray Rwanda as some kind of tropical human-rights paradise. Regardless of the fact that it was a dictatorship that the UK had condemned for human-rights violations. Then he tried to claim the programme would be a bargain. Ignoring the fact that some Tory MPs had estimated it would be cheaper to put all the refugees up at the Ritz. But he saved the best till last. The plan was necessary because he was a firm believer in the rule of law. From the man who has shown a spectacular disregard for it since he became prime minister. Keep those fixed penalty notices coming.

Johnson kept the bullshit going when it came to questions. He merely repeated that he was probably treating refugees with too much kindness. Britain would be overwhelmed with asylum-seekers desperate to be interned in Rwanda. Maybe he should try to make the new regime more punitive.

As for his own criminality, he merely smirked and tugged the toddler haircut. If it was all the same, he would fail to answer the questions sometime next week. He's taking the whole country for mugs. We have a criminal in No. 10, and he refuses to explain himself. The Tory wankocracy in overdrive. He also said Rishi Sunak was safe in his job. So that means he's toast. Rishi must be wishing he had the self-worth to resign.

About an hour later, we disappeared through the looking glass. Here we had Patel, as vicious as she is half-witted, in Kigali. Back in the 1960s, her parents had fled Uganda. Now she was proposing to send terrified refugees to a neighbouring country whose own citizens seek sanctuary elsewhere. Priti Vacant looked a bit glum as she read out all the positives of the programme but cheered up when she remembered they were all lies and that the refugees would be banged up in a hostel after all. This was her life's work, and she could die happy.

* * *

It wasn't just Boris Johnson and the Tories who were under pressure, though. It had been discovered that Keir Starmer had had a £200 curry with some of his aides while campaigning in Durham during lockdown. All of which was perfectly legal, but the Daily Mail *reacted as if this was the height of criminality. Every day, for more than a week, the paper devoted its front-page story – and several inside* pages – to Labour's Currygate. Anyone might think the non-dom owner of the Mail was upset that Labour planned to remove non-dom tax status. It didn't help that Starmer always seemed rather shifty when asked about it, rather than just giving the straightforward reply that it was a confected story from a desperate government. Starmer did eventually claw back the moral high ground by promising to resign if he was given a fixed penalty notice by the police – something Johnson and Rishi Sunak had not done.

In early May, local elections took place. The Tories were annihilated in London and did poorly elsewhere in the country. Not that you would have known it, as Robert Jenrick and Oliver Dowden – the Dumb and Dumber of the Tory party – were sent out onto the airwaves to say that everything had gone swimmingly. Jenrick managed to say he had been at his local Asda at five in the morning – the store later confirmed it had been closed – while Dowden claimed that no one had asked him about Partygate on the doorstep; instead, all anyone wanted to talk about were the enormous benefits of Brexit. Both concluded that losing so badly in London was a positive sign, because it meant they were alienating the metropolitan elite. Brilliant. The way to win elections is to lose them. Dialectical stupidism in action.

Elsewhere, the Rwanda plan continued to unravel, and various Tories were accused of sexual misconduct. It was almost enough to make you forget that everything else was falling to pieces. Almost.

Michael Gove causes havoc on breakfast TV – but at least he's not Priti Patel

11 MAY 2022

As a health warning about the dangers of taking illegal drugs, it couldn't have been improved. Quite who in No. 10 decided Michael Gove was the right person to front the government's morning media round was unclear. But it must have been someone willing to gamble that the minister for levelling-up would be more impressive than most of his colleagues, even if he was clearly off his head.

Unfortunately for the news anchors, they were somewhat obliged to take the overly chatty Gove seriously. It made for an excruciating couple of car-crash hours of TV and radio. First he was asked if Downing Street being the most law-breaking street in the UK during lockdown, along with Keir Starmer's offer to resign if fined, meant that Boris Johnson should do the decent thing.

The Govester started spewing drivel. The Convict had worked extraordinarily hard during the pandemic and had got most of the big calls right (really?), so he deserved a break. Regular all-night parties were the least that the prime minister should have been allowed by a grateful nation. Boris was born to be indulged. Kay Burley tried to get a word in edgeways, but Mikey was sure he was the most fascinating person in the room and just talked over her. Rushing on his run.

Even so, that proved to be the most sense Gove spoke all morning. Over on *BBC Breakfast*, he started speaking in silly voices. 'Oh, Big News story in capital letters,' he said, when asked why the Convict had insisted the government was going to do more on the cost of living if he hadn't really meant it. 'Calm down, calm down,' he added, channelling Harry Enfield's 1990s scousers in a terrible Liverpool accent, before wandering onto the set of *Good Morning Britain*, where he happily contradicted himself. When he caught up with the Michael Gove who had once said that reducing VAT on fuel would help the less well-off, he would be sure to give him hell.

He ended his trail of destruction on the *Today* programme, where he said that the manifesto promise of building 300,000 new homes a year was a load of old bollocks. Far better to build just one that everyone liked rather than a whole load that most people were indifferent to. Thank you and goodnight. Or good morning. Whichever it was – it's hard to tell when you've been up all night. He stumbled off to have a lie-down, oblivious to the havoc he had caused.

Still, at least the Govester had the excuse that he had been completely out of it. Priti Patel merely proved she was naturally that stupid as she opened the second day of the Queen's Speech debate in the Commons. Though, like many naturally half-witted people, she harbours the belief that she's actually very bright. So she smirked and patronised her way through what turned out to be a long litany of failure. Her speechwriter in the Home Office must be a secret Labour supporter.

Priti Vacant doesn't do nuance. She has only one mode of engagement, and that is to pick a fight. She's as vicious as she is vacuous. So she kicked off by insisting that the Labour Party were all either murderers, paedophiles and rapists or they had friends and family who were.

Having got her insults in early, she then got down to the nitty-gritty. Crime was up 18%, and prosecutions were down 18%. So the government was clearly doing something right. Yvette Cooper, the shadow home secretary, tried to intervene several times to point out that Vacant had got the wrong end of the stick, to save her from embarrassing herself further. But Patel just waved her away imperiously.

'Beating crime is the plan to beat serious crime,' Vacant announced. Though she didn't seem any the wiser about how it would work. 'We are going to stop people locking on to each other.' Everyone looked blank. Understandably.

She then went on to say she was going to spy on spies. Labour's Holly Lynch wondered whether she might want to start with the Convict, who had gone to Italy in 2018 to meet ex-KGB agent Alexander Lebedev. Patel ignored that and talked up the bill of rights – aka the bill of wrongs – which she hoped would prevent any kind of peaceful protest. People should just learn to be more grateful for everything the government was doing for them.

In reply, Cooper tried to explain to Vacant that she had just delivered a long suicide note on law and order on behalf of the government. This was too much for junior Home Office minister Kit Malthouse, who said that some crimes had gone down last year.

Cooper gently reminded him that it would have been a surprise if more people had been out on the streets robbing one another during lockdown. But not to worry, the figures had reassuringly picked up in the last few months. Malthouse looked as if he might burst into tears. Working for one of the dimmest people in government can do that to you. Still, at least he could console himself he wasn't as mindless as Tory Lee Anderson, who suggested food banks were a waste of space and that the poor would be better off in a chain gang. Vacant gave him the thumbs-up.

Over in Stockholm, the Convict was busy showing that he too embraced his government of all the talentless. As part of the new defence pact with Sweden, he happily signed up to an agreement that committed the UK to defending European institutions. From a prime minister who has undermined most European institutions and plans to ignore international law by triggering Article 16. Anyone would think he hadn't read the agreement he had just signed. Or was counting on no one else bothering to read the small print.

Sociopathy and stupidity worn like badges of honour in cabinet of all the talents

12 MAY 2022

On days like these, it's hard to know if the government is criminally insane or just criminal. Perhaps it's both. After telling parliament several times that the very idea of illegality in Downing Street was unthinkable, Boris Johnson was forced to admit that a further 50 fines had been handed out to members of his staff. That takes the total amount of fixed penalty notices well into three figures, with the police barely having begun their investigation into the 12 parties.

Other than the prestige of being the main resident of the most law-breaking venue in the entire country during lockdown, the only comfort for the Convict was that this time he wasn't among those who got collared by the Old Bill. Though his time will surely come again. Instead, it was just his underlings – who had gone to the parties only because they had been assured they were perfectly legal by the prime minister – who got a criminal record. Yet again, Johnson was the go-to man for laying down his friends for his life.

The news of the latest police fines appeared just in time for the arrival of Jacob Rees-Mogg and Oliver Dowden at the cabinet play-date in Stoke. Rees-Mogg greeted the news with a sense of rapture. The FPNs proved that the Convict was a man of utmost probity, and his only regret was that the police hadn't issued more of them. The Moggster is completely abject in his needy devotion. Dowden took one look at the waiting press mob and dived into a doorway. Of a bunker. It was some time before he guiltily did the walk of shame.

It was fortunate, however, that the fines had come too late for Johnson's LBC interview with Nick Ferrari, which had been recorded on his trip to Scandinavia the day before. Still, there was just enough time for him to say he didn't approve of a windfall tax, but if everyone else wanted one, he'd probably do it as he'd never given much of a toss about anything anyway. Though it would break his heart to knowingly do the right thing. He's a man whose convictions are strictly criminal.

Come the cabinet meeting, the best he could say was that he was delighted with the growth figures. An economy that is only flatlining is now apparently a Tory aspiration. By the end of the day, Johnson was blocking the publication of the intelligence services' advice he had received on Evgeny Lebedev. Advice he was obliged to hand over after a binding Commons vote. The Convict never did think any of the rules applied to him. Least of all these ones. His amoral sociopathy is his strongest asset. Having a conscience can drag you down.

Elsewhere in government, Northern Ireland seems to bring out the stupidest and the worst. First off, we had the attorney general, Suella Braverman, declare that she was perfectly OK with the UK breaking international law. Just as long as we didn't make a habit of it. Or even if we did, come to think of it. Braverman is just another apparatchik whose job depends on her willingness to do whatever Johnson wants. She likes to boast of how well qualified she is, but her actions only make you think it can't be too hard to become a top lawyer. No one has yet seen her approximate any cognitive ability.

Still, she keeps good company. Step forward Liz Truss, who declared she was feeling tetchy with the EU after Maroš Šefčovič hinted there would be a trade war if the UK decided to trigger Article 16. Our quarter-witted foreign secretary has yet to realise that the Northern Ireland protocol was negotiated and agreed by her own government just a few years ago in order to get a Brexit deal through the UK parliament. Somehow, in her barely functioning synapses, she has reconfigured events to an altered reality in which the EU duped the Brits into signing something against their will.

Then there was Conor Burns, a junior minister for Northern Ireland, who had gone to the US merely to post photos of himself on Twitter with a huge wad of paper, while observing that this formed the documentation now required to facilitate trade between the UK and the EU. Er, yes, Conor dearest. That's precisely what so many people were warning your government about back in 2016, when they suggested that Brexit wasn't a particularly good idea. Give it a year or so, and Conor might come to realise that leaving the EU has caused a 4% hit to the UK economy.

One member of the wankocracy not on view was Michael Gove. Though he should have been in the Commons to open the second day of the Queen's Speech debate on 'fairness at work and power in communities'. But after his cocaine binge the day before – any minister can fuck up one media interview, but it takes a certain genius to fuck up all five – the Govester was lying down in a darkened room, nursing his nose and on the phone to his sponsor. 'Thing is, Mikey, you still haven't quite got the hang of Step One.'

So it was the perfectly nice but wholly unremarkable junior business minister Paul Scully who was left to pick up the pieces of what passed for a levelling-up agenda. He was looking forward to the economy growing a bit, he said hopefully. Aren't we all? Though there is little sign of it. Nor could Scully offer any clue as to when it might happen. He also looked forward to the UK bene-fiting from a flexible workforce, though not quite so flexible as P&O's. And we'd be levelling up somehow or other at some unspecified time in the future. Thank you. I'm here.

Labour's Angela Rayner wasn't sure whether to take pity on Scully – it wasn't his fault he was so useless – or go for the jugular. So she pitched her response somewhere in between. A semi-detached contempt. Was that really it?

Where was the employment bill? The Tories were making no effort to disguise the fact that they had no interest in working people. Theirs was a miserable vision, whose highlight was bus passes for elderly people so they had somewhere to keep warm. An old people's crèche.

Next, they will be having gala dinners to open food banks. Tinned beans as finger food. Scrub that. They're already doing that, if they can get there in time before Lee Anderson closes them. Just another day in the life of a necrotic government. *Viva* the Twatterati. Lucky us.

* * *

Towards the end of May, Sue Gray published her full report. Boris Johnson seized on it gratefully. There was little doubt Gray had pulled her punches. She was a career civil servant, after all, who had spent a lifetime covering up other people's messes. Yes, there were some telling details in it – the wine stains, the puke, the brawling, the dodging out of sight of CCTV cameras at 4 a.m., the altered invitations – all of which suggested that everyone knew they were acting against the law. But there was no smoking gun. Or not one that could flush out a prime minister devoid of shame. Gray had even concluded there was not enough evidence to investigate the ABBA party in the Downing Street flat, despite the noise, the guests and the booze that countless people had witnessed. That some concluded Gray's report was damning is merely indicative of how widespread the rule-breaking was. When the Met came to issue more fines, it was the junior members of staff who took the hit. You know, the ones who hadn't been given access to top legal advice. In total, 126 fixed penalty notices were issued. Johnson claimed absolution and said the country now needed to move on. Some hope.

Rishi Sunak, meanwhile, was trying to keep his head down and deal with the cost-of-living crisis. For weeks, he had been saying there was no more money for further bailouts to help people with their fuel bills. Eventually, he was forced to look down the back of the sofa and, in yet another improvised mini-budget statement, concede that there was some money after all. He also did another U-turn. Having declared that Labour's plan for a windfall tax on the oil companies would not be feasible, he promptly introduced a windfall tax on oil companies. He even tried to make out it was all his own idea. The fact that Labour had come up with something similar long before him was entirely coincidental.

But Johnson couldn't postpone his day of reckoning indefinitely. After days of speculation, Graham Brady declared enough no-confidence letters had been submitted to trigger a vote.

Day of pleading and threats ends with Boris Johnson in post. Just about

6 JUNE 2022

Only last week, every cabinet minister was insisting that there would not be a vote of no confidence in Boris Johnson. That such an idea was pure media confection. Imagine their surprise, then, when they woke up this morning and heard Graham Brady announce that the number of letters needed to trigger a vote had been exceeded. Nice to have a government with its finger on the pulse. A fifth day of the jubilee celebrations.

Within minutes, the Convict had drafted a letter to all his MPs listing his achievements. Largely imagined. He had got all the big decisions right. Apart from the ones he had got hopelessly wrong. It was time to move on from Partygate. It was what the public wanted. Apart from those militant monarchists who had booed him at St Paul's. '**PLEASE** VOTE for **ME**,' it ended, with a liberal sprinkling of bold capitals. Not forgetting the PS that everyone who voted for him would be guaranteed a ministerial post in the next reshuffle. At this rate, the total number on the government payroll would be well over 300. Luckily, no one would be capable of doing the maths. No one became prime minister by underestimating the collective stupidity of their MPs.

Then came the threats. Anyone who didn't immediately tweet their support for the prime minister would be sacked from whatever job they happened to hold. Almost immediately, Liz Truss duly obliged. Even though she was almost bound to vote against him. She still imagines she's in with a chance of winning the leadership contest. Sketch writers are backing her all the way. For the lols. Rishi Sunak was next to tweet, even though he knows everyone hates him and that he's finished politically. But then he's a bit pathetic and has no self-worth.

Other cabinet ministers followed throughout the morning. Even Penny Mordaunt, though her support was decidedly lukewarm. Her focus was on the anniversary of D-Day. Remembering the sacrifices of others. Expecting Boris to sacrifice himself for the sake of the country and the Tories was clearly a non-starter. She also fancies her chances.

Priti Patel was the one refusenik. She still hasn't forgiven the Convict for depriving her of sole responsibility for deporting asylum-seekers to Rwanda. She misses the look of abject fear as people are put on the plane. But the overall message from the cabinet was that they were all completely shit and couldn't be trusted to take over from a man who wasn't trusted by the country.

A few of the rebels put their heads above the parapet. First Jesse Norman. Then John Penrose, Johnson's own anti-corruption tsar. What took you so long, John? Which bit of industrial-scale law-breaking did you miss? Lastly came Jeremy Hunt with his own leadership bid. Theresa May just purred quietly. This was by far her best day as an MP since becoming prime minister herself.

This was all too much for Nadine Dorries, who threw herself to her inamorato's defence. Jeremy was just a complete bastard. Worthless. And he'd completely fucked up the health service, which is why 150,000 people had died of Covid. A great start to Johnson's 'health week'. And could she just shout to the world, 'I LOVE BORIS!' It was completely unhinged. She has no idea that every time she speaks she creates another couple of rebels.

Every time the Convict is in trouble, he makes a point of phoning President Zelenskiy. To ask for advice from someone who is genuinely loved by his country. Today was no exception. It's turning into a very one-sided relationship. The Ukrainian president should start billing Johnson for therapy sessions. God knows what advice Zelenskiy gave him, but by 4 p.m., when Boris went down to address the 1922 Committee, he appeared to have completely forgotten that he was in deep trouble and needed the help of his MPs to bail him out of his latest fix.

There was a loud banging on desks as Johnson entered the Boothroyd room in Portcullis House – there always is: duplicity comes as second nature to most MPs – but rather less noise as he made his way out. No one was going to publicly say that Boris had lost the room, but it was far from clear that he had done enough to win back those intending to vote for a new leader. The never-shy-and-retiring Steve Baker was first out to speak to the media huddle. Enough was enough. The prime minister had broken the law and had to go. It's no more than any organisation would expect of its leader.

As the other MPs made their way to various corners of Westminster, Johnson's top spinner came to deliver the official verdict. An architect of chaos very much in the image of his master. It had been a complete triumph, he said. The MPs had fallen down to worship in front of their leader. Not that they had any choice, because there was no one worth having as leader instead.

This had been serious Boris, the spinner said. 'There had been a lot of detailed policy stuff in there.' Though, when pressed, he couldn't remember any of it. Details. Details. There would also be tax cuts. But he hadn't a clue what kind. More details. Details. He ended by saying that Boris really wasn't sorry for anything. Least of all his lies. And that the vote was pretty much a waste of everyone's time. Boris: a sociopath to the last.

'Who here doesn't get pissed? Who here doesn't like a glass of wine to decompress?' I put my hand up but was ignored. Boris would go to all the parties again if he had the choice. It was totally tone deaf. No recognition of breaking the law. Contrite Boris was last week's Boris. It was almost as if he had nothing but contempt for his MPs and was goading them to vote against him. An elaborate game of dare.

The queue to vote was a steady 12 metres long for the first hour, with almost every MP moaning at being made to wait. Ocado shoppers the lot of them. They were, though, surprisingly cheerful. Either they weren't aware their party was suicidal or death was a merciful relief. Douglas Ross had just jumped ship for the second or – maybe – third time. He's a man of flexible principles. But how could the Convict ever go into another election with all of his Scottish MPs at his throat?

Edward Leigh muttered something about Banquo's ghost. May came dressed in a ball gown. She means to party. Michael Gove insisted he had voted for Boris. So that's one in the 'no' column. Hunt chatted to me about his recent event at Hay. He reckons his talk with Rachel Clarke ended in a draw. He'd settle for a similar result today. Everyone had their phones confiscated at the door. No one trusts the whips not to demand proof of loyalty.

A rather troubled-looking Convict emerged shortly after 7 p.m., when the queue had died down. Perhaps it's finally dawned on him that his whole premiership has long since stopped being a joke. That his options are rapidly running out. That the populist leader is no longer popular and has nothing left to offer anyone. That he has even lost the support of a large number of his most myopic constituency: his MPs. He probably voted twice – once for and once against – just for old times' sake.

At 9 p.m. on the dot, Brady announced the result. 211 for, 148 against. As expected, the Convict had won the vote but lost the leadership. Worse even than the Maybot back in 2018. Johnson said he was going to hang on – he's a bad loser – but there is no coming back from this. It may be weeks, it may be months, but Boris is toast. And the Tories will spend the time fighting each other to the death. While the country is on its knees. At a standstill. What a legacy. Johnson must be so proud.

* * *

Things fall apart. Loyalists, like Nadhim Zahawi, tried to claim that Boris Johnson had won a great victory in the no-confidence vote. A great victory, as in had done worse than Theresa May and Margaret Thatcher. Both of whom had been forced to resign within a matter of days. The only real question was how long Johnson would hold on.

Things fall apart. As well as the train strikes – transport secretary Grant Shapps had tried to make out it was Labour's fault that the strikes had gone ahead; some day he might realise that the Tories had been in power for 12 years – the cost-of-living crisis continued to erode trust in the government. It had become increasingly hard for people to think of anything that worked better now than it did in 2010. On top of this, the Tories had suffered two crushing by-election defeats: to the Lib Dems in the normally safe Conservative seat of Tiverton, and to Labour in Wakefield.

Things fall apart. Johnson had allowed himself two final outings on the international stage: a last hurrah at the Commonwealth Heads of Government conference in Rwanda, and then the NATO summit in Spain. He made little impression at either. Upon his return, he found himself embroiled in further scandals. One involved his then girlfriend Carrie Symonds, whom he had tried to install as his head of staff when he had been foreign secretary. The other was over what he had known about his deputy chief whip, Chris Pincher, who was caught up in a sex scandal.

Things fall apart. You know things are shaky when even Oliver Dowden resigns as party chairman. The whole point of MPs like Dowden is that they will put up with almost anything. They exist to have no principles. When he went, we knew the game was almost up.

Boris takes a battering in what may be his last PMQs

6 JULY 2022

The Sky News helicopter hovered above Westminster, the constant thrum an insistent death knell for any incumbent prime minister. Down below, a steady stream of junior ministers and parliamentary private secretaries — many of whom were barely known even by their own families – offered their resignations, while many no-mark backbenchers wrote letters of no confidence.

When you've lost faithful toadies like Robert Jenrick and Tom Hunt, as well as 2019 red-wallers such as Lee Anderson and Jonathan Gullis, then the game is up. At this rate of attrition, Boris Johnson is going to have trouble filling all the available ministerial posts.

Inside the Commons, the Tory backbenches were paralysed by existential despair. There were just minimal cheers when the Convict arrived for prime minister's questions, and these only a reflex of collective memory. They weren't even sure what they were shouting for. That Johnson had repeatedly broken the law and lied about it, while they had just sat by and applauded? Or that the Rwanda Panda had given a job to a man he knew to be an alleged serial groper? So proud. So brave.

Johnson took his seat and smirked. It's what he does. A nervous tic. Even when the shit hits the fan, he can't help taking everything as a joke. The masochist in him loves the attention. Even when it's all negative. He'd rather people were still talking about him than ignoring him. It's about the only way he knows he's still alive. He looked to his right and left. There were Dominic Raab and the newly promoted Nadhim Zahawi, who had just spent over £20 billion in his first media round as chancellor. He could get to be an expensive habit. But both were fine as they were. Useful idiots. Loyalists who knew they would never get a job in any other government. Good thing they had no idea of the contempt in which he held them. No sign of Michael Gove. The ever-treacherous snake was bound to stab him in the back sooner or later. Just a matter of time. Well, sod him. They'd have to carry him out of No. 10.

Keir Starmer had one job. And he did it well. He was the best he's ever been at PMQs, honing in on the Convict's decision to appoint Chris Pincher, despite knowing of his alleged history of groping. He even managed to get in a couple of killer lines. The charge of the lightweight brigade. The sinking ships fleeing the rat. Johnson just did what he always does when under pressure. The default Boris. He lied. Not cleverly, but obviously. The sort of lie even a child wouldn't hope to get away with. He'd acted when he first heard of the allegations, he insisted. He hadn't. No one even pretended to believe him.

That was just the start of his troubles. Tory backbenchers Tim Loughton and Gary Sambrook called for him to go before he took the party any further into the sewer, but it was Sajid Javid's resignation speech that proved the killer. Javid is no natural orator – his chances of making leader are virtually nil – but he had a powerful story to tell. The Convict had lied to him. Had lied to everyone. Enough was enough. Doing nothing was no excuse; it was an active decision. The entire Tory front bench looked dead ahead, refusing to catch each other's eye. They were also busted. Nothing left but hollowed-out ambition. A cry of 'Bye-bye, Boris' accompanied Johnson's exit from the chamber.

Shortly before the start of the liaison committee meeting, Angus Brendan MacNeil was doing a poll of his fellow committee members on whether Johnson would turn up. Of course he did. It was never in doubt. His pride and vanity would not allow him to stay away. To do so would mean that he accepted the game was up. His denial was total. So what followed was one of the more surreal two hours of everyone's lives. Almost politics expressed as interpretive dance, with Boris the sole person in the entire room seemingly unaware that he was finished. That wasn't the only irony. If this was to be the Convict's last act as prime minister, it was to be a peculiar kind of hell for him. Johnson hates details, yet here he was being pressed on policy he knew little about and which he has no chance of implementing. Ukraine, the size of the military, education and road pricing would all be someone else's problem.

All the committee members acted as if they too were in a dreamlike state, only capable of connecting with reality by staring at their mobile phones for updates on the ongoing resignations. Huw Merriman took the performance art to new levels by posting his own letter of no confidence about 30 seconds before quizzing the prime minister in person. Stephen Crabb decided to update the Convict on the MPs who were quitting and ask who was left to fill the vacancies.

Labour's Darren Jones adopted an almost caring tone. This must be a painful moment, he said. This was too much for Johnson. The contempt and dislike he can take. What destroys him is the pity. The reminder of his own weakness. So he just rocked back and forth in his chair – primal, childlike – and smirked. Asked about something he had written concerning oblivion setting in, he could merely joke that it must have been penned by Cicero or Aristotle. Only he laughed. It was too much of a private grief.

Things turned darker when the subject switched to ethics and standards. The confidence visibly drained from the Rwanda Panda's face, highlighting the rings around his eyes. He tugged the toddler haircut, pulled faces and lapsed into near incoherence. He couldn't really answer anything. Truth and accuracy were a foreign country. He mumbled something non-committal about Pincher, appearing to blame the booze rather than the person. He was confused about Lord Geidt's resignation.

It ended with committee chair Bernard Jenkin asking if Johnson would rule out the nuclear option of calling a snap general election. The Convict just couldn't do it. There was always a 'yes', followed by a 'but'. He'd rather tear down the government. Tear the Tories apart. Anything but relinquish power. His whole life had been geared to becoming prime minister. He'd hang on, even if it meant appointing Dilyn the dog to the cabinet. Without the trappings of office, he'd be nothing. Goodbye to Lord Brownlow and dreams of a £150,000 tree-house.

Back at No. 10, a cabinet delegation – including Zahawi, soon to be the shortest-serving chancellor in history – gathered to tell the Convict it was over. Only the ever-deluded Nadine Dorries still believed in the Thousand Year Reich. Boris, meanwhile, hid in a fridge. Hoping everyone would just disappear. Hoping for just one more night in Downing Street. Waiting. Waiting. Waiting. Waiting on a miracle.

* * *

Finally. Enough was enough. Boris Johnson had run out of rope. The only question was, how gracefully would he go? Actually, scrub that. He was never going to go gracefully. This was Johnson. An entitled narcissist to the last.

The Convict remains true to himself with a very on-brand resignation

7 JULY 2022

It's hard to pinpoint the exact moment Boris Johnson knew his time was up. After all, he'd already outstayed his welcome by hours. If not days. If not weeks. If not months. If not years. But hearing that Chris Philp had resigned as digital minister must have come as a killer blow.

Ministers don't come more stupid or more loyal than Philp. There is literally nothing he won't do or say to

112

get noticed. To be loved. His neediness is matched only by his limitless appetite for humiliation. Without Philp, the Convict was down to the real dregs: Peter Bone and Michael Fabricant. Even he could see that wasn't going to fly.

After that, things unravelled quickly. More resignations. Michelle Donelan had come and gone as education secretary inside 36 hours. A record. She's destined to end up as a question on *Pointless*. Liz Truss had booked herself on the first flight out of Indonesia, while doing her bit by tweeting. For the good of the country, you understand. Not to start on an early leadership campaign.

Suella Braverman combined taking attorney-general questions in the Commons with her own leadership bid. Nadhim Zahawi couldn't make up his mind whether he was meant to be preparing his own leadership campaign or working on his joint speech with the Rwanda Panda on the economy. It was politics on acid. A Peppa Pig world, where all the usual norms are thrown off-centre.

But someone, somehow, managed to talk Johnson down briefly. A momentary break in his narcissism to get him to focus on the mechanics of his departure. Even as he was busy appointing some new ministers, on the condition that neither they nor he would do anything. A sort of first version of his resignation honours list, presumably. You dread to think who may appear on the second one. Welcome, Lord Dacre. Hello, Dame Lulu Lytle. There will be a race to save the wallpaper. The bits of it that haven't already peeled off the No. 10 walls. Saved for the nation. A remembrance of times past.

Long before midday, Downing Street was a media scrum, with everyone jostling for the best view. If this really was the end for Johnson, people wanted the best possible seat. This was a collector's item. The Convict had dodged a bullet so many times before, no one could be certain the greased piglet wasn't going to wriggle free again.

At one end of the street stood a few dozen No. 10 staffers, along with Joy Morrissey, Johnson's most loyal parliamentary private secretary. She looked lost in private grief. A true believer to the last. Loyal to the death cult. An anthem to futility. On the other side of the building, there was another small huddle. A sad group of the half-dozen or so Tory MPs who could be bothered to pay their respects. Andrea Jenkyns even shed a tear and appealed to the crowd for dignity. No one had ever cared that much about Johnson. It was almost touching. Almost.

At about 12.20 p.m., out came the praetorian guard of Jacob Rees-Mogg, Nadine Dorries and Carrie Johnson, with baby Romy in a papoose. Carrie looked surprisingly chipper, as if she was relaxed about the whole thing. Maybe she is. Maybe she too has had enough of it all. It must be exhausting having to remember what lies you are supposed to forget. Or maybe she was just pleased that Johnson had won a stay of execution, and she was going to be able to use Chequers for her long-delayed wedding party at the end of the month.

There was a round of applause from the devoted and the damned as Johnson walked out of the front door and approached the lectern. His opening words were drowned out by the serial protester Steve Bray singing, 'Bye-bye, Boris,' but it wasn't hard to get the gist. The Convict wasn't going to go down with any fake displays of piety. He was going to remain true to his narcissistic self. This was his show, and his essential message to the country was: 'Fuck the lot of you. I'm the best you're ever going to get.' An unusual approach, but very on-brand.

Previous prime ministers have departed with displays of emotion. David Cameron and Theresa May had been in tears, choked that their ambitions had not survived contact with reality. Johnson was peculiarly disengaged. Almost as if he was unbothered and was just enjoying the cameras. Any attention and all that. He was as careless with the office of prime minister as he was with everything else.

Or, more likely, he was in denial and had not yet processed that this was the end, and was gaming some way in which he might hang on. Maybe there would be a war. Maybe the Tories would do something so spectacularly stupid, like electing Braverman as leader, that they would beg him to come back. Maybe. Maybe. Maybe. It was telling that in his resignation speech he did not use the word 'resign' once.

The Convict began by listing his greatest triumphs. The Brexit deal that wasn't oven-ready. Flying to Kyiv twice. Not building 40 hospitals. Not levelling up. Coming out of the pandemic at about the same time as everyone else. Having the second-lowest rate of economic growth in the G20. He was a serial winner, and the Tories had been lucky to have him. He had been the best prime minister the Conservatives had ever had. And they had just tossed him to one side ungratefully. The herd mentality of a brain-dead mob. He knows how to make friends.

There was not a single suggestion that he might have been the author of his own demise. That telling lies for a living eventually catches you out. That breaking the laws you expect others to keep is never going to end well. That covering up sexual abuse scandals in the party and blaming groping on the alcohol and the victim was a very 1990s look. No, it was just that the Tories had lost their nerve and been ambushed by the media. Yup. The *Mail*, the *Sun* and the *Telegraph* have always been his sternest critics.

'Them's the breaks,' he shrugged. Grudgingly. And yes, he'd do his best to support the next idiot the Tories chose. Though his best might not actually be very much. Why would he bother to go out of his way for someone else? Especially someone for whom he had no respect. Which was everyone, really.

Johnson tugged the toddler haircut and scratched his arse one last time. Determined not to let anyone see that he cared. That his fragile ego had been shattered. He would survive, he told himself. Books and columns to write. Proper money. And he was sure he would find a way to ensure Lord Brownlow still stumped up for a £150,000 tree-house. Even if he didn't have a garden to build it in.

He sloped back into Downing Street. Dilyn the dog wisely gave him a wide berth. Maybe it was time for him to be rehoused too. Out on Whitehall, Bray was playing the *Benny Hill* theme tune. *La commedia è finita.*

* * *

It felt like the end of an era. Surely we could now rely on politics to return to something approximating normality? Think again . . .

As Tories queue up to fill the Convict's shoes, we are now officially in game-show territory

11 JULY 2022

You might say it's a long-standing Conservative tradition to suspend reality throughout the party's leadership elections, only the Tories have been struggling with reality for years. Just think. The Ukrainians voted for a comedian and got a serious leader. Three years ago, the UK voted for a comedian and got a sociopathic end-of-the-pier clown. Someone who visibly recoiled at the truth.

The whole country is now in urgent need of treatment for PTSD as a result.

Even so, we are now officially in game-show territory. Aka the Tory party having a collective orgasm as it exposes its deep dysfunction, with countless deluded halfwits deciding they want to be prime minister, while making promises they haven't a hope in hell of keeping. I mean, Rehman Chishti. Not even his family knows who he is. Why waste everyone's time? It's not as if anyone is going to bung him a cabinet post.

And Grant Shapps. You know the party is really screwed when Grant Baby is one of the more serious candidates. And his only promise – apart from the obligatory unfunded tax cuts – was that he could help get a few MPs re-elected. Because that's the big picture. The way to take the country forward is to make sure Chris Pincher's constituents vote for him next time round. That will do it. Things are so bad that Rishi Sunak's commitment to bankrupting the country marginally slower than any of his colleagues is looking quite attractive.

Still, we are where we are. So we might as well sit back and enjoy the shitshow, watching a ragtag collection of Tories crash and burn while competing with one another to appear the least competent. Hell, Wimbledon's over, the World Cup has been delayed until November, so we might as well get in the popcorn and look on the leadership race as this summer's entertainment. Sort of a third-rate reality show. Only with more laughs. And lies.

The fun began in the Churchill War Rooms in Westminster, where Steve Baker was launching his latest pet project, Conservative Way Forward. The ideal bunker for the bunker mentality. They will never take Steve alive. The CWF is not really a think tank, as no thinking is ever involved with anyone who aligns themselves to Baker's derangements. It's more a nostalgic journey back to pure Thatcherism, where the market and low taxes solve everything. The opening video, which somehow left Boris Johnson off the list of recent Conservative prime ministers, was pure *Little Britain*.

Baker's slogan was 'happiness through freedom'. Or something. It made the Bruges Group look like intellectual heavyweights. He was backed by the irredeemably dim Lord Frost, whose attempts to wrestle with the mind/body split has led him to attempt a full frontal lobotomy on himself. He now has no idea he was the man who negotiated the Brexit deal. He mumbled along in a monotone, while steadily losing his audience, who were suffocating in the heat. 'I'm excited,' he said. While flatlining.

Then came the first contender: the chancellor of the exchequer for the next 10 minutes or so, Nadhim Zahawi. It was painful. Nadhim is clearly totally unaware that the main reason he got the job was that the Convict was completely desperate and anyone with any self-worth would have said no. He was also virtually incoherent. Sentences were mangled and died without meaning. Whoever had told him he would make a good leader can never have heard him speak. Being marginally more familiar with word formation than Liz Truss isn't the vote-winner he might have hoped it was.

Zahawi first committed himself to abolishing planned tax rises immediately, seemingly unaware he was part of a lame duck administration that was prohibited from doing so. Like I said, not the sharpest. He then promised to cut yet more taxes and reduce departmental budgets by 20%. Nothing like taking a wrecking ball to the NHS and schools.

As the word salad continued, a young woman passed out in the heat. It was the most intelligent response of the day, though Tobias Ellwood, one of Zahawi's surprise backers, pushed a few people out of the way to offer his help. Not that he wanted anyone to notice, of course. Meanwhile, Nadhim just carried on spluttering. Oblivious to the drama. Oblivious to everything. Other than getting to the end. It had effectively been the shortest leadership campaign of the season. Even if he didn't know the game was up, everyone else did.

Suella Braverman was among her people – her tribe – and her appearance at the lectern was greeted with whoops and cheers. She began by saying she was totally signed up to cutting taxes – she didn't mention how she intended to fund this, but we can all play fantasy economics these days – before insisting she wanted to preserve the Good Friday Agreement by leaving the Northern Ireland protocol and the European Convention on Human Rights. Her grasp of the law is tenuous. Even for an attorney general.

It was fitting, she said, that we were in the Churchill War Rooms because it was thanks to Churchill we were having this leadership election. You could have fooled me. I could have sworn it was because the Tories were mired in sleaze and the party had finally realised the country had got fed up with Johnson's lies. She went on to say she hoped old people would do the right thing and not use too many of the NHS's services. 'I have a clear vision,' she said. There again . . .

The day's final launch took place in the private dining room of the Cinnamon Club, where Sajid Javid was making his appeal to the party. He wasn't going to go on about being a bus driver's son, he said, while going on about being a bus driver's son. Because going on about being a bus driver's son hadn't worked so well for him when he stood for leader three years ago. And he didn't have any flash videos or promo materials. Though he did have a glossy manifesto that didn't look as if it had been knocked up in the past five days.

We need a leader in the national interest, he went on. Though he couldn't quite explain why it took so long for him to realise that the Convict was a wrong 'un. Nor why he had been happy to support tax rises that he was now determined to undo. 'The best prime ministers surround themselves with people cleverer than them,' he declared. Javid, though, appeared to be surrounding himself with complete lightweights. Sitting in the front row were Chris Philp, Rachel Maclean and Robin Walker, who can't boast a neuron between them.

'Only two candidates are really fit for this contest,' he ended. Without telling us who those two might be. Though presumably none of him, Braverman and Zahawi, who appeared to have done their best to disqualify themselves. But the rest of the week would almost certainly reveal some fresh idiocies. On with the motley.

* * *

Right from the start of the leadership contest, there were two front-runners: Rishi Sunak and Liz Truss. Sunak was a former Goldman Sachs hedge-fund analyst, married to Akshata Murty, the daughter of an Indian billionaire, and far richer even than the Queen. He had been chancellor under the Johnson regime – he had been given the job when Sajid Javid had resigned after the prime minister had sacked his special adviser – but was deemed to be suspect by Tory party loyalists as he was thought to have plotted to remove Johnson.

Truss, the foreign secretary who was thought to embody the libertarian right of the party, was the clear favourite. There had been no doubts about her loyalty to Johnson. She had been far too busy having photos of her driving a tank in Estonia uploaded to her Instagram account to have any time for disloyalty.

I was ready for Rishi, but he wasn't ready for me

12 JULY 2022

An email arrives from the Ready4Rish! media team late on Monday afternoon. Would I like to go to Rishi Sunak's leadership launch at the Queen Elizabeth II conference centre the following morning? Hell, yes. I can't think of anything better. I am Ready 4 Rish!

Only it turned out that Rish! was far from Ready 4 me. An hour or so later, I got a reply. Thanks, but no thanks. The venue was already at capacity. Another time. Maybe. Or maybe not.

Several hours later, I heard from a colleague on a more Tory-friendly paper that he applied to go long after I'd sent my email and had been welcomed in with open arms. I wrote back to complain and give Sunak's media team the chance to reconsider. Instead, they doubled down. They didn't seem bothered that they had lied to me about the room being full. I wasn't invited. End of.

Things got worse when I found out that two sketch writers from other, less critical papers were let in on the nod. And they hadn't even bothered to go through the process of applying. The room was crowded but far from at capacity. There was space for plenty more. Including me.

So it was personal. And the front-runner to be our next prime minister was running scared. Rish! was so thin-skinned he couldn't even take a bit of criticism or gentle piss-taking. And at heart was against a free press. So much for the man who claims to love democratic values.

Shortly before Rish!'s event went live, Grant Shapps announced he was abandoning his own campaign – a loss to entertainment, if not the country – and would be backing Sunak. He was greeted with loud whoops by enthusiastic apparatchiks waving 'Ready4Rish!' placards. Sunak kept rather more silent about his endorsement from Norman Lamont. No former chancellor really wants the backing of the architect of Black Wednesday. There again, you wouldn't have thought you would want to make a show of having a total psychopath as your right-hand man. But Rish! happily allowed himself to be introduced by the angriest man in politics.

'Vote for Rish!, FRIENDS,' Dominic Raab snarled menacingly. If you didn't, you'd have no one to blame but yourself. And the body count could rise exponentially. Rish! had the courage of his convictions, he went on. That's why he had implemented tax cuts to the tax rises he had recently introduced.

Shortly afterwards, Sunak peeked over the lectern. He wanted to have a grown-up conversation. Though not one that might involve anyone talking back at him. This was to be strictly a one-way conversation. About how we had got where we were. A three-year trajectory in which he had no recollection of ever being involved. It's astonishing how bad the economy has got in the week since he resigned as chancellor. We were doing just fine till Nadhim Zahawi came along.

Then Rish! went for the party-loyalist pitch. Boris Johnson had been a great, great leader. So great that Sunak could no longer remember why he had plotted to get rid of the Convict. It had just been a coincidence that the Ready4Rish! website had been registered back in December. Yes, he had written a resignation letter, but that had been just for fun. There were no serious points of disagreement over the direction of government. That had just been a slip of the tongue. Yes, Boris was a flawed individual, Sunak went on. But then so was everyone. Even him. Hell, which one of us hasn't lied to everyone we've met, cheated on every woman with whom we've had a relationship and broken every law in sight? Just traditional Tory values. And he was the man with a plan. Though he couldn't tell anyone what it was, other than that he would continue to carry on as normal. Because that was obviously all working just fine.

Rish! took a quick question from a Tory councillor – 'I don't know how to love you. You complete me' – and then a couple more from the media, which he made no effort to answer, before scurrying off to count his votes.

Like Rish!, the launch had been slick and vapid. Much ado about nothing. Just the sort of vacuity that could have been designed to please the hollow neediness of Matt Hancock. Within hours, he had tweeted his support with a moody, oh-so-sincere video. The Gina look of lurve. The vote they all wanted. The game-changer. Some men have greatness thrust upon them . . .

Just down the road on Millbank, Tom Tugendhat was having his own campaign launch. One from which potentially unfriendly journalists weren't banned. Unlike Rish!, he is open to criticism.

Everyone was half expecting Tug to abseil from the ceiling of the four-storey atrium – he's never worn his military background lightly – but instead he appeared from behind a giant sign saying 'Tom'. Like a game-show host. Polished with freshly cut hair. Tough times call for etc. . . .

Tugendhat has one distinct advantage over all the other leadership contenders: he's never been in government – indeed, he's often sounded more like the opposition – and is not contaminated by sleaze, incompetence and failure. Unfortunately, this might not be a positive for Tory MPs, who tend to trust only other people's lies. So his pitch of clean-living dependability, stitched together with plenty of extended military metaphors – did you know he had been in the army? – may have fallen largely on deaf ears. But Tug did go into a lot of policy detail – he claimed to have discovered a £100 billion stash of dead money he was happy to spend (me too) – but there was something rather distracted about his performance. Either it was too rehearsed or his mind was elsewhere. He almost committed news by saying an election was essential, before later clarifying that he meant an election to decide on the last two in the contest, and then he just suddenly drifted away midway through the Q&A. No one could quite believe he had left.

The third launch was that of the eccentric Kemi Badenoch. Her pitch was that everyone should be allowed to do pretty much as they pleased. Why bother with a police force when people can just go and shoot criminals themselves? And hospitals were just for wishy-washy liberals. Things were much better when people with cancer just shut up and died.

In an ideal world she would burn down the entire country and start again. Her biggest bugbear was the woke warriors. What was wrong with bullying in the workplace and the odd racist joke? Predictably, she went down a storm. Michael Gove applauded enthusiastically.

Meanwhile, Liz Truss's campaign was being derailed even before it had formally started. Liz fancies herself as the new voice of change. Just why that might be is anyone's guess. But then she is entitled to be delusional: she's never knowingly had an original thought. Which is why she is the natural person to be the Boris continuity candidate. But even she recoiled when Nadine Dorries and Jacob Rees-Mogg endorsed her. The backing nobody wanted.

Truss perplexes her fellow MPs with a robotic pitch for Tory leader role, upstaging the Maybot

14 JULY 2022

I eventually found confirmation of my accreditation for the Liz Truss launch bash in the spam folder. Perhaps my email was trying to tell me something.

It was again standing room only for the last of the Tory leadership campaign launches, and the mood was flat. There was no buzz, no momentum. Just a feeling of going through the motions. That Liz Truss was less a person, more an idea whose time had been and gone, if indeed it had ever existed. That as foreign secretary she had already been promoted well beyond her talents. And being prime minister was a fantasy. An aberration. A category error.

Still, at least the air con was working. So it wasn't all bad. Before the start, a gaggle of MPs hung around at the front of the room, as if unsure what they were supposed to be doing or, more importantly, why they were doing it.

Things had moved at lightning speed. A week ago, being the continuity Boris candidate had seemed like a viable pitch. A keeper of the sacred flame for *Daily Mail* readers. But things had moved on. Now the Convict was not even an irrelevance. That might have been survivable. Rather, he had turned actively toxic. Distance from the poisoned legacy is a necessity. Which is a problem if, like Liz, it's just about your only selling point.

Nadine Dorries, Thérèse Coffey and Dehenna Davison took selfies together. Perhaps they'll look back on their pics in five years' time and ask themselves what they were doing in the summer of '22, the year the Tory party went even more bonkers than usual. There must have been even more drugs flying around than they remembered. The seat reserved for James Cleverly went unfilled. Perhaps he had come to his senses and run for the hills.

It was left to Kwasi Kwarteng to make the introductions. He kept it short and sweet, before welcoming Liz to the podium. Only she didn't turn up. We waited. And waited. And waited. It was all getting very awkward. There were even a few sniggers. Then eventually Liz made it to the front. She had literally got lost after walking through the door. It wasn't the best of starts.

Truss looked blankly straight ahead, her body rigid with fear, and started misreading her script. She stumbled over words and left pauses mid-sentence. If she was hoping to sound statesmanlike, then it misfired badly. She was robotic, brain-dead, managing to make Theresa May sound engaging, animated and personable. A laugh a minute. If this is the prime minister the country has been waiting for, then we have all been lobotomised.

'I delivered on Brexit,' she began. Which was news to those still waiting for the government to show there had been any benefits. Or perhaps she just meant she always knew Brexit was a bad idea – she voted remain in the referendum – and was thrilled to have been proved right.

Still, Truss was big on delivery. She said so, over and over again. She had delivered all the good things that people liked and hadn't delivered the things that people didn't. These had all been delivered by someone else. The Convict. Or the snake Ready4Rish!. Not that she was going to bad-mouth any of her colleagues. She was bound by collective responsibility. Loyal to the last. Though she was quite happy for her supporters to trash-talk anyone. Only that morning she had been devastated to hear Lord Frost accuse Penny Mordaunt of not taking her job seriously enough. This from a man who has spent the last six months running away from his own Brexit deal. That level of denial will get you a long way . . .

What the country really wanted was a modern Conservative Party, Truss concluded. This left most people nonplussed. Because if they did, what was she doing standing for leader? All that she could promise was a bit more of the same. Though even she could sense the writing was on the wall, that she was haemorrhaging support. All she really had to offer was the one thing that no one wanted: the Convict. So she mumbled on, until no sounds at all came from her mouth. A rabbit in the headlights.

As she left the room, she headed for . . . the window. The launch may have been bad, but it hadn't been that much of a disaster. Eventually, as she walked through a cluster of camera tripods, a snapper took pity on her and directed her to the door. *Classico*. She couldn't find her way into the room and she couldn't find her way out. I've never loved her more. Obviously, she would be a total disaster as prime minister, but she'd be great material for the sketch. Someone worse than the Maybot. Sign me up for Team Liz.

Elsewhere, other candidates were also on manoeuvres. Tom Tugendhat was living his best life. He seemed to have realised he had no chance of making it to the last two and was just hoping to get as far as the TV debates, where he would have a chance to shine. He'd visibly relaxed over the last two days. He now takes the piss out of his near-constant references to his military background and is enjoying being courted by the other teams eager for his vote, like a prom queen. Welcome to the next cabinet.

Rish! was in full-on defensive mode on the *Today* programme. He seemed taken aback by how many people disliked him. And that was just his colleagues in Westminster. He didn't even let the BBC broadcast video footage of his appearance in case he was caught crying. He now trusts no one but his teddy.

Suella Braverman went batshit mad, with a hostage video on Twitter in which she blew up the entire Good Friday Agreement by promising to pull out of the European Convention on Human Rights. Might as well go down fighting, I suppose.

Shortly after 3 p.m., the results of the second round of voting were announced. Sunak and Mordaunt were both comfortably ahead. Truss was desperately scrabbling to scoop up any spare votes from the other right-wing candidates, while Simon Clarke, one of her minders, tried to persuade everyone things were absolutely on track . . . Anything to avoid the humiliation of not making the final two.

Kemi Badenoch was comfortably in fourth. Going nowhere, but happy enough with that. Result. Tugendhat had lost votes but had made it to the TV debates. Result. Braverman was out. One less nutjob for the country to worry about. Result.

The Tory leadership debate: desperate as a political sales pitch, worse as entertainment

15 JULY 2022

Hard to believe, but it's only just over a week since the latest Tory psychodrama began. It feels longer. So much longer. Time bends and stalls when you're in the parallel universe of a Liz Truss speech. She leaves audiences begging for a lethal injection. The other leadership contenders are little better, registering mostly as absences on the space–time continuum. Negative energy.

But we are where we are, and we have moved on to the first of the televised debates, a weird game show where the only audience that counts consists of the 360 or so

Tory MPs who may or may not be watching. The rest of us are merely voyeurs, having no say in which two clowns will still be standing by next Wednesday evening. This is apparently how the UK likes to choose its prime minister these days. Very on-brand for a country that has become a laughing stock.

First, though, there was a warm-up Zoom hustings on the Conservative Home website. Think a weekly meeting of junior sales reps. Just infinitely more boring. It's almost as if no one really wants the job. Which would actually suit the rest of us.

The only highlights were the flatlining Truss forgetting to unmute herself – she's at her most articulate when you can't hear her – and Ready4Rish! suggesting that his biggest fault is his perfectionism. I'd say a far greater fault was being in charge of an economy that is predicted to have the second-lowest growth in the G20. If he was a real perfectionist, he'd have made sure we were bottom. The other three – Penny Mordaunt, Tom Tugendhat and Kemi Badenoch – said nothing memorable at all. Which meant they easily came out on top.

Come 7.30 p.m., the Fatuous Five were lined up like *The Weakest Link* in the Channel 4 studios, with Krishnan Guru-Murthy as guest presenter. And what a dismal 90 minutes it was. Desperate as a political sales pitch, worse as entertainment. On this showing, the gene pool of talent in the Tory party isn't even a puddle. A great night for the Labour Party, if no one else.

The first question was one of trust. 'I've delivered the impossible,' said Truss, blinking rapidly and sounding like a superannuated 1980s Amstrad computer. As AI goes, Liz makes the Maybot look human. At least Theresa May was vaguely aware there was a reality from which she was detached. Truss is just some free-floating atoms in search of a personality and ideas. Virtually nothing she said made any sense. And if it did, it was entirely accidental. She is everyone's preferred comedy candidate.

Not that Rish!, Mordaunt or Badenoch could come up with any better reasons for why they should be trusted. Resigning from the government months – if not years – after the rest of the country has concluded that Boris Johnson is a lying, narcissistic sociopath isn't going to win anyone any brownie points. Tugendhat won the first applause of the evening by shaking his head and saying the Convict was dishonest. He went on to quote *Harry Potter*, and thereafter chose to play the part of the outsider. The wise younger man who was outside the system and who could afford to tell the truth. Not that it mattered much, as he is going to be out of the contest on Monday.

Nor did anyone pay much attention to Badenoch, after she had had her five minutes kicking lumps out of Mordaunt over the culture wars, as she too isn't a bona fide contender. So most of the rest of the debate consisted of Liz fantasising about uncosted tax cuts and trying to sound human – next time out, someone should restore her to her factory default settings – and Mordaunt sounding surprisingly wooden and clueless. Someone should teach her to smile and not talk in banalities. She even forgot her own promises to cut tax. Just trying not to screw up on live TV is setting the bar a little low for a wannabe prime minister.

All of which left the hopeless Rish! sounding like the voice of experience and the only person you might conceivably trust with running the country. Because the rest were no-hopers or out of their heads on Mogadon. Terrifying, really. Still, we can only hope that Tory MPs are stupid enough to coalesce around Liz. After all, we're fucked regardless. So we may as well go down with a laugh.

Shapeshifter Liz Truss on a roll as version 3.0 hits Tory sweet spot

21 JULY 2022

Listen to Liz Truss for long enough and she'll tell you she's been on a journey. The inexorable rise of a girl who went from a rough Leeds comprehensive to front-runner for next Conservative prime minister. Via a brief spell in the Lib Dems. We all make mistakes.

Examine the journey more carefully, though, and it begins to look even more remarkable. The human flotsam that just happens to have been carried downstream towards the doors of No. 10. A journey undertaken without any ideas or purpose other than to allow her adapt to her surroundings and rise to the top. The failures have been spectacular, yet also spectacularly successful. Each time, she emerges into a more powerful iteration. Samuel Beckett could only stand back and applaud. She is literally living his dream.

Take version 1.0 of Radon Liz. She's a gas, but she's inert. This was back in the early days of David Cameron's leadership. No one was more socially liberal than Truss. No one ever hugged a husky tighter. Or embraced austerity harder. As and when required.

This Liz was also an ardent remainer. I can remember meeting her in the spin room of a televised debate during the referendum campaign. She bent my ear at length about how Vote Leave was based on lies and that remain was going to win at a canter. No sweat. No bother. That was probably the first time I seriously entertained the idea that the UK was going to leave the EU. Her reward for failure was promotion.

Radon Liz 2.0 turned out to be a passionate leaver. Far more so than many people who had supported Brexit all along. It wasn't that she now reckoned what was done was done, there was no going back and we just had to make the best of it. It was that remaining in the EU was wrong. A thought crime. A mortal sin. This was the Truss who draped herself in the Union Jack for photographs at every available opportunity. Who was never happier than when cosplaying Margaret Thatcher in a tank. While the economy also tanked. This version was also rewarded with ever more governmental baubles.

The newest version, Liz 3.0, is almost incomprehensible. She has slid so far through the looking glass to the Tory right that in some parallel universes she appears to have adopted Marxist economics. Dialectics have never been so confusing. She both reveres Boris Johnson's memory, saying she wouldn't have changed a thing, yet trashes the record of the government. Her prescription for getting the economy back on track is to reverse the national insurance hikes and cut personal and corporation tax. How she would do this, she hasn't said. Right now, it's enough just to talk in riddles.

It is exhausting, though. To keep up with Radon Liz's journey, you have to be able to run fast. She is the anti-ideologue. The anti-conviction politician. Not so much a set of ideas looking for their natural home as vaulting ambition in search of some ideas. Any ideas. If you don't like hers, she's got some others.

Because here's the thing. Truss is a *tabula rasa*. A dodgy 1980s computer with a screen that is permanently buffering. Someone capable of reinventing herself almost at will. And it just so happens that every time she needs some new ideas, she comes up with a set that exactly mirrors those that are needed to enable her to rise still higher in the Tory party. It's one hell of a coincidence.

Imagine one person having that much luck. It's almost as if she doesn't believe in anything at all. The ultimate shapeshifter. 'Tonight, Matthew, I will be whatever you want me to be.'

For reasons not entirely clear to anyone, Truss has struck paydirt with version 3.0. It's all but a certainty that her journey is now complete. No one is calling the next seven weeks a pointless extended coronation yet, but we're not far off that point. Radon Liz's latest incarnation has hit the Tory members' sweet spot. Partly by not being Rish! – there are plenty who will never forgive him for betraying the Convict – but mainly by telling them what they want to hear.

Were she a bit brighter, she too would be amazed that so many people could forget that Rish! didn't increase public borrowing and increase taxes because he's a social-ist. He did so because the country was falling apart in a pandemic. But when you're on a roll, you're on a roll. And Liz is living her best life as the prime-minister-in-waiting. So much so that she's almost relaxed. As relaxed as AI gets.

Her interview with Nick Robinson on the *Today* pro-gramme passed off with few alarms. She even found her way into the building and navigated her way out without having to call security. A vast improvement on her launch event the previous week. And she even managed to talk the usual bollocks without sounding too robotic. Close your eyes and you could almost imagine she was human.

She knew her plan for unfunded tax cuts wasn't inflationary because Patrick Minford had told her so. This was the economist who had forecast that Brexit would increase GDP by 7% and that food prices would fall. Bring on the Nobel Prize.

Later on Thursday afternoon, Radon Liz was at Little Miracles, a charity for children with life-limiting and other disabilities, and looked quite at ease. She must have made countless visits like this as a constituency MP. She chatted to the kids for a while about the hassle of being followed around by the media, looking pointedly at the collection of sketch writers. But there was kindness and laughter in her eyes. She can at least see the absurdity of someone like her becoming prime minister. And she does believe in a free press. Unlike Rish!.

Truss then moved on to the parents and listened as they shared their experiences. Afterwards, I asked two of them, Wendy and Brian – neither a Tory voter – what they thought. Nice enough, they said. Though the proof would be in the delivery. If Truss were to spend proper money on social services, that would be a first.

By then, Radon Liz had moved on. She just had time to say she was all in favour of a new royal yacht, provided it was funded by Tesco, and that she was Labour's worst nightmare. Wet dream more like. But she's entitled to her delusions. And with that she was off. Job done. It had been the quintessential Liz experience. Charmingly superficial. Little Miracles would still be short of funds, and the parents would still struggle to get the services their children needed. But, more importantly, Truss would be in Downing Street. She left as she came. Without a trace. On-brand to the last.

Tory hustings: a fresh circle of hell where we don't even get to enjoy Rish! and Radon Liz fighting

28 JULY 2022

Welcome back, my friends, to the Show That Never Ends. The Tory leadership contest is only just into its third week but it already feels interminable. Timeless, even. As if it's almost impossible to imagine life without it. First we had a series of unedifying debates, in which Liz Truss and Rishi Sunak – with occasional contributions from three other, long-since archived contenders – picked fights and traded fantasies with one another. Now we have entered a fresh circle of hell. Twelve hustings where Radon Liz and Rish! each face an hour's worth of questions from party members, one after the other. So we don't even get the pleasure of seeing them disagree with each other. Rather, they do battle to feed the delusions of the 160,000 or so Tory members who are the only voters that count for this particular election with ever more far-fetched right-wing policies. If you can call them that.

We began with an event hosted by LBC's Nick Ferrari in front of an audience of 1,400 at the Centenary Pavilion, opposite the football ground in Leeds. Not more than a long stone's throw from the Roundhay school Truss attended while she was growing up in grinding middle-class poverty. Fed on a diet of beetroot quiche. It's a wonder she can now read and write. Let alone that the school failed her so badly that she went on to do PPE at Oxford.

Just like Rish!. Fancy that. His only connection with Leeds is that his constituency is in the same county. So he knows all about the hassle of trying to get planning permission for a tennis court, swimming pool and gym. Just one of the hardships of being worth three-quarters of a billion. He feels the country's pain.

Or not. It was Rish! who won the coin toss and got to go first in making a 10-minute opening pitch from a platform in the centre of the auditorium. He did so without notes, but came across like an empty vessel. Davos man, full of slick superficiality. Completely oblivious to the fact he had been in government and was responsible for the dire straits in which the country found itself.

'I'm having the time of my life,' Sunak began. Well, that's nice. Because millions of people are struggling with the cost of living and using food banks. But as long as Rish! was having a good time, all was well. He went on to make a joke about his skin colour that died on its feet. Thank you and goodnight. He'll be here all week. Sadly for us, he'll be here for the next five weeks. Though that gag should be dumped from his next 11 gigs.

We then got the imaginary backstory about how his parents hadn't had two Mogadon to rub together at their Southampton pharmacy. But he loved this country for what it had given him. Which is why he wanted to stop other refugees getting here. Rish! had done his homework on the priorities of the Tory members. He ended by talking about honesty – he couldn't explain why it had taken him so long to realise that Boris Johnson was pathologically unable to tell the truth – and the need to rebuild the economy and reunite the country. He said this with no sense of irony. Or responsibility. Time and again he paused for applause that never came.

Radon Liz also spoke spontaneously without a script. Or as spontaneous as a late-1990s computer with obsolete software can manage. Often she seemed to stop mid-sentence. Not because she couldn't remember how it was meant to end, but because she seemed to think she had already finished. It made for a staccato 10 minutes. Not that the audience seemed to mind as Truss did a whirlwind tour of soundbites. Her time as a local councillor. Northern Powerhouse Rail. Don Revie. Standing up to Putin. Anti-wokery. All got applause. She may be awkward but she had done her homework.

After a short interval, Rish! reappeared, this time to be interviewed for 15 minutes by Ferrari and the audience. The LBC presenter didn't pull his punches, but

Sunak was well prepped. Up to a point. His panicked U-turn promise to reduce VAT on fuel bills that was un-Conservative last week was now a well-considered, time-limited policy. Hmm. Margaret Thatcher would have done exactly what he was doing. They might as well be soul siblings. Hmm. He hadn't stabbed Boris in the back. He had been totally cool about Boris lying about parties and ignoring allegations of sexual assault; he had just had a difference of opinion on the direction of the economy. Hmm. He even voiced his enthusiasm for grammar schools. Yes, it was that bad. The applause was almost audible at times.

Things didn't improve much when Truss got her turn under the spotlight. She claimed that she was public enemy no. 1 of President Putin – apparently, she is the most feared woman in the world – and she too insisted she was a blood sister of Maggie. After that, everyone seemed to tune out rather. It was all just a wee bit flat. Dull, even. But for all her weirdness, Radon Liz was the one who charmed the audience most. Imagine that.

Rish! must be in despair. The boy with the golden touch, to whom life has effortlessly bestowed everything on which he sets his heart, is going to be denied. The Tory members have spoken, and they just don't like or trust him enough. And the rest of us will be lumbered with Radon Liz as prime minister. There is no coming back from the hubristic road to perdition. We can only forget our patriotism and succumb to satire. Sit back and enjoy the ride. So we beat on, boats against the current, borne back ceaselessly into the past.

Finally, the Truss vs Sunak psychodrama comes to an end – for now at least

31 AUGUST 2022

Finally. This is the end, beautiful friend. The end. Well, let's hope so. For now at least.

In the absence of the government doing any actual governing, we've been forced to endure the tedium of a drawn-out Tory leadership contest. A niche psychodrama for the 160,000 people allowed to vote. One with very little actual drama, as we've all known who was going to win from the moment MPs reduced the candidates down to the final two. Given a choice of a halfwit with half an idea and a flatlining ideologue with no actual ideas, the Conservative members were always going to vote for the most hopeless. There's even less to Liz Truss than meets the eye.

But all mediocre things have to come to an end, and the six weeks of hustings finally limped to a close in London. Not that anyone cared. It was possible I was the only one watching. It certainly felt like it. There was not even a hint of celebration about the proceedings. No sense of excitement at a new beginning. Rather, just relief at the absence of chronic pain. Still, at least it's not as if there's been anything much going on that's more important than the leadership contest. Like cost-of-living and energy-price crises. Or a war in Europe. Otherwise the last few months might look very much like a dereliction of duty.

As it is, this government is no more! It has ceased to be! It's expired and gone to meet its maker! It's a stiff! If you hadn't nailed it to the perch, it'd be pushing up the daisies! Its metabolic processes are now 'istory! It's kicked the bucket, it's shuffled off its mortal coil, run down the curtain and joined the bleedin' choir invisible!! THIS IS AN EX-GOVERNMENT!!

Take the prime minister. Please. Anywhere. You'd have thought that Boris Johnson might have wanted to use his last two months in office to shore up what was left of his already tattered reputation. But no. His main achievement has been to make sure he used up most of his holiday allowance. Though most people would be asking, 'Holiday from what?' as it's not as if the Criminal has done much to be proud of.

Then there's the chancellor of the exchequer. The crème de la crème of futility. Which is quite the achievement: there's been tough competition to see who is the most useless cabinet member. But Nadhim Zahawi has been on a mission not just to do nothing, but to be actively seen to have done nothing. So every week he has been sure to let everyone know that he hasn't done anything. Now he's even nipped off to the US to let everyone know he isn't doing anything

Over at Wembley, Gyles Brandreth was trying to warm up the crowd for the last hustings. But even the permanently chipper smooth talker couldn't generate much enthusiasm. Though he did say he loved the Tory party for what it had done to the country. Hmm. Not sure the country feels the same way.

Then we got the deathly dull Iain Duncan Smith and Michael Gove trying to explain why they were backing Liz Truss and Rishi Sunak respectively. IDS merely put himself to sleep, while the Govester looked washed-out, as if on the comedown from a cocaine binge. He especially wanted to thank Johnson. For having been so corrupt that even the Tories had had enough of him.

Then came the two main players. Both were in their comfort zones, having been here and done it many times before. There isn't a question they haven't been asked, and they have their shtick off pat. Well, almost off pat in Radon Liz's case. She still sounds surprised if she makes it to the end of a coherent sentence.

As well she might. She is an intellect- and charisma-free zone. She mumbled about her grinding middle-class poverty and the UK being an 'aspiration nation', and continued to activate the culture wars, before she was asked by LBC's Nick Ferrari to explain what she was doing. It wasn't fair to call the government a 'zombie government', Radon Liz insisted. Because that implied the government had been asleep while doing nothing. In fact, it had been very much awake while doing nothing. There was a big difference between dozing and actively choosing to do bugger all. That was us told. And she would go and visit Ukraine. Probably during the Labour Party conference.

Ready 4 Rish! was slightly more chilled than on previous outings. He seemed less brittle and was less willing to openly criticise his opponent. Perhaps he knows the game is up and has relaxed a little. Playing the long game of waiting for Truss to screw up and trying to pick up the pieces in a couple of years' time. Or maybe he'll just head for the hills with his billions. Mind you, despite all the practice, he's still none the wiser as to why inflation spiralled to record levels while he was chancellor.

What cheers were on offer all seemed to be headed Rish!'s way. Some reward for his slightly greater competence. But not enough. All the polls suggest that Radon Liz is a certainty to become the new Tory leader on Monday. What on earth have the rest of us done to deserve her?

Radon Liz romps home in a pyrrhic victory

5 SEPTEMBER 2022

O brave new world, that has such people in't. Or not. William Shakespeare clearly had never imagined a clusterfuck on this scale. Given the state of the country right now, he would be in need of a long lie down. It would take more than a few prayerful tweets from Justin Welby to sort this one out.

On the road outside the Queen Elizabeth II conference centre, a few environmental protesters glued themselves together, while Steve Bray competed with a group of evangelists to provide a backing track. Some things never change. Just inside the main entrance, James Cleverly held court. The meeter and greeter with a smile for everyone. A man at peace with himself. Someone who knew he had backed the right horse.

In the foyer, Iain Duncan Smith wandered around in search of a camera to say something to. He's not fussy. No day is complete without him having recorded some dull opinion for posterity. Over in the corner, a grinning Liz Truss shuffled herself into a lift, accompanied by Thérèse Coffey, who is tipped to become health secretary. There was no sign of Rishi Sunak.

The excitement was almost excitement. No one was expecting any surprises. All the polls conducted over the past two months had indicated that the leadership contest would be a protracted coronation rather than an election. So those Tory MPs who had bothered to walk over from Westminster were only really there for the hell of it. And to be seen. It never hurts to look as if you've always backed the winner. Or, in the case of Dominic Raab, a vocal Sunak backer, to kiss goodbye to the rest of his political career. A Truss government isn't all bad, then.

Shortly after 12.30, the lights went up, and Andrew Stephenson, the Tory party co-chair, took to the stage. The Conservatives had been in good voice and good strength during the hustings, he said. He must have been watching a different election campaign from the rest of us. He then thanked Boris Johnson for . . . being Boris Johnson. It seems to have been long forgotten that the Convict had been the architect of his own downfall. That he had broken the law, protected sex pests and lied and lied and lied. Now he is a latter-day Tory party saint. For the first time, the applause felt genuine. Just weird. The Tories were electing a new leader while still grieving one they themselves had deposed.

'I'd like you to welcome Liz Truss and Rishi Sunak,' Stephenson said in winding up. Truss bounced in. Sunak, not so much. He looked as if he would rather be any-where else than at the scene of his final humiliation. He also seemed confused, as if he still couldn't work out why he had lost to someone so obviously less competent. He had been ready to be leader. How come no one had been Ready 4 Rish!? There was no logic. No sense. You only needed to listen to her staccato, robotic voice to realise just how useless she was. The country had already worked her out. A new poll showed that the Labour lead grew by seven percentage points when people realised Radon Liz was in charge of the Tories.

In a nice twist, most of the humiliation was reserved for Truss herself – almost all of it of her own making.

First, though, came the announcement by Graham Brady, the always-pleased-with-himself chair of the 1922 Committee, that Truss had won. Of course she had. We didn't need to be told that. But it was a victory so small, so pyrrhic, that there was no glory.

IDS punched the air. He was no longer the most disliked Tory leader of all. That was quite some title for Liz to live down to. It wasn't just the entire country and two-thirds of her own MPs who didn't want Truss; it was over half of the Tory party membership. Of a possible 170,000 votes – assuming all Tory members are actually alive – Radon Liz had secured just 80,000. But that was apparently enough to make her the UK's next prime minister. Good luck to us. Democracy moves in mysterious ways.

Then came the speech. If you can call it that. More a word salad. Imagine it. You've known for two months that you're going to win. And all you've got to do is make a five-minute acceptance speech. Just something anodyne and uncontroversial. Something that proves you're at least semi-sentient. Yet all Truss could come up with was a mumbling monotone that would have been booed at a fringe meeting at a Tory party conference.

'I think we have shown the depth and breadth of talent in the Conservative Party,' she began. Really? Are you mad? What it's really shown is that the Tories are a spent force. And that they are scraping the barrel in their search for a new leader. What were the chances of finding someone worse than Johnson? Actually, quite high, considering the diminishing gene pool.

Truss then went on an amnesiac's tour of Boris highlights. 'You are admired from Kyiv to Carlisle,' she said. Yup. And hated in Scotland and Northern Ireland. And, actually, in Carlisle, which has just elected a Labour council. There was an awkward few seconds' pause as Truss waited for applause. Eventually, a few Tories put her out of her misery and obliged.

The rest of the speech was even more pitiful. Some achievement. She was going to deliver. And deliver. And deliver. She had no idea what. Nor, indeed, any comprehension that she had been in the cabinet since 2014 and might have been expected to deliver in the intervening years. The clockwork ran down, and Radon Liz slurred her way to a stop. There had been nothing about uniting the country. Nothing on the cost of living. Just a vague hope she might win the next election in 2024, if Labour refused to take part.

It could hardly have gone any worse. You could see panic in the eyes of some Tory MPs. They had somehow imagined that Truss might miraculously transform into the coherent, plausible leader they had been promised during the campaign. Yet here she was, flatlining before their eyes. If she lasts a year, it will be a miracle. Then we'll all be back in the QEII centre to anoint someone even worse.

* * *

Just a few days into Liz Truss's premiership, the Queen died. She was 96 years old. Immediately, the country went into a 10-day period of mourning, and normal parliamentary business was suspended. It was a time for Westminster to show its better side, and MPs rose to the occasion.

Politics gives way to history as news from Balmoral reaches parliament

8 SEPTEMBER 2022

It was a moment impossible to forget. A time when icy shards of reality forced their way into the national psyche, and politics had to give way to history. A time we all knew would one day come but which had somehow still caught us unawares. The death of the Queen was always something for a tomorrow. Tomorrow and tomorrow and tomorrow.

The first sign that anything was wrong came early on in the energy debate in the House of Commons. It was about 12.15 p.m., and Keir Starmer was replying to the prime minister's opening remarks. A continuation of their disagreement at prime minister's questions the day before over whether the government should impose a windfall tax on oil and gas producers to part-pay for the £150 billion guarantee on energy costs. A necessary and urgent argument, the outcome of which would affect people for years to come. Then, in an instant, it became a news-in-brief.

Nadhim Zahawi entered the Commons and hovered hesitantly behind the Speaker's chair. He then had a few words with Lindsay Hoyle, before edging his way along the government front bench to sit down between Liz Truss and the chancellor, Kwasi Kwarteng. His arrival initially provoked a few raised eyebrows from the opposition benches – was it possible that last week's chancellor was better briefed on energy costs than this week's chancellor and had come to update the prime minister? – but nothing more. Starmer pressed on, oblivious to the distraction, asking why previous Tory governments had done so little for solar, onshore wind and nuclear energy.

Zahawi passed Truss a note, and the pair began an intense conversation. Then the prime minister seemed to send the chancellor of the Duchy of Lancaster away, as if she had asked him to get more information. The debate continued, with Theresa May talking about the benefits of home insulation. She never could pick her moments.

Minutes later, things became more frenetic as Zahawi returned. People had put two and two together. Zahawi was a royal conduit after all. He went back to Truss to update her further, before returning to the Speaker's chair. He passed a note down the Labour front bench to Angela Rayner. She nodded and informed Starmer, who immediately left the chamber for a few minutes.

Meanwhile, the press gallery emptied. The rumours had started. The Queen had died. The Queen was dying. For once the rumours were on the money.

Truss appeared rooted to the spot, as if unsure of what to do. Of all the things she had dreamed of doing in her first few days in office, this wasn't one of them. Should she stay or should she go now? This was well above her pay grade. Except it wasn't. You could sense her telling herself to get a grip.

The rest of those in the know were just grateful the Queen had lived long enough to accept Boris Johnson's resignation. The last thing the country needed was a narcissistic prime minister who would make a monarch's death all about him. Starmer returned to his place, his expression giving nothing away.

Hoyle clutched a note of his own, anxiously waiting for Buckingham Palace to release official confirmation of the rapid decline in the Queen's health. When it came, he interrupted the SNP's Westminster leader, Ian Blackford, to make a short statement. 'I know I speak on behalf of the entire house,' he said, 'when I say that we send our best wishes to Her Majesty the Queen, and that she and her family are in our thoughts and prayers at this moment.'

After that, the Commons all but emptied. All noise and passion spent. For most MPs, a row over how the energy price cap would be paid for could wait another day. And those that did stay, like the Lib Dem leader, Ed Davey, admitted that their hearts were no longer really in it. Starmer and Truss left together, deep in conversation. This could be one of the less dysfunctional relationships between party leaders.

Truss returned to No. 10. First to tweet her sadness about the Queen, then to tweet about the energy price cap. Even on a day like this, she couldn't quite bring herself to accept that her big policy announcement had been overshadowed. Come the winding-up speeches, most of the front benches had returned to the Commons. There were a few nervous jokes – received with forced laughter – but no one was really paying attention. Just filling in time. Awkwardly.

When the debate ended, everyone gradually disappeared, knowing that something seismic was about to happen to the country, but with no idea what form the upheaval might take. The Queen had somehow always seemed immanent. Now she was flesh and blood in a state of imminence. Nothing for anyone to do but wait. There would be no miracle. Waiting, waiting, waiting.

After an afternoon of time suspended, in which the minutes seemed to loop back on themselves, the waiting was finally over shortly after 6.30 p.m. The Queen was dead. Half an hour later, a visibly emotional Truss spoke to the nation from Downing Street. Several times her voice caught on her words as she tried to capture the scale of the loss of someone who had been queen for longer than most of us have been alive and had helped to shape the direction of the country.

It was the end of a second Elizabethan era, and the beginning of one as yet unknown. As yet undefined. A period of crushing uncertainty. A pillar of our lives had crumbled. There was, perhaps, too much of Truss herself in the speech. We didn't really need to know that the Queen had been an inspiration to her and that it had been nice to see her on Tuesday. But at least she was trying to connect with the country. Something she has never yet managed to do.

This was a long way from Tony Blair's speech about Princess Diana, one in which the Labour leader caught the mood of the country and made a common grief felt heard. But it was far better than it might have been. The Queen is dead. Long live King Charles III.

Starmer pitch perfect on love and grief as Commons meets to pay tribute to Queen

9 SEPTEMBER 2022

Death takes us to unusual places. Who would have imagined that Boris Johnson could have reinvented himself as the voice of the nation? Or that Theresa May could turn out to be a gifted after-dinner speaker, with a nice line in gags? Or that the Met Office would decide to stop weather-forecasting for the next 10 days? We can all just get wet instead. As a mark of respect. It's what the Queen would have wanted. Apparently. Cancel culture.

After a minute's silence at noon, a packed Commons met to pay its own tributes to the Queen. To try to find the words the rest of us couldn't. To explain why a death that had been so anticipated had still come as such a profound shock. To make sense of the deep affection so many people felt for someone they had never met. Someone who for almost all her 96 years had kept her real self private to allow everyone else to impose their own needs and truths on her. The Queen had been whatever we wanted her to be.

It fell to Liz Truss to open the speeches. The best that could be said was that she was serviceable. Then again, it was never going to be any different, even if she had had more than three days in the job and had had more than passing contact with the Queen. The prime minister is not in touch with her own emotions, so how can she possibly connect with the nation's? She can only report her feelings, not experience them. So her grief inevitably feels second-hand.

Not that she didn't say all the right things. Truss echoed Churchill, describing the Queen's death as 'stilling the clatter of modern life'; she declared that the Queen had more than fulfilled the promise she had made to the country on her 21st birthday; she joked about James Bond and Paddington; and she looked to the future with thoughts of the new king. A new Carolean age.

But it was all somehow flat and profoundly unmoving. Unintentionally deaf to the public mood.

Keir Starmer was pitch perfect. Emotionally and verbally literate. When he spoke of love, you felt it. He understands grief. That when we are grieving for the Queen we are allowing ourselves to grieve for ourselves. For the mothers and grandmothers we have lost. Or never even met. For the hopes and dreams that will never be fulfilled. For the family that remains out of reach.

The Labour leader gets the Freudian subtext. Death's psychological meaning. That no matter how we may try to fill the gap of someone's death, part of us will remain inconsolable. Which is how it should be. As that is how we perpetuate the love we do not want to let go of.

At times, Starmer sounded spiritual – almost religious – as he talked of the capacity for the Queen to dwell with us in our pain. Almost as if he was inviting us to make the comparison between the empathy of a monarch and the coldness of an uncaring government. He was so powerful, so convincing, that even the Tory front bench nodded along when he told us she was the person to whom we turned for comfort during the pandemic. She was a leader we could trust.

There was no chance Johnson was going to miss out on a chance to make his own tribute. Even if he wasn't going to bother to brush his hair or find an uncrumpled suit. Why break the habit of a lifetime for his first return to the Commons since he was kicked out of No. 10? These are the occasions he lives for. He may have been a disaster as a prime minister, but he can write and deliver a speech. More than that, what made him unsuitable for No. 10 makes him a great speaker. Like all narcissists, he suffers from a deep wound to the psyche. One that will never heal. So when he speaks from that wound, as he did here, he allows us to feel our own wounds.

Johnson unashamedly acknowledged the love he felt for the Queen. Unlike so many others, he talked in specifics rather than generalities. It was psychologically impressive. Though, as so often, it did all come as a stark contrast to how he had behaved. His staff had partied on the night before Prince Philip's funeral. He himself had lied to the Queen over the prorogation of parliament. Here was the classic Johnson mind–body split. The man who believes his motives to be pure, yet whose stock-in-trade is personal advantage and betrayal.

It was ironic that the next person to speak was Harriet Harman, the MP in charge of the privileges committee that will ultimately determine whether Johnson has to stand down as an MP. But now was not the time for point-scoring. Rather, she was gracious enough to congratulate Johnson on his speech, before going on to extol the Queen as a role model for women.

The big surprise was May. She had predictably started off disconnected and without affect. Monotone, dull and boilerplate. Going through the motions you would expect of a former prime minister. Service, duty, war record and longevity. The Queen didn't just know most of the world's leaders; she also knew their fathers. The Queen had touched her, she said. Though you would never have guessed it from the way she spoke.

Then she told three cracking anecdotes and didn't screw up the punchlines. Not even once. Who knew? Most unlike her. The Commons loved her. As much for the relief as anything. Johnson had made them feel too much. And most MPs don't like that. They prefer to operate as insentient beings. May allowed them to release the tension with laughter.

After that, many MPs began to drift away. All that had needed to be said had long since been said. Though that didn't stop many from queueing up to repeat themselves. MPs can never resist the sound of their own voices. Even when the most moving sound is silence.

Pageantry and absurdity abound as the King comes to Westminster

12 SEPTEMBER 2022

Sail on, O Ship of State! . . . You'd have thought that King Charles would have wanted a little down time. A little me time. A time to grieve his mother privately and to accustom himself to his new role as head of state. But constitutional monarchy allows no rest. There are procedures and protocols to be observed. Preferably with as much pageantry and absurdity as possible. Brits like history to come as costume drama.

So on Monday morning the new sovereign came to Westminster Hall to receive the condolences of both houses of parliament and make his first speech to them as king. And, in fairness, if you're going to do this sort of thing, there is nowhere better to do it. The 900-year-old hall is genuinely awe-inspiring – it makes the Commons and the Lords look tawdry – and has been a pivotal scene in British democracy. Our history has grown up around it, the physical intersection of the monarchy and the people. It's also where Charles I was tried. Though this probably wasn't the day to bring that up.

The band of the Royal Household Cavalry played the 'Eriskay Love Lilt' as MPs and peers made their way to their seats. Even Jeremy Corbyn was there, having missed the meeting of the accession council on Saturday, despite having been invited. Perhaps it had been a busy day down on the allotment. Keir Starmer, Rachel Reeves and Angela Rayner all arrived together. Liz Truss came in alone, almost unnoticed.

Someone with a sense of humour had seated Theresa May next to Boris Johnson. May pulled her hat down over her right ear so she couldn't catch a glimpse of him by accident and studiously ignored him. A crumpled and dishevelled Johnson – he couldn't even be bothered to make an effort for a state occasion like this – had to make do with some small talk with Suella Braverman. The shortest of short straws. Still, be grateful for small mercies. At least the ceremony took place before Johnson had been given the chance to demean it with his resignation honours list.

Shortly before 10 a.m., one of the doormen made a brief housekeeping announcement, ending by urging everyone to enjoy themselves. Though not too much. Then eight Yeomen of the Guard with giant spears processed up the central aisle, their spurs echoing on the stone floors, followed by a decidedly elderly and sweaty group of Gentlemen at Arms in floppy hats. Only in Britain. Next up was the Speakers' procession, led by Lord McFall, the Speaker in the Lords, and ending with Lindsay Hoyle.

Having made it up to the south end of Westminster Hall, the Lord Great Chamberlain – who invents these titles? – scurried back down to the other end to meet King Charles and Camilla, the Queen Consort. He had a bit of a wait as Charles hadn't even left Clarence House. Presumably, the delay had some massive constitutional significance rather than just being a failure to synchronise watches.

Once Charles and Camilla were in place, both Speakers made their addresses on behalf of their members. Their voices briefly brought us back to the 21st century. McFall grew up in Dumbarton, the son of a caretaker, and left school at 15; Hoyle grew up in Lancashire, the son of a

Labour MP, Doug Hoyle. Both men expressed their sadness at the death of the Queen and how difficult it must be for the new king at such a time. But they also tactfully, but firmly, articulated the expectation that Charles should treat parliament in the same way as his mother had.

Hoyle mentioned the ceremony the Queen had attended in 1988 to celebrate the 300th anniversary of the 1688 revolution. It may have seemed odd, he said, to mark a revolution with an address to the Queen, but those revolutions had protected people's liberties and created a stable monarchy. King Charles laughed awkwardly. He didn't seem entirely sure if he had been given a welcome or a warning.

Then it was Charles's turn to reply. He began by quoting Shakespeare. Like the other Elizabeth before her, his mother was a 'pattern to all princes'. He went on to talk about the physical marks left on the parliamentary estate to celebrate her visits to it over the years: the sundial, the fountain, the stained-glass window. His message was clear. The Queen had known her place. And he did too. The will of parliament was paramount. He wouldn't be rocking the boat.

After a quick rendition of 'God Save the King', the ceremony was done and dusted. All in well under half an hour. The more obsequious MPs and peers bowed and curtseyed – Michael Gove would have prostrated himself on the floor if he had been given the chance – as the royal party made its way back down the aisle. Others just enjoyed the spectacle, while wondering what the hell it had all been about. The machinery of constitutional monarchy in progress? The continuation of hundreds of years of history? Or just a nice day out for everyone, to remind them of their places. Your call.

* * *

With the end of the 10-day period of mourning, parliament returned to normal. 'Normal' meaning 'chaos'. Liz Truss, it seemed, was on a mission to undo almost every Johnson policy . . .

Tories usher in their brave new world of half-arsed fantasy

22 SEPTEMBER 2022

Liz Truss isn't going to die wondering. She's only been prime minister for just over two weeks, most of which she spent touring the country in mourning for Queen Elizabeth II, and already she's ripped up large chunks of her predecessor's agenda. It makes you wonder how she ever managed to agree with a word Boris Johnson said. I guess ambition takes you to some dark places. No matter. Fiscal rules are for wimps! National Insurance contributions are to be nixed! She's been surprisingly active for someone whose normal delivery tends towards the comatose.

The latest U-turn is on fracking. The 2019 Tory manifesto committed the party to a moratorium until such time as the science indicated it could be done without causing earth tremors. But that was so three years ago. Needless to say, the science hasn't changed at all, but that's not good enough for our Librium Liz. She thinks it ought to have done. So she's had a look at the science and decided that the science has got it wrong. What's needed is new science. One that agrees with her. And guess what? She's now redefined the science and we're all systems go. The power of magical thinking.

It was left to the business secretary, Jacob Rees-Mogg, to explain the change of heart in answer to an urgent question from the shadow climate change minister, Ed Miliband. The Moggster was in his element. He's never happier than when indulging his 19th-century fantasies. If he could bring back coal mining, he would. Anything to escape from reality.

There was a brief hiatus, though, as Rees-Mogg couldn't find his script. Hardly surprising, as he didn't seem to have one. All he really had to say was that fracking was back on the agenda, whether people liked it or not. Like Librium Liz, he seems to be under the delusion that all you have to do is bore a hole somewhere in an area of outstanding national beauty and you get unlimited supplies of gas. Enough to lower the price to a matter of pennies and end global reliance on Russian gas.

Miliband treated Rees-Mogg as if he was a halfwit. Most people do these days. Long gone is the time when MPs were impressed by his faux politeness and smug self-confidence, poured into an oversized undertaker's suit. Now people see him for the needy fraud that he is.

What was he trying to prove? asked Miliband. There was almost no chance of any of this going ahead. Most Tory councils won't give planning permission for a garden shed, let alone a fracking site. And even if they did, it would change nothing. The gas price wouldn't fall, and it would just alienate voters everywhere. It was nothing less than a charter for earthquakes. What happened to the Tory commitment to renewables?

Rees-Mogg merely shrugged. People were far too hung up about earthquakes. What was wrong with a bit of seismic activity? It never did any harm to San Francisco. Well, apart from in 1906. We should all get used to some vibrations. How would we know it wasn't safe unless a few people had died?

The Tory MPs Mark Menzies, Greg Knight, Scott Benton, Ruth Edwards and Paul Maynard were all furious at this casual trashing of the manifesto and sought reassurance that the government was still sticking to its promise that nothing could go ahead without local consent. Rees-Mogg pointedly did not answer this. You can never trust local people to come to sensible decisions. It would be far better if the drilling companies tried to bribe a few choice residents.

Give us a break, Rees-Mogg pleaded. 'We've only been in government for two weeks.' Er, make that 12 years. Besides, he suggested, most of the anti-fracking protests had been funded by Putin. And this coming from someone who was part of a Brexit campaign tainted by Russian influence.

At least there was less revisionism taking place in the health secretary's statement on her plan for the NHS. Mainly because Librium Liz never had a plan for it in the first place. Other than to make it slightly better than it currently is now. Somehow or other. She'll be furious when she discovers who has run it into the ground. But she has at least chosen her new health secretary wisely. Because when you've got no ideas, who better than Thérèse Coffey? A woman of no imagination and no great brain. But someone who can be relied on to come up with some nonsense on the back of a cigar packet.

Sure enough, Coffey did not disappoint, coming up with – in the absence of a plan – a memory game. A was for Ambulance. B was for Backlog. C was for Care. D was for Doctor. And E was for total fucking Eejit. Poor Thérèse. She didn't realise how shabby and half-arsed her ideas were. She didn't seem to even realise that she had moved the goalposts from people being able to see a GP in 48 hours under Labour to a fingers-crossed two weeks under Librium Liz. And, she said sternly, people could move to another GP who also wouldn't be able to see them, if they had no luck with the first one. Failing that, they could do everyone a favour and die.

Did Coffey really imagine setting some more targets that wouldn't be met was the answer? Thérèse looked miserable. Because it turned out that's precisely what she did believe. Truly, we are screwed.

* * *

During her leadership campaign, Liz Truss had promised to make her close friend Kwasi Kwarteng chancellor of the exchequer, in return for his support. Now it was time to see if he could steady the economy as he delivered his mini-budget . . .

Kwarteng throws UK on sacrificial altar of Trussonomics, where only bankers win

23 SEPTEMBER 2022

Kwasi Kwarteng. What a guy! On Monday, he put the fun into funeral with a few gags at Westminster Abbey. On Friday, he put the fizz into fiscal with an event – we would call it a budget, were it not for the chancellor having gone out of his way to make sure the Office for Budget Responsibility couldn't supply any figures to fact-check his economics – that was so high and wild we may never see another like it. To infinity and beyond! A mini-budget that was anything but mini. Faith-based casino economics on which he'd bet the bank. The biggest tax giveaway – primarily to the rich – in 50 years, while increasing government borrowing to record levels. Time was when Labour used to get it in the neck for uncosted public borrowing. That's now so last month.

All you have to do now is believe, and everything will be OK. It's the new economics for Brexit Britain. You want growth, you get growth. And if you don't, then it will be everyone else's fault for talking Britain down. The country has just been turned into a laboratory experiment for a plan dreamed up by the right-wing Institute of Economic Affairs. Kwarteng does believe. Primarily in himself. His self-confidence is remarkable for a man of relatively ordinary talents. Someone who had always got by with a few glib words. Who could talk the talk but had never been asked to walk the walk. Now was his time to put up. To throw the country on the sacrificial altar and keep his fingers crossed that he hadn't blown it. To boldly go where no man had gone before. Primarily because it was so obviously disastrous.

But this is the brave new world of Trussonomics. It's like turning on all the taps at once and being surprised when you flood the house.

The Commons was still packed, but this was no normal budget statement. There were no flourishes, no long build-up explaining how brilliant the government had been. And no loud cheering from the Tory benches. Most MPs looked sick. Apprehensive even. Unsure of how they were going to sell this latest Tory iteration to their constituents. Half of the personal tax cuts going to the richest 5% might not be quite the policy to win the hearts and minds of red-wall voters.

Kwarteng got down straight to business. So much to announce, so little time to do it. Tax was too high! Growth was too low! The government had let the economy stagnate. He wasn't sure what the government had been doing over the past 12 years, but he and Librium Liz had definitely played no part in it. Which was odd, as most of us could remember them both having been cabinet ministers who had voted for measures they were now trashing. And who had several times made a point of highlighting the dangers of government debt.

Like Truss, Kwasi is a *tabula rasa*. Free to reinvent himself, unmoored to the past. 'We are at the beginning of a new era,' he said. Weirdly, he even sounded as if he believed it. That people really are ready to forgive and forget. To consider this government as Year Zero rather than the continuation of the several failed ones that preceded it. No one else in the chamber seemed to share this view. Some Tories had the grace to look embarrassed. Librium Liz just looked blank. But then she often does. Maybe she too couldn't quite accept that she was getting away with it.

The chancellor moved on to the remedies. First up was loads more borrowing. He couldn't say how much. And it would be rude to ask. Then on to deregulation. It must be easier to treat workers worse. After all, if people weren't earning enough, it was entirely their own fault for not having a better-paid job. And what about the poor bankers? They hadn't been able to afford their second homes while their bonuses had been capped. Time to free the Goldman Sachs elite.

Then Kwarteng got on to tax. There was far too much of it. If he had his way, no one would be paying a penny. It would be up to everyone to either sink or swim. There were far too many people idling around, relying on schools and the NHS. But he couldn't bring himself to cut taxes completely. So he was just going to do so for the most well off. Because that was obviously the fair thing to do.

This was a budget devoid of moral purpose. Even Boris Johnson hadn't sunk this low. It's come to something when Kwarteng now finds himself lower on the ethical balance sheet than the Convict. Though it's all of a piece. Every time you think the government couldn't possibly sink any lower, it finds new, creative ways of doing so.

Labour's Rachel Reeves put in a decent reply – her highlight was chucking the six previous failed Tory growth plans across the dispatch box and asking why the new one should be any better – but she lacked a bit of edge. Almost as if her whole speech had been pre-written and she wasn't able to grasp just how reckless the Tories were being. A little more ad-libbing wouldn't have gone amiss. Sterling was down by two cents against the dollar to a fresh 37-year low.

For the Tories, only John Redwood and Richard Drax were wholly enthusiastic. This was all their wet dreams come true at once. Others, such as Mel Stride and John Glen, were openly sceptical. Of Johnson, Rishi Sunak and Michael Gove there was no sign. They are now non-people. Long before the end, every Tory MP had melted away, and Kwarteng was left to take questions from opposition backbenchers.

The chancellor looked increasingly lost and lonely. His self-confidence had definitely taken a hit over the past two and a half hours. Not least because the markets had responded to his mini-budget with a resounding thumbs-down. Now not even Kwasi could wholly convince himself that he knew something no other financial analyst did. Though give him a day or so . . .

* * *

With Liz Truss in hiding, Labour was living its best life. Previous party conferences had been marked by back-biting and division. Now everyone was falling over themselves to agree with one another. And not to smirk too broadly at the pound being in freefall, thanks to Kwasi Kwarteng's budget. For the first time in years, Labour actually believed they might be a government-in-waiting.

Not a hint of a heckle for the least Labour thing you'll see at a Labour conference

25 SEPTEMBER 2022

Stick to what you're good at. It's in the nature of things – especially during a party conference – that opposition leaders find themselves put under the microscope for character flaws. For reasons why they may never make it to prime minister. Keir Starmer is no exception. No matter that he has been consistently ahead in the polls for months now, or that Liz Truss has spectacularly failed to secure the traditional new-prime-minister bounce – she seems to be taking her desire to be unpopular extremely seriously – as she tries to crash the economy. Starmer gets it in the neck from left and right. He's too timid. He's too vague. He never says anything.

Except that over the last few weeks we've found something at which Keir genuinely excels. In fact, he's probably one of the best, if not *the* best, in the business. He's just an exceptional mourner. Were I to pop my clogs in the not too distant future, I hope that my family fall to their knees and beg him to organise the 10 days of national psychosis. There would be tears. There would be pomp.

There would be circumstance. Chopin's funeral march on repeat. And more and more tears.

When the Queen died, our lantern-jawed superhero with the sensitive, middle-distance stare suddenly came into his own. Come the tributes in parliament, he was note-perfect. While Librium Liz couldn't even connect with herself, in a drab, monotone speech that said everything about her and nothing about the Queen, Starmer was emotionally literate enough to convey the nation's feelings. He touched us. He held us. Acknowledged our loss. And then, during the rest of the ceremonies over the next nine days, he was strong and silent. Present but unobtrusive. Not trying to game the situation for his own political advantage. If one of the pallbearers had fainted, Keir would have been the first to step up.

All of which goes some way to explaining why this year's Labour Party conference began with the singing of the national anthem. Now anyone in the Commons last Friday for Kwasi Kwarteng's asset-stripping suicide note would have realised politics was well and truly tribal again. You'd have needed a heart of stone not to have enjoyed the sight of free marketeers not quite grasping what a free market actually means as the pound sank without trace. Not so much Britannia Unchained as Britannia Unhinged.

No matter. Starmer wanted to get the conference off to a good start – he'd navigated the traditional leader's interview on the Sunday-morning politics shows without taking much collateral damage, though sometimes you wish he'd learn to lie a little better; it wouldn't hurt him to say he'd freeze energy prices for longer than six months, given that he's never going to be in a position to do so – so he was determined to play to his strengths. Doubling down on mourning it was.

Just before 11 a.m., Starmer took to the conference stage in front of a packed hall. Above him was a giant video screen with a black-and-white image of the Queen. Behind him was a new Labour logo of a swirly Union Jack. There's sometimes a fine line between patriotism and nationalism. But if some people had their reservations, they kept them to themselves.

This was to be a theme of this year's party conference. There might have been a few angry members on the periphery, but everyone else was determined to put on a display of unity. Labour has now decided it's in with a genuine chance of winning the next election and will do whatever it takes. These days, it's the Tories who are the real political psychopaths. Imagine trashing the economy just because it's something you've always wanted to do, and finally all the grown-ups have left the room and there's no one left to stop you.

Starmer kept it short and sweet, sensing that not everyone might share his enthusiasm for mourning and that they might have come to Liverpool to talk politics. She wasn't just Our Queen, he said, ripping off Emmanuel

Macron's high-class tribute. She was The Queen. The Queen of the World. The very best Queen we had ever had. The very best Queen there ever could be. We had been blessed. Keir's eyes half closed in a moment of zen-like calm. He gulped. Perhaps he was laying it on a bit thick.

Cut to the national anthem. Starmer, Angela Rayner, Anneliese Dodds and John Ashworth all dressed in black. Ashworth looking as if he had a magnificent soprano, as the broadcast footage focused on him rather than the woman leading the singing. The audience all standing and singing along. They didn't even need the printed sheets of the words that the ushers had thoughtfully left out. It was about the least Labour thing you'll ever see at a Labour conference. But everyone was on message. Not even a hint of a heckle. This was an unashamed land grab for the now vacant middle ground. A siren call to the red wall.

Stranger things still were about to happen. In her speech as deputy leader, Rayner twice made reference to 'rising to the occasion' of this 1997 moment. Normally, any mention of Tony Blair is the kiss of death in the conference hall. Then, in the afternoon, at a session on winning the next election, the same video screen that had hosted the Queen showed images of Blair and Gordon Brown. Weirdly, members of the audience started clapping and cheering. Unheard of. Most disturbing of all, there was even a fleeting sighting of Peter Mandelson on the display. Birnam Wood has come to Dunsinane.

* * *

Now it was the Conservatives' turn. The sensible ones made sure to stay away from the conference. From a car-crash Liz Truss interview with the BBC's Laura Kuenssberg at the beginning to the very end, it was an excruciatingly painful four days for the government. A collector's item.

Half-witted, reckless Librium Liz may be even worse than May and Johnson

29 SEPTEMBER 2022

First, an apology. I should never have christened Theresa May 'the Maybot'. With hindsight, she appears positively emotionally present. Touchy-feely. Almost functional. If not entirely competent. Certainly not the piece of 1980s Amstrad junk she always seemed like when she was running the country. If you can call it that.

But the Tories were just playing with us. It's as if the members had said: 'So you think David Cameron is useless? Just wait until we give you Theresa.' And once we'd all had about enough of May, they gave us a narcissistic, sociopathic liar instead.

Now to top it all – at least we hope so; surely there can't be another one who is even worse? – we've been landed with Liz Truss. Someone who is not just half-witted and robotic, but reckless enough to bankrupt the country. The ideologue with only a tenuous grasp on reality. There's always a job waiting for Truss in an automated call centre – a deathless loop that sucks the life out of you.

I'm not sure who was stupid enough to suggest starting the reclusive prime minister's media rehabilitation with a tour of the BBC's regional radio studios, but they won't be doing it again in a hurry. If they thought they were going to ease Librium Liz out of her week-long hibernation with a series of short 'lifestyle' interviews – think author flogging new book on PR junket – that would reach a smallish, local audience and fly beneath the radar of the national media, then they badly miscalculated. Local radio presenters are no mugs, and they weren't going to look a gift horse in the mouth.

Inevitably, they all asked more or less the same questions. After all, there really is only one game in town. What the fuck did you think you were doing? Didn't it occur to you that your mindless mini-budget could wipe £500 billion off the markets, putting pensions at risk and increasing the cost of borrowing? Thanks very much for the £100 or so tax cut that the least well off will be getting, but did you know that you've just made most people even more broke?

But there was a virtue in hearing the same question asked on eight separate occasions. Because it reinforced the key message that Librium Liz doesn't have any coherent answers. She really didn't seem to have any idea of the scale of the damage she had done. She was in total denial. Like an arsonist caught with a can of petrol. It also said much about Truss's limited capacity for rational thinking. Most artificial intelligence is programmed to learn from its mistakes. So you'd have thought she would have got better and better as the hour went on – that she might even have sounded half human and half intelligent by the time she came off air.

Only she didn't. She got worse and worse. Out came the same absurd answers, and the pauses as she tried to think of something credible got longer and longer. She is the embodiment of the circle of doom on a laptop that's crashing. She is not AI. She is Artificial Stupidity, programmed to carry on repeating more and more errors until she collapses in on herself. A dead cert to win this year's Darwin award for those who have contributed to human evolution by selecting themselves out of the gene pool. Wire Truss up to an ECG, and you'd find no activity. Just a flat line.

The circus began at Radio Leeds, where presenter Rima Ahmed cut to the chase. Why had Truss crashed the economy, and what was she going to do about it? 'Um . . . er,' muttered Librium Liz, apparently astonished to be asked about why the country was in crisis. 'We took decisive action.' Thousands of people shouted at their radio. You took decisive action to wreck the economy. To make everyone significantly less well off. The one thing you weren't supposed to do. What we really want to know is what 'decisive action' you are going to take to reverse your child-death-squad-style mindless destruction. Doing nothing isn't an option. 'Nothing,' said Truss.

It was like this, she said. It all went wrong because we were trying to help people out with their energy bills. Are you stupid? everyone screamed. Of course it didn't. You had announced the energy bailout in early September, and no one had batted an eyelid. The markets had taken it in their stride. It was only when you and Kamikwasi Kwarteng announced your unfunded tax cuts that benefited the most well off that the pound nosedived. It was an entirely self-inflicted crisis that only the ever-delusional John Redwood and the batshit-crazy Institute of Economic Affairs welcomed.

On and on Librium Liz went. Through Radio Norfolk, Kent, Lancashire, Nottingham, Tees, Bristol and Stoke. Each time sounding less and less convincing. Detached, emotionally dead, intellectually wanting. Careless with other people's lives. Not even curious to find out how people were experiencing her calamity economics. The dead-air silences became so long I presumed she was trying to communicate by telepathy.

It was Putin who had crashed the economy, Truss insisted. Which was weird, because no one could remember the Russian president having delivered the budget in the Commons. Then it was the fault of the Marxist International Monetary Fund for sticking their oar in. Go back to North Korea! Finally, it was all down to the Bank of England. Mortgages getting more expensive was all their fault. They were the ones who had put up interest rates. Out of pique. Not in response to the budget.

Come the end, Truss was little more than a puddle on the floor. A pool to be mopped up and taxied back to Downing Street. She couldn't even answer any of the local questions she was asked. Who would have guessed local journalists might ask local questions? She was clueless on fracking. Clueless on everything. When she was talking to her own local radio station in Norfolk, she didn't just seem unaware that the roof was falling in on the hospital in King's Lynn, she also seemed to have forgotten she was prime minister and in a position to do something about it.

It could have been worse. She could have spoken to 10 radio stations rather than eight. If there was a way out of this mess, Librium Liz wasn't letting on. At present, her only plan seems to be to hang on and hope for the best. Much the same goes for Kamikwasi. He spent the day in Darlington doing not very much. At this rate, our two star-crossed lovers could be the only Tories to show their faces at the party conference in Birmingham next week. Let's hope they've thought of something better to say by then.

Kamikwasi Kwarteng delivers his excruciating career suicide note

3 OCTOBER 2022

Not waving but drowning. Days like these are coming round with increasing frequency. Days when the sketch is little more than a transcription service. Days when there is no way to improve on the sheer madness of the Tory party. Its capacity for self-harm has become compulsive. An addiction almost. The only way most Conservatives can reassure themselves they are in government is by noting the chaos surrounding them. Their lives – and ours – are unmanageable. Interest rates rising, the pound tanking, public infighting: yup, that's the way Tories know they are still relevant. Even if they are on life support.

We all knew Liz Truss was going to be hopeless. That was a given. We just didn't know she was going to be so hopeless quite so quickly. Or that she would be given so much enthusiastic support from the half-witted collective that make up her cabinet. Step forward Kamikwasi Kwarteng and the skin-crawlingly needy Chris Philp, everyone's favourite punchbag. We imagined Radon Liz might spread out the fun. A managed decline of her party. Instead, she has gone for broke, daring the Tories to get rid of her little more than a month after electing her. She is the queen of the clusterfuck. The Trussterfuck.

Sometime between Liz Truss telling a near-catatonic late-night party of Tory donors – the applause was one hand clapping – that the 45p tax rate was being abolished and the next morning, the prime minister did a U-turn. At some point between Kamikwasi briefing extracts of his conference speech about 'staying the course' on Sunday night and 6 a.m. on Monday morning, the chancellor did a reverse ferret. It was shabby, desperate stuff. The stuff of a government that was entirely clueless. Politically and economically completely illiterate.

Just after 7.30 a.m., Kamikwasi appeared on *BBC Breakfast*. It felt more like a hostage video. The normally arrogant, over-confident facade had given way to fear. You could sense a man who was now out of his depth and playing for time. Trying to wind down the clock by bluffing. Everything was fine. Never better. Reinstating the 45p tax rate was no big deal. It was just a distraction, he said time and again. It wouldn't affect the overall plan. Largely because there wasn't one.

Kamikwasi was slightly more verbal when he appeared half an hour later on the *Today* programme. But not much. He knew he had been so busted. Not so much a chancellor, more a chancer. Someone with a smattering of undergraduate bluster who had somehow been let loose on the UK economy. And he had now been seen. He had no clothes.

It was only a matter of time before he was gone. What credibility he ever had totally shredded. He may have reversed a tax giveaway to the rich, but there were still billions of pounds of other unfunded tax cuts. And just as importantly, he had shown his hand. He might have been forced into a humiliating climbdown, but now everyone knew he was completely relaxed about extra tax breaks for the most well off. The optics were shite either way. Though Kamikwasi was too dim to appreciate it.

Nick Robinson was brutal. Who was responsible for the U-turn? Truss, Kwarteng or the useful idiot, Philp? You could almost hear Philp's squeals of pleasure at having a purpose in life as a fall guy. A place in history as a government patsy. Why had Kamikwasi rubbished the Bank of England, sacked the permanent secretary to the Treasury and sidelined the Office for Budget Responsibility? Because they would all have thought he was batshit crazy. And what about spending cuts?

He couldn't bear to hear the truth. And now he'd finally had to bend, just 10 days after delivering the mini-budget, when reality became unavoidable. Was he going to apologise? He wasn't. Though he would mutter something about humility and contrition. Those words were squeezed out through gritted teeth. His budget was all about growth, he insisted. Except, as ever, Kamikwasi had missed the point. His budget was the exact opposite. Anti-growth. It could have been designed to make people worse off.

It was just Kwarteng's bad luck that he was due on the conference stage to give his keynote speech in the afternoon. He spent the intervening hours holed up with the reclusive Librium Liz – they cancelled a planned outing to Selly Oak – watching ITV news clips of her insisting that the 45p tax rate would not be abolished. Both were equally confused. Unsure if these were clips that had been pre-recorded or whether there had been yet another U-turn. It's getting hard to keep up.

After a brief video of the chancellor meeting young people whose in-work benefits he was about to cut, a visibly sweaty Kamikwasi appeared from the wings. He looked terrible. Anxious, nervous and keen to be anywhere but Birmingham. It soon became clear why. He had nothing to say beyond a few half-arsed platitudes that even he didn't seem to believe. He was merely going through the motions, with a speech that was intellectually empty. It could have been a career suicide note.

He began with a jokey reference to the U-turn. Or 'turbulence', as he put it. Not the most sensitive way of acknowledging that his wilful imposition of untested libertarian ideology had cost homeowners thousands in extra mortgage interest payments. Kwarteng then went on to say the government was 'getting Britain moving'. Some hope. The only people moving anywhere in the next few years will be those in the process of having their homes repossessed. You couldn't make this stuff up.

The speech lasted barely 20 minutes but felt longer. It was almost painful – excruciating even – to watch Kamikwasi die on his feet. He missed his punchlines, such as they were, and openly contradicted himself. There would be a plan, he promised. Just as soon as he had thought of one. But fingers crossed for late November.

At one point, he said it was all Labour's fault that the UK had low growth. Then, in the next sentence, he blamed it all on the Tories. Next, he claimed the Tories were the party of fiscal responsibility. Wait till he finds out who caused the Bank of England to spaff £65 billion on protecting pensions. It was embarrassing. The applause – if you can call it that – was sparse and sporadic. Not even sympathetic.

Kwarteng staggered off the stage. Thrilled just to have survived the ordeal. Then reality bit. His wasn't even a heroic failure. It was bog-standard hubris. The inevitable end point for someone whose ambition exceeded his talent. Radon Liz offered him a hug and her undying support. That was just too much. Now he knew he was finished.

Liz Truss says nothing at all, and says it really badly

5 OCTOBER 2022

Well, what would you have said? You've tanked the economy, your government is in meltdown and you're 30 percentage points behind in the polls. Just think how much worse it could have been had you not had to suspend all government activity for 10 days of national mourning after the Queen's death. 'Sorry' might have been a start. Or even 'I resign.'

Liz Truss took a different approach. One with no empathy, no understanding of the occasion. Oblivious to the fact that the Tory party conference had morphed from mayhem to abject chaos. Don't mention the war! Or maybe she was stuck in the denial stage of grief. Unable to accept the reality.

So all she could do was offer an extended-highlights reel of the same speech she had delivered to Tory party members during the summer's leadership hustings. No acknowledgement that things had spiralled out of control. Or that she was in any way responsible. This was safety-first stuff. Damage limitation. Say nothing too controversial. Better still, say next to nothing at all. Just fill the hall with a sound cloud and hope to get out unscathed.

The queues for the hall had started early, but there was plenty of room for everyone. There were almost no MPs left in Birmingham. Most were thrilled to use Wednesday's rail strikes as an excuse to get away from a toxic political war zone. Scenes like the last chopper out of Saigon.

The Tory party chair, Jake Berry, took to the stage to begin the last rites on a harrowing few days. 'What a conference it's been!' he announced. Even the Tory members couldn't resist laughing out loud. Berry looked surprised.

Shocked even. 'You weren't meant to laugh there,' he said, sounding hurt. It's one thing to try to ignore a conference that's been an unmitigated disaster from beginning to end; it's another to try to spin it as a resounding success. But in JakeWorld that's what it had been. He never really recovered from that.

Next up was Nadhim Zahawi, who appeared – like so many Tories in Birmingham – to be operating in a different space–time continuum. Slipping effortlessly between different time zones. Some in the past, some in the future. He too had been having a blast. It had been great to meet so many activists ready to get rid of the last dreadful government, which had been holding the country back for 12 years, and replace it with this one, which would drive it onto the rocks. This Zahawi was not the same Zahawi who had been a minister under Boris Johnson. That one had been a clone from a parallel universe.

There was polite applause as the cabinet filed in – it looked like a Ceaușescu line-up from circa 1989, with a similar career life expectancy – and then a video of Truss saying she had always wanted to help the little people with their energy bills was played on the big screens. Which was odd, because most of us could remember her having said that people were going to have to suck it up and get better-paid jobs if they wanted to heat their homes this winter, and changing her mind only when it became a political necessity. But perhaps that had been another Liz Truss.

Then the hall lit up, and Truss walked to the centre of the stage, accompanied by M People's 'Moving on Up'. This earned Radon Liz her first standing ovation. So far, so good. She had made it to the lectern without falling over. And none of the scenery had collapsed. A distinct improvement on Theresa May.

The problems started when she tried to speak. She still hasn't learned the basic rhythms of language. Understood the purpose of punctuation. Sentences collided with one another, so that any sense was lost. Her delivery was awkward, as she tried to escape the monotone by putting the stress on random words. She frequently looked towards the wings as if begging for help, and her hands chopped the air as if she were a 1960s TV puppet. If you looked closely, you could see the strings. Mostly, she looked nervous. As if she knew she wasn't cut out for these gigs. She grasped a glass of water with two hands to stop herself from spilling it.

Librium Liz then returned to familiar ground: her backstory. She was the first prime minister to have gone to a comprehensive. She wasn't. But who cares about details? She knew people who had taken drugs. Leave Michael Gove out of it. People had always tried to stop her from fulfilling her potential. But not nearly hard enough. It had always been obvious she wasn't the sort of person you would want running a country, but somehow she had made it to the top. The Dunning–Kruger effect has a lot to answer for.

Bizarrely, things looked up for Truss when two Greenpeace activists staged a protest. The audience became protective of their lame-duck leader and started clapping wildly at everything she said. Even when the applause was entirely inappropriate. So Radon Liz ploughed on, underwhelming everything that got in her way by listing everything she didn't like. People who didn't like her style should have listened harder to her before. Er . . . we did. It's just that we weren't allowed to vote in the leadership election. That pleasure was reserved for the people in the hall.

'I'm for growth, growth, growth,' she declared. Which is exactly what Keir Starmer had said in a speech in the summer. Though maybe he wanted a different type of growth. Or it was a different type of Keir. It's not just the Tories who can time-slip. Mostly, though, she wanted to declare war on 'the anti-growth coalition'. Which seemed to be anyone who had taken a taxi from north London to the BBC. Along with anyone else who thought she was a halfwit. Which is almost everyone in the entire world. Including most of the Tory party. The IMF. The RSPCA. Anyone with a brain. So count me in.

It was all bonkers. But it was good enough in its way. Because mediocrity had been all that had been expected. No one had thought she might actually save her career. That was a fantasy too far. Even for this conference. She stopped mid-sentence. No one knew if she had come to the end or not, but they applauded all the same. And as

Truss didn't know if she had finished either, she took their cue and wandered off. As she left, the pound lost 1% of its value and two-year fixed-term mortgage rates hit 6%. It seemed the financial markets were also part of the anti-growth coalition. Who knew?

Labour glee as Librium Liz twists and U-turns her way through PMQs

12 OCTOBER 2022

No words were needed. Their faces said it all. Penny Mordaunt looked like someone who had just been told her house was about to be repossessed. You reap what you sow. James Cleverly kept his eyes closed for the most part. Wishing he was anywhere but here and hoping he would wake up somewhere else when he opened them. Thérèse Coffey just remained in her usual stupor. She has yet to work out just what she has done to become deputy prime minister. She and I both.

That was just the cabinet. If anything, the Tory backbenchers – those who had made the effort to turn up – were in an even more pitiful state. Most appeared to be suffering from acute post-traumatic stress disorder. Clutching their heads. Staring vacantly ahead. Talking to themselves. Unlike those on the front bench, almost none of them had actually wanted Liz Truss in the first place.

They had been given no baubles, no offices of state to feed their ambition. They had always known Librium Liz would be a Trussterfuck.

Yet even in their darkest moments, few had realised just how bad Truss would be. Or how quickly. Most had thought she would take her time to reach maximum uselessness. Most new leaders get a short honeymoon period. Time for even the sceptics to reserve their judgement. Not Radon Liz. She had driven her party off a cliff in a matter of weeks.

So the Tory cheers sounded barely half-hearted – more a death rattle – as Truss entered the chamber for her second outing at prime minister's questions. Chronicle of a death foretold. She was to give her Tory MPs precious little to be happy about. Librium Liz could almost have been a Labour plant. The Tory leader that the opposition would have chosen if it had been allowed a vote.

Even when Boris Johnson was blustering, there was a thread of an argument. Even if it wasn't always rooted in reality. Truss can't even manage that. Her answers may be more direct, but there is an air of hopelessness about her from which she can't escape. Truss is the loser's loser. At one point, she said: 'I am genuinely unclear.' Which was probably the truest thing she's said in months. A cry of pain. A brief realisation of her own hollowness. The Labour benches merely laughed. It's not often you get a Tory leader who feeds them all their best lines.

And it probably won't last, as most Tory MPs are desperate to get Librium Liz out of No. 10 as soon as possible. So the Labour benches will enjoy it while they can. And what did Truss do? She repeated herself. 'I am genuinely unclear,' she sobbed. This time, some of her own back-benchers couldn't help joining in the laughter. Labour's highlights reel of Truss soundbites for the next election is going to be a director's cut.

There's only one game in town at the moment. So, after Truss had performed her first U-turn of the day on no-fault evictions in answer to Labour's Graham Stringer, Keir Starmer predictably went in hard on the economy. Did she agree with the half-witted Jacob Rees-Mogg that the turmoil in the markets had nothing to do with the budget? Er . . . yeah, but no, but yeah, but no, but yeah, but we've taken decisive action. Decisive action to spook the markets and tank the pound.

Starmer tried to talk Librium Liz down. It was Labour that had voted against the rise in national insurance earlier in the year. It wasn't the energy bailout package that had sent the pound tumbling and interest rates rising. And to not implement a planned rise in corporation tax was still a tax cut. Even if you would rather pretend it wasn't.

It was all basic stuff. Economics 101. But still way beyond Liz. Oxford must be so proud of her achievements. No wonder the university has dropped down the world rankings. Instead, she merely doubled down on everything. Hers was a budget for growth – she did at least refrain from calling Labour 'the anti-growth coalition'; presumably someone has told her it makes her sound ridiculous – and she wouldn't be making any spending cuts. She was going to carry on doing all the things that had already cost the government £65 billion in bailouts. God stand up for Trussonomics! Or Trussian roulette. Amazingly, this level of idiocy didn't send the pound tumbling further.

Maybe it's all been a cunning plan to confuse and wrongfoot the markets. Now they've no idea what she's going to do. She's just as likely to U-turn on her budget as she is to see it through. Who knows? Within a week, Kamikwasi could be an ex-chancellor – that's what you get for doing what Truss wants – the mini-budget could be ripped up and tax rises and spending cuts could be imposed. You just never quite know . . .

As if to confirm this, Radon Liz used PMQs to perform yet another U-turn. This time on a government advertising campaign on energy efficiency. Whoever had said she was against the idea was a liar. Though she did categorically rule out another general election. Which probably means there will be one before Christmas.

Truss left the chamber to cries of 'More!' from Labour and widespread indifference from her own side. That was the closest to enthusiasm the Tory benches could manage. She left behind the creepy Chris Philp – the Nose in Search of a Bum – to answer an urgent question on why the economy was even worse on Wednesday than it had been on Tuesday. The Labour benches were full, the government's nearly empty. It was almost as if the Tories couldn't bear to revisit the scene of the crime.

Philp was up against Rachel Reeves. It was no contest. Philp is a lightweight. An inveterate people-pleaser. A crawler to those in power. Someone in cabinet only because the government is morally bankrupt and there is no one else left. His idea of making an argument is merely to shout bollocks very loudly.

'THE CHANCELLOR IS AWAY AT A ROUTINE MEETING OF THE IMF. I SAID, "ROUTINE",' he yelled. And no, he didn't know what was going on – this was very much above his pay grade – but the budget definitely wouldn't be reversed, unless it was. Nor would the next fiscal event be brought forward, unless it was. Everything was worse somewhere else, even if it wasn't. And spending cuts would go up with inflation. Though it depended on what inflationary index you were using.

Christ. Why does anyone bother with the Nose in Search of a Bum? That was the question even those Tories who had stayed behind to make a plea for sanity, such as the Treasury committee chair Mel Stride, were asking themselves. But Philp was rushing on his run, his elevation just one of the eternal mysteries of the Truss regime.

* * *

Chaos upon chaos. U-turn upon U-turn. By now, the Tories were in complete meltdown. Every time Liz Truss appeared in order to try and explain herself, she only made the situation five times worse. There was another disastrous prime minister's questions. Even the new king could sense things were going badly wrong. When Truss turned up for their weekly meeting, he was overheard saying, 'Dear, oh dear.' The sort of thing he normally says when told Prince Harry has signed a new book deal or Prince Andrew has given another interview to Emily Maitlis.

There was only one thing for it: it was time to chuck her friends overboard. No greater love hath any woman than this, than to lay down her friends for her life. Now it was only a matter of time. How long till Liz had the self-worth to sack herself?

Kamikwasi takes Librium Liz's offer to consciously uncouple from the train wreck

14 OCTOBER 2022

On Thursday afternoon, Kwasi Kwarteng told reporters in New York that he wasn't going anywhere. As an expression of physical intent, it turned out to be well wide of the mark. The chancellor was back in the UK a day early, on Friday morning. But as a statement of existential despair, it was spot on. Kamikwasi is going nowhere.

His political career is finished. His credibility trashed. He's destined to become the answer to a pub-quiz question about the shortest-serving chancellor who didn't die in office. Still, at least he got a lot done in his 38 days: forced the Bank of England into a £65 billion bailout of pension funds and increased everyone's mortgages. Nice work, if you can get it.

After landing at Heathrow, Kwarteng took his last ride in a ministerial Range Rover back to Downing Street, where Liz Truss would administer the last rites, the prime minister having apparently switched sides to the 'anti-growth coalition' and decided to sack her pro-growth chancellor. It turns out there are limits to how unpopular Librium Liz is prepared to be. She hasn't seen anything yet.

Their conversation must have been awkward. Not to mention surreal. 'I'm going to have to sack you for doing all the things we agreed in the mini-budget. I just can't tolerate that level of loyalty from my chancellor. Imagine if every minister did exactly what I wanted. What kind of state would the country be in? Surely you must have realised I was batshit crazy and not to be trusted. But anyway, I'm demanding of you a futile gesture. If you resign, then suddenly my credibility will be restored. People will begin to realise I know exactly what I'm doing.'

The exchange of letters was equally bizarre. Kamikwasi's was a model of restrained politeness. With an undercurrent of passive aggression. Understandable in the circumstances. 'Your success is the country's success,' he wrote. Twisting the dagger. Shame about the financial markets and all that, but you live and learn. And people shouldn't have bought houses they couldn't afford, Kwarteng went on. No one could have predicted that things would get worse after 23 September. Just mad. Still no understanding that it was his budget that created the chaos.

Librium Liz's reply was no more grounded in reality. She began by praising him. As if crashing the economy was a tremendous achievement. Then she wrote that she respected his decision to resign. Hang on. He didn't have a choice. You just sacked him, so he could hardly have remained in office. It made it look as if she wasn't sure exactly who had sacked whom. Maybe it had been a conscious uncoupling. Gwynnie would have been proud.

Then came the press conference. If you can call something that lasted eight minutes that. Best to call it for what it was: a train wreck. Beyond awful. More like a short suicide note. One that radiated anxiety and insecurity. One that screamed that Truss wasn't up to the job. Never had been. Never would be. The Tory members had signed their own death warrant for the next election by making her leader. It had been obvious to everyone else that she would be a disaster. And she hadn't let us down.

Truss opened the train wreck with a brief statement. She sounded even more robotic and disconnected than usual. Out of touch with herself. Out of touch with her party. Out of touch with the country. It would have been kinder if her minders had put her out of her misery and pressed the 'off' button. It was excruciating to watch. A postcard from the edge. A tacit admission that she was incapable of being prime minister.

Librium Liz then regressed to her childhood. The grinding middle-class poverty of being brought up in a nice area of Leeds. Previous Tory governments of which she had been part had let the country down. She was still committed to growth. She would do everything all over again in a heartbeat, if given the chance.

Her one mistake had been to try to do everything too quickly. So she was going to do yet another U-turn on her budget and increase corporation tax after all. And hopefully that would do. But if the markets were still unimpressed, then she had some other unfunded tax cuts she could reverse. And to prove she was serious, she had appointed Jeremy Hunt as the new chancellor. Quite what was in it for Hunt was less clear. His economics are not that much different to Kamikwasi's, so perhaps he's just hoping to break his predecessor's record for length of time in office. A race to the bottom.

It was all bonkers. Delusional. As if Truss still didn't quite understand the seriousness of the situation. She also looked terrible. Washed out. There was a part of her that was terrified, a part she was struggling to suppress. She could barely even read out the names of the four journalists to whom she was prepared to grant questions.

First up was the *Telegraph*. Usually a safe port in a storm. Not this time. Could she say why she should stay as prime minister and her chancellor should go? It was a joint project after all.

'I took decisive action,' she stumbled, seemingly unaware that her decisive action had caused the chaos in the first place. Everything since had been reactive and defensive. Her voice petered out. Next, she turned to Harry Cole of the *Sun*. But even her authorised biographer didn't give her a break. Perhaps he's already rewriting the final chapter. He too wanted to know why she wasn't resigning as well. There was a long pause before she mumbled nonsense about decisive action. Her artificial stupidity needed a reboot.

There were two final questions that went unanswered before Librium Liz dashed for the exit. The journalists left in the room were shell-shocked. Unable to process the shambles. It was the Trussterfuck of all Trussterfucks. There was literally no point to her premiership. All her leadership promises had unravelled. The only thing left was to implement someone else's plan. Anyone's. She was a laughing stock. The Tories were a laughing stock. Give it a week or two and she would be gone. This press conference had merely been the Chronicle of a Death Foretold.

Up was down, night was day. And was the prime minister OK?

17 OCTOBER 2022

It was a very British coup. So polite that you could almost have missed it. So restrained that Liz Truss actually had to mastermind her own dismissal. If Librium Liz can be said to mastermind anything. It was like asking a death row inmate to administer their own lethal injection.

But it was a coup nonetheless. There may have been no military berets, but we might as well have had a TV announcer saying: 'We interrupt this programme to inform you that the United Kingdom has a new junta. There is no need to panic, but we advise you, for your own safety, to remain indoors. What the country now needs is stable government. Liz Truss is not – I stress not – being held under house arrest. She is just being kept hidden for her own good. She hasn't been gagged. She has just become an elective mute. And now a quick word from your new prime minister.'

Cut to Jeremy Hunt, draped in his own flags. The same Jeremy Hunt who had been a disaster as culture secretary. The same Jeremy Hunt who had taken the NHS to the brink while health secretary. The same Jeremy Hunt who had twice campaigned to be Tory party leader and had twice been rejected, most recently in the summer, when he had finished eighth out of eight, with only 18 Conservative MPs thinking he was worth voting for.

Yet this new, improved version of Jeremy Hunt was being paraded as a safe pair of hands. Despite the fact that he had no experience of working in the Treasury. But then he wasn't just the new chancellor of the exchequer; he was the de facto prime minister. The new leader of our Brave New World. Truss was sidelined. Silenced. Only nominally in place. Just for as long as it took for her party to work out how best to dethrone her. You'd have thought they had regicide off pat by now.

Hunt looked straight at the camera. You have to hand it to him. He has the style. The blag. He sounds plausible. Then again, right now it's hard not to. A child of 10 could make a decent fist of being chancellor at the moment. All you have to do is the opposite of everything Kamikwasi and Librium Liz did in their mini-budget three weeks ago.

It was an open goal, and Hunt happily took advantage. Along with the measures he'd announced last Friday, he reversed the 1p cut in the basic rate of tax and cut short the energy price guarantee by 18 months. The most brutal U-turn in government policy in living memory. And he made it sound so matter-of-fact. As if it was an everyday event. Which, in fairness, is what it is rapidly becoming.

Normally, when a government can't get its budget through parliament, it calls a general election. Hunt had other ideas. It was a measured act of stability. He didn't care to say why the economy had crashed in the first place.

What everyone needed to do was take a deep breath and wait for the cuts to public services. They'd seem like light relief compared with the chaos of the past few weeks. At least, that was the hope. Up was down. Night was day.

Meanwhile, Labour was still worried about the state of the ex-prime minister. The prime minister formerly known as Liz. Was she OK? Was she being looked after? Did she need a human rights lawyer? By lunchtime, Keir Starmer was so concerned that he tabled an urgent question, inviting Truss to come to the Commons to explain why she had felt the need to sack Kamikwasi rather than herself. And to give her life some meaning. Now that her government's entire ideology and purpose had been trashed, she was in a death spiral of existential despair.

Only it turned out that Librium Liz was in no fit state for anything. She didn't want to speak. She didn't want to do anything. She was in a deeper state of catatonia than ever before. Her captors had seen to that. And Penny Mordaunt was more than happy to answer the UQ on her behalf. In fact, she was desperate to. The coup might be well under way, but they are still jostling for position. Mordaunt is keen to be seen as a possible next leader. And what better way of achieving this than by appearing to be loyal to Truss while also gently ridiculing her?

It had been a hugely courageous thing Truss had done to sack one of her best friends, Mordaunt insisted, just about keeping a straight face. It had been a far, far better thing Librium Liz had done that she had laid down a friend's life for her own. So brave that she couldn't even be bothered to turn up to the Commons to explain in person why she had done it. Or to say sorry. Mordaunt, though, was happy to apologise. Sort of. On the whole, she would rather the country hadn't been made a great deal less well off as a result of the government's actions. But what could she do, if the Tories had chosen a halfwit?

The opposition still wanted to know what conditions Librium Liz was being kept in. Mordaunt became even more gnomic. First she said that Truss had been desperate to take the UQ but had been prevented from doing so. Volodymyr Zelenskiy had left her on hold, presumably. Then she said she was dying to be able to say why Liz was incapacitated but would have to kill herself and everyone else if she broke the *omertà*. Then she declared: 'The prime minister is not hiding under a desk.' So she was under the bed then. Or in Boris Johnson's fridge.

At which point, Librium Liz meandered into the chamber. Her eyes vacant, unblinking. A rigid smile. As if her minders had overmedicated her somewhat. As if she had no idea she was now starring in her own hostage video. She took her place next to Hunt, her captor, and just sat there vacantly, devoid of emotion, as Rachel Reeves rubbished her reputation. The markets may have been reassured, but the Tories would still be punished by the voters. They wouldn't forget.

As silently as she had arrived, Truss pootled off after less than 20 minutes. It had been a Scandi noir cameo, with the killers in plain sight. A few Labour MPs shouted after her. Was she really OK? Just give us a sign. Any sign. A mere word.

Nothing. The Tories ignored her. She was an aberration. A past tense. The last few weeks had just been a bad dream. Onwards with the new regime. To oblivion.

Laughter fills the pauses as a blank Liz Truss is let out to play leader

19 OCTOBER 2022

It was excruciating. Of course it was. It was never going to be otherwise. Liz Truss is finished. Her MPs know it. The country knows it. We're all just filling in time as we wait for a definite sell-by date, wait for the Tory party to do the humane thing.

So much for compassionate conservatism. Right now the kindest thing anyone could do is switch off Librium Liz's life support. Instead, they let her stagger on, humiliating herself more by the day. And all because they have still to work out how to replace her. Or with whom.

And yet, weirdly, it could have been so much worse. Truss didn't die. Or knock over her glass of water and electrocute herself. The bar really is that low. The Speaker didn't call a premature end to prime minister's questions to prevent further embarrassment. Her artificial stupidity didn't buffer at inconvenient times. So her jerky arm movements almost synchronised with her robotic delivery. Almost.

Her own MPs didn't publicly abuse her. Sajid Javid, who had been granted a question on the order paper, didn't bother to show up. Rumour had it that he had been bought off, with No. 10 suspending the aide who allegedly told the media that Truss had always thought Saj was shit. As if. The idea that Truss has sufficient insight to tell if someone else is crap is patently absurd. Like getting primitive AI to review the latest iPhone.

Best of all, Jeremy Hunt didn't intervene. He could have said enough was enough at almost any time. That the new regime had tried to be an understanding, benevolent regime. Which is why it had allowed Truss out from under the desk where she had been held hostage so she could play at being team leader for half an hour. But having seen just a few minutes of her in action, it had decided to cut short the indulgence. It was time for the regime's actual leaders to take over and reassure the country. Or try to, at least.

Five minutes before PMQs were due to begin, Thérèse Coffey took her place on the front bench. She reached into her doctor's bag and started handing out large quantities of mind-bending psychotropic prescription drugs to other members of the cabinet. Though not to Hunt, who appeared to be tripping already. Watching his face melt in the reflection of his glistening, patent-leather, thigh-length boots.

The others wolfed the pills down eagerly. By the fistful. Anything to ease the pain of their shared existential futility. To momentarily forget they had allowed their ambition to be linked to someone so obviously flawed, intellectually and emotionally. To obliterate the inevitability of them also becoming a past tense.

Then Librium Liz appeared. Smiling inanely. As if she was unaware of the temporary nature of her condition. That this could well be the last time she was given a starring role at PMQs. It was as if she too had been at the narcotics goody bag. Though not for her the usual heavy-duty tranquillisers and barbiturates. Instead, she'd gone for the quaaludes, somehow contriving to reduce herself to a zombie state, while reaching dizzying heights of disinhibition. A disturbing proposition.

There had been no cheers to speak of to greet the Leader in Name Only's arrival. Rather, her own backbenchers had gathered like gawpers at a road traffic accident, appalled by their own ghoulishness, but not wanting to miss the action. Within minutes, we got the first laughs. All it took was for Truss to say she had spent the morning meeting with ministerial colleagues. Something that gets said at every PMQs. Only this time everyone knew she didn't have any colleagues. Just captors and minders.

From there on, it was just a painful, slow decline. Labour's Justin Madders wanted to know why she had sacked her chancellor rather than herself. After all, Kwasi Kwarteng had only been doing exactly what she had promised the Tory party. 'I've been clear,' said Quaalude Liz. She really hadn't. She never is. The syncopated pauses mid-sentence provided a vacuum that was only filled with yet more laughter. Truss grinned blankly again. She has no emotional antennae, so she can't read the room, unable to tell if people are laughing with her or at her. Someone should help her out.

Then Keir Starmer stood up to inflict further wounds. None fatal. It suits Labour to have an ersatz prime minister whom everyone knows is on life support. This was the Labour leader at his most surgical. His most forensic. Good gags, better soundbites. Short and not so sweet. Truss had nothing to say. Other than 'Sorry,' 'I take the tough decisions' – she really doesn't, all the tough decisions are made on her behalf – and 'What has Labour done about the economic crisis?' Er . . . a word to the dim. Labour hasn't been in government for more than 12 years. It didn't cause the chaos nor is it in a position to do anything about it. Not yet, anyway.

On it went. Quaalude Liz did go on to tell the SNP's Ian Blackford that the pensions triple lock would be retained. Only no one knew if she had cleared that with her captors or if she was just freelancing. Just the day before, Reichsmarschall Hunt had rather suggested he was keen on pensioners dying. And even if her claim were true now, there are an infinite number of parallel universes in the Truss space–time continuum in which things could be both true and untrue at the same time. Today's promise is just a lie waiting to happen.

There were no cheers as Quaalude Liz left the chamber.

Just an empty silence as she was led back to Downing Street to be put back in her cage. 'We can't let this happen again,' said Hunt. 'Cancel her engagements this afternoon and keep her indoors. The new regime has been too kind. Too benevolent. It's time to do another Kwasi. Someone get rid of Suella Braverman. Somehow. Just for the hell of it. To show we can. It's about time we had a home secretary who isn't half-witted and vicious. We need someone with at least one brain cell.'

'What took you so long?' said Grant Shapps, flicking through his spreadsheet.

'It's a stitch-up,' sobbed the useless Suella.

No one expects the *Guardian* Anti-Growth Coalition. *Viva* the Wokerati!

At peace with herself, Librium Liz re-embraces her own mediocrity

20 OCTOBER 2022

The agony was finally over. The week-long battle between Liz Truss and the *Daily Star* lettuce had been won. The lettuce had romped home at a canter, with only a few leaves showing any sign of wilting. In the end, it hadn't really been much of a contest.

Shortly after 1.30 p.m., Truss emerged from the front door of No. 10, closely followed by her husband. She walked to the lectern and started speaking in her familiar, disconnected monotone. She had come into office at a time of great political and economic instability. Weirdly, she forgot to mention her part in adding to the instability. But the country will be paying for it in increased mortgages and borrowing for years to come.

Truss went on. She had delivered some fantastic achievements for the country. An energy package that literally any other prime minister would have introduced. And the reduction in national insurance contributions that Labour had first proposed. Amnesia prevented her from mentioning her U-turns. But her achievements had been so remarkable that it was best she went out on a high. The record for shortest-serving prime minister was hers. Though she would hang on for another week while the Tory party hastily scrabbled around for a new leader.

Her statement lasted barely a couple of minutes. Yet by the time she had finished she looked almost relieved. At peace with herself. No more trying to conceal her shame. Her humiliation. The shame and humiliation that had become the country's own shame and humiliation. A lightning rod of despair. The pretence of trying to appear competent could be abandoned. No further series of time-slip adventures in which she could enter parallel universes where she was a successful prime minister would be called for. She could re-embrace her own mediocrity. The authentic voice of those guaranteed to get most things wrong. Doomed to be forgotten. A footnote in the country's history. A question in a pub quiz.

It had been quite the 24 hours. At prime minister's questions on Wednesday, Librium Liz had insisted she was a 'fighter, not a quitter'. So what had changed? Mostly, she had allowed reality to finally intrude. It had been obvious to the rest of us for weeks that she was hopelessly out of her depth and that the Tory party and country were falling apart around her. Indeed, she had been a leader in name only since Colonel Jeremy Hunt assumed control of the country last week. From then on, she had in effect been a hostage inside No. 10, with various captors having to give regular updates about her well-being to an incurious nation. 'Liz has had a very productive day, sleeping under her desk.' 'Liz has been allowed out to sack Suella Braverman.' Truss had tried to send messages by blinking desperately in Morse code, but her pleas for help had gone unnoticed.

Lino Liz might still have been cooped up in her Downing Street gilded cage had not Thérèse Coffey – Dr Feelgood – rushed down to the voting lobbies on Wednesday night with a bag stuffed full of mood-altering drugs. Tory MPs had surrounded her and Jacob Rees-Mogg, and everyone had bundled one another through the No lobby during the fracking vote.

People were so wired that no one had a clear recollection of anything. No. 10 couldn't even be sure if Liz had remembered to vote for herself in a confidence motion. Or, indeed, if it had been a confidence motion. It would have been the most on-brand thing Truss had ever done, to vote for her own removal. There again, she wasn't entirely clear if the chief whip had resigned or not. This was the tipping point for Tory MPs. Truss had to go. Blame the drugs.

With Liz out of the picture, the new regime rapidly unravelled. So much for a smooth takeover. Col. Hunt tried to steady the ship by saying he would remain as chancellor and wouldn't be standing for leader again. Probably just as well. His key policy had been to reduce corporation tax to 15%. In yet another space–time continuum shift, of which the Tory party is increasingly fond, the new Hunt 2.0 had reinstated corporation tax at 25%. The wonders of quantum physics.

Next up came the chair of the 1922 Committee, Graham Brady, who had called a press conference to say that he didn't really have much to say. Other than that the Tory party would try to stitch up the election process by the end of next week. He couldn't provide any details as yet, as it wasn't clear right now what rules would need to be bent. But there would be two candidates going through to the members' ballot. Unless, that is, there turned out to be only one candidate. Then all bets were off.

We can see which way this one is going. The new regime going to its default position of a failed state. Yet another prime minister with no general election. No mandate. We used to laugh at Italy. Now the joke's on us. The UK is far more chaotic, far more corrupt, than anything the Italians could dare dream of. Now it's just a case of 350 Tory MPs who are more concerned about holding on to their jobs for another two years than doing the right thing for the country. O brave new world . . . To have such people in it. People such as Braverman, Rishi Sunak and Penny Mordaunt. MPs who had tried and failed to become Tory leader only months ago. Wannabes who had been rejected by either their own MPs or the Tory gerontocracy now suddenly fighting each other for another shot. People such as Boris Johnson. A dozen or so Tories, led by the deranged Nadine Dorries, thought it was time to give the Convict another shot. To forget that he had been disgraced for his criminal behaviour. That more than 50 ministers had resigned from his administration just months ago because he was unfit for office. Now they wanted him back. The venality. The desperation. The neediness. All just nauseating.

This was a Tory party that was treating the country with contempt. It was only a matter of time before someone suggested Lino Liz had another go. After all, she'd been out of office for a few hours. Surely that was long enough? Theresa May called for a candidate to unify the party. Some hope. Has she seen the state of it? Everyone hates each other. The only thing holding them together is the fear of being in opposition.

But maybe there is a saviour. Someone who has the unwavering support of himself. Step forward Rehman Chishti. Your time has come.

It was déjà vu all over again. Just months after the last Tory leadership election had thrown up Liz Truss as leader, we were now facing a second. Weirdly, Boris Johnson was seen by many as a serious contender, but the runaway favourite was Rishi Sunak. The man who had come second last time round and whose policies had been roundly rejected by the Tories. You couldn't make this stuff up.

Gagging for Rish!. It's a second coming for Sunak, the silent messiah

24 OCTOBER 2022

It all panned out about as well as the Conservative Party could have hoped. A new leader – the right leader, as far as MPs were concerned – elected in a matter of days. No general election. Heaven forbid. A failed state couldn't be doing with that level of democracy. Never trust the people you're intending to govern.

Not even a parochial, controlled election involving the Conservative gerontocratic membership. That hadn't worked out so well the last time they tried it. No, now was the time to reduce the electorate down from 180,000 party members to 357 MPs. That was the way to govern the UK. The only men and women who could be trusted to put the interests of themselves and their party ahead of those of the country. A higher calling than simple patriotism.

Mind you, it hadn't been entirely plain sailing. Boris Johnson had flown back from his holiday – how thoughtful of him to take a break when the rest of parliament was not on recess – to announce that he thought he had served his time in the wilderness. In his mind, a couple of months' hard vacationing was more than enough punishment for criminality, serial lying and general incompetence. To be fair, it had also been enough punishment in the minds of 102 MPs. Enough to have secured the Convict a place on the ballot. That's if you trust him not to have double-counted at least 20 of his supporters. Not many people did. Most just thought he hadn't got the numbers and was trying to put the most positive spin on a failed comeback.

This time his MPs had looked him in the eye and said: 'Thanks, but no thanks.' The country and his party had moved on from his comedy bullshit routine. Well, not quite all the Tories. There had been time for Nadhim Zahawi to make a complete idiot of himself – something that appears to be becoming a bit of a habit. Back in July, Zahawi had called for the Convict's resignation. Now he was his biggest cheerleader again. Up until Johnson dropped out and he switched to Sunak. Half-witted doesn't do him justice. The anti-career careerist.

Johnson pulling out left just Penny Mordaunt to take on the Chosen One. But she too couldn't scrape together the numbers that would require the involvement of the Tory membership. The 1922 Committee – along with the Conservative grandees who had spent all weekend begging MPs to do whatever it took to avoid a democratic vote – had got what they wanted: a coronation for Rishi Sunak.

Back in August, it had turned out that the Tories weren't Ready 4 Rish!. But now, just seven weeks later, Rish!'s return was being treated as the second coming. We weren't just Ready 4 Rish!. We were now absolutely Gagging 4 Rish!. Not that anyone had a clue about what particular policies he had in mind, because Rish! had negotiated the entire three and a half days of the leadership campaign without actually saying a word to anyone.

He could have been standing on the same leadership manifesto as last time. Or he might have a completely different one. You decide. Presumably, he now acknowledges it had been a mistake to raise national insurance contributions by 1.25 percentage points. Or perhaps he is now going to reverse the cut in National Insurance contributions, which was about the one thing Liz Truss had done that didn't crash the economy. And we can only assume that he's going to admit that he had been a fairly hopeless chancellor and would now try to implement a growth programme that didn't involve rampant inflation and higher interest rates.

Rish! was the silent one. After the anarchic, punk rock, 'Let's trash the establishment' of Trussonomics – 'We mean it, maaan' – we were moving into a new era of the carefully curated, bloodless boy band, with Sunak as the frontman. Rish! says it best when he says nothing at all. Just seven years from becoming an MP to the top job.

He was to be the first person of colour to be prime minister. He was also going to be the richest. Working at Goldman Sachs and marrying the daughter of a billionaire – a woman keen to maintain her non-dom status at that – has its benefits. Rish! spends more on his gym and swimming pool than many people do on their homes. Keeping it real for the little people.

Only a handful of MPs were in committee room 14 to hear Graham Brady's proclamation. Probably because everyone already knew the result, with Mordaunt having withdrawn 10 minutes earlier. Those who did turn up were the real adrenaline junkies. The ones who thrive on the fix of voting for a new leader as frequently as possible. The clinically insane who keep on doing the same thing expecting a different result. The dealers waiting for a card that was so high and wild, they'll never need to deal another.

Half an hour later, the same room was a great deal fuller as Tory MPs gathered to hear from their new messiah. Mordaunt arrived looking quite shaken and bruised. 'I'm good,' she insisted. She sounded anything but. 'I'm going to support the new PM.' There was a banging of tables as she entered the room. More out of sympathy rather than regret she didn't make the ballot. There was no sign of Johnson. He's always been a notoriously bad loser. Though perhaps he was just busy doing constituency work. Jacob Rees-Mogg, Zahawi and James Cleverly were also no-shows. Their days in government might well be over.

After a quick false start, Rish! sauntered down the corridor, before entering the room without saying anything to the media. After giving a five-minute speech that was received with more banging and wolf whistles – he must have been kissing the badge – Rish! left, still not saying a word. Clearly, he's decided it's his short cut to success. The trick will be to carry on saying next to nothing for the next two years.

The Tory MPs then emerged. Most were in a state of rapture. Or perhaps it was relief. After four or five attempts, they could finally pat themselves on the back for choosing someone who vaguely resembled a grown-up as their new leader. 'He spoke about unity,' swooned Alex Chalk. As if that had come as a revelation. Even Truss had used that line. But then few people have shorter memories than Tory MPs.

Rish! then went to Conservative central office, where he was greeted by more adoring MPs, among them Matt Hancock. 'Give us a job, give us a job, I love you, I love you,' screamed Needy Matt. Sunak blanked him, giving hugs instead to John Glen and Jake Berry on either side of Hancock. Matt looked as if he was about to burst into tears.

There was just time for a brief, wooden clip for TV – he could have got his media training from Truss – in which he talked about unity and stability. Then Rish! went back into hiding. That was the easy bit. Convincing the country he can fix the economy and make the Tories re-electable? That will be a whole lot trickier.

* * *

Yet another new prime minister meant yet another new cabinet. Suella Braverman was reinstated as home secretary, just six days after being forced to resign for breaking the ministerial code after leaking sensitive Home Office policy using her private email. Time was when ministers used to have to spend years doing charitable works in the East End of London to remove the shame of breaking the ministerial code. Now you could be forgiven in under a week. Braverman herself was completely shameless. Couldn't see what all the fuss was about.

But Rishi Sunak's desperation to have Suella back in the cabinet was telling. When he first became prime minister, he had stood outside Downing Street and said he would govern with 'integrity, professionalism and accountability'. Many had looked at Sunak's calm manner and Goldman Sachs background and assumed we were in for a period of middle-of-the-road centrist conservatism. It was a mistake people would go on mak-ing for many months. The appointment of Braverman indicated that Sunak was spiritually at home on the far right of the party.

Tories unite in their perforated defence of Leaky Sue

27 OCTOBER 2022

This one is going to run and run. If Rishi Sunak had hoped that his somewhat confusing explanation at PMQs for Suella Braverman's special interpretation of national security was going to end doubts about his decision to reappoint her as home secretary, then he was in for dis-appointment. Unsurprisingly, not many MPs – including some Tories and probably even Rish! himself – were convinced by a garbled 'She done nothing wrong, but even if she had, at least she owned up, and besides six days is more than long enough for her to have learned her lesson.'

Come Thursday morning, things were looking a whole lot worse for Rish! and Leaky Sue. First the sacked Tory party chairman, Jake Berry, told TalkTV that, far from coming forward and admitting her mistake, she had only 'fessed up when confronted with the evidence. Moments later, another Tory MP, Mark Pritchard, popped up to suggest that MI5 lacked confidence in her and the situation needed sorting. So much for Rish! uniting the Conservatives.

Inevitably, these revelations prompted a whole load of new questions, and the hopeless, hapless Nadhim Zahawi, the newly appointed party chairman, was sent out on the morning media run to see if he could come up with a passably inventive explanation. After all, if Zahawi could demean himself by posting tweets supporting both Boris Johnson and Sunak last Sunday – there is nothing he wouldn't do to prolong what passes for his career – then he should be able to talk himself out of this one. He couldn't. He crashed and burned horribly. But hey, he did turn the news round into a comedy circuit. A public service.

First off, Zahawi tried to claim that the original version had been true. If there was a victim in all this, it was Leaky Sue herself. She had just been minding her own business in copying government business to her personal email account. As you do. She had then tried to forward it to her old mucker, the notoriously trustworthy Tory MP John Hayes, a man far to the right of the ERG. As you do. Only Hayes was having problems with his email, so Braverman sent it to his wife for her to print it out for him. As you do. Her sole mistake was to send the confidential document to the wrong address. As you do. To a member of staff of another Tory MP. Who promptly reported the breach of the ministerial code. As you don't.

Braverman had been absolutely shocked – appalled, I tell you – to find out that she had committed an error and had raced to report herself when confronted with the evidence of her own lapses in security.

To his credit, Zahawi didn't really labour the point. There are limits to the bullshit to which even a professional bullshitter can descend. He was prepared to go through the motions of the 'Free the Leaky Sue One' line, but no more. Instead, he went for the absurdist, Dadaist defence – aka the alternative space–time continuum hypothesis.

It was like this. Six days might not seem very long between getting sacked and reappointed to the same job. That's because ordinary civilians experience six days as six days. But MPs and ministers experience six days as six months. In some cases as six years. So actually Leaky Sue had been sacked for an exceptionally long period of time. More than enough, in fact, for her to have been fired and rehired for further breaches of the ministerial code. She had been frozen out for far too long.

Zahawi was warming to his theme. He believed in redemption. Let him who was without sin cast the first stone. Poor Leaky Sue! Cast out into the wilderness for six long days and nights. How could anyone do that to a woman of the utmost compassion? Someone whose every dream was a loving romp with drowning asylum-seekers? Whose only mistake had been to serially break the ministerial code that she was honour-bound to obey?

Surely now was the time also to release all offenders. Hmm. Suella died for somebody's sins, but not mine. With that, Nadhim died on his arse.

Next to defend what was left of Leaky Sue's reputation was Oliver Dowden, the new Cabinet Office secretary. That did not go well either. First he had to fend off a question from Labour's Chris Bryant about Leaky Sue being a possible target for Russian spies, given her known lack of interest in national security.

Dowden bobbed nervously from side to side. He's desperate to make a good impression with the new Sunak junta and was squeaking with anxiety. He was sure the Russians would never consider targeting a home secretary who was a known security risk. But he would try to make sure she emailed all confidential documents to the entire country in future. That way there would be no *kompromat*.

Dowden tried a coquettish giggle when Angela Rayner asked much the same question. They were very similar, he smirked. They were both gingers and liked Glyndebourne – Tories clearly consider both to be an insult. But he couldn't comment on anything. Not on whether any future ethics advisers – neither Johnson nor Liz Truss felt the need for one – may consider Leaky Sue's reappointment a mistake. Nor whether the cabinet secretary had advised against reappointing her. So we can assume he did.

But all this leaves the government with a home secretary who can't be allowed out in public. Leaky Sue avoided answering an urgent question on her six-day hell on Wednesday. And she avoided answering another on conditions inside the Manston asylum-seeker processing facility – aka an overcrowded concentration camp ridden with disease. You'd have thought Braverman would have wanted to take the credit for that. But it's one thing for the prime minister and his outriders to lie on her behalf. They can claim they were misinformed. But it's a bad look for the home secretary to lie on her own behalf. So she's holed up indefinitely, waiting for the crisis to pass.

Also out of view was Penny Mordaunt, still sulking about her failed leadership bid and being left in the job of leader of the house, which she never wanted in the first place. First she failed to turn up on time, telling the Speaker that she was busy doing her nails. Then, when she did appear 50 minutes late, it was with a face contorted into a rictus of self-hatred. I'm not fucking unhappy to be here, she snarled. No one believed her. Even her colleagues thought it best to give her a wide berth. It clearly wasn't the best of days. Or best of lives. Meet the new regime. One big happy family.

Just when refugees thought Manston couldn't get any worse, here comes Leaky Sue

3 NOVEMBER 2022

It never rains . . . Rishi Sunak must have been hoping for at least one day when his home secretary didn't dominate the headlines. He could just about cope with her being malicious and vindictive. What he hadn't banked on was her being hopeless with it.

So there was no chance for Rish! to plan ahead for his day trip to COP27 on Monday. Not that he needed time to mug up on climate change. He'd already made it clear that he had little interest in that. No, his main concern was that he got more photo ops with other world leaders than his arch-rival, Boris Johnson. Hint: that just wasn't going to happen.

Even though Macron, Biden and co. know that the Convict is totally amoral, they'd rather spend time with him than with a no-mark like Sunak, someone who couldn't be counted on to still be in office at Christmas. The UK is now officially the world's laughing stock. Here's the thing: while there may be any number of Tory multiverses in which manifesto promises are both kept and broken, there are none in which the government is even halfway competent. A connecting synapse in cabinet is a wish too far. We have gone from full-on

Trussterfuck to completely Sunakered in a heartbeat.

As it was, the firefighting in the Home Office restarted on Wednesday night and continued throughout Thursday. First the immigration minister, the baby-faced five-year-old Robert Jenrick, announced that there would be a judicial review into his department's handling of the refugee crisis, as the Manston asylum-seeker processing facility was being run illegally. You'd have thought not breaking the law was the minimum requirement for a home secretary. But we live in unusual times.

Then came the news that the Home Office had driven a minibus of 11 refugees in flip-flops up to Victoria Station and just dumped them in the street. *Sayonara, losers!* Weirdly, a departmental spokesperson had said the refugees had not been dropped off in error. Which rather suggested it must have been done on purpose. It's a look. Finally another clarification. The refugees had said they were being met by family and friends, and no one had thought to check if they were telling the truth. Why would you? It's not as if the government has a duty of care or anything.

Leaky Sue chose not to apologise. Rather, she came out fired up to make life even more miserable for asylum-seekers. She was fed up that her £200-million-and-counting plans to export undesirables to Rwanda had so far delivered precisely no one onto the streets of Kigali. So she now briefed the right-wing tabloids that she was going to try out the same trick on

Paraguay, Peru and Belize. Surely they wouldn't mind. Except it turned out they did. Belize was horrified at the thought of taking in refugees who had ended up in a Third World country like the UK. A place where diphtheria, scabies and MRSA were rampant. The foreign minister insisted Braverman must have got the wrong end of the stick. It was the UK that was the designated recipient of people Belize didn't want. People like Lord Ashcroft. There were only so many tax exiles a country could take.

By now Rish! had had enough. Leaky Sue was sent down to Kent to do a tour of Manston. She took an RAF Chinook helicopter from Dover to the facility. Just so she didn't have to meet any refugees who had broken out. Quite what the prime minister thought the visit might achieve was anyone's guess, but he had to look as if he was doing something. Braverman remained tight-lipped throughout. She couldn't see what all the fuss was about. Surely it was a sign of how well things were being run if a facility designed to hold 1,600 people for 24 hours was taking 4,000 for a month or so? She refused to meet the media and take questions, so that insight died on her lips.

It wasn't just the asylum system that was failing. Not to be outdone, the police service was also falling apart on the Tory government's watch. And so the newly demoted – and never was a demotion more earned – junior Home Office minister Chris Philp was forced to come to the Commons to explain why a recent report had found that police vetting procedures were failing to detect misogyny, sexual misconduct and criminality in potential recruits.

Philp didn't have a lot to say. What could he? The report had been both damning and depressing in equal measure. It rather looked as if the only defence was that for more senior roles in the police, vetting procedures were rather more stringent. To become a superintendent you needed to have been convicted of aggravated burglary as a bare minimum. All the minister could do was apologise and insist that the three recommendations made to the Home Office would be acted upon. If only there were a precedent for the department obeying the guidelines.

At lunchtime on Thursday, Leaky Sue could breathe a little easier. The focus was off her for a while, as the Bank of England announced it was raising interest rates by 0.75%, to their highest level since 2008. Inflation needed to be battled, and the UK was heading for a two-year recession. And after that we could look forward only to barely noticeable bottom-feeding growth.

It was about now that Jeremy Hunt started regretting making his comeback as a replacement chancellor for yet another failing Tory prime minister. You only know you've hit the bottom of the barrel when the splinters begin to show. The first few weeks in the job had been the easy bit, just undoing everything that Liz Truss and Kwasi Kwarteng had proposed. You or I could have done that and looked competent. It was undoing the last 12 years of Conservative economic mismanagement that was more tricky.

Hunt gave a brief TV interview. It wasn't a Tory-made disaster. It was just a disaster the Tories had made. And the really great thing about this recession was that it had happened on the Conservatives' watch. Because the Conservatives could be trusted with the economy. If the same recession had occurred when a Labour government was in power, then the country would have been totally screwed.

'Er . . .' said the chancellor. It was all going to be tough. Especially for the prime minister, who stood to see millions of pounds wiped off his £730 million net worth. So we should all Pray 4 Rish!. 'Will that do?' asked Hunt, desperate to get away. It wouldn't. It really wouldn't. But it was all we were going to get. Welcome to Breadline Britain.

* * *

Worse was to follow. Gavin Williamson had also been fired by Theresa May – remember her? – for breaking the ministerial code by leaking details from national security council meetings. Sunak felt Gav was due for redemption and appointed him as minister of state without portfolio. It was never going to end well.

Williamson devotees rally behind Britain's finest fireplace salesman, but Gav goes – again

8 NOVEMBER 2022

Alas, poor Gav . . . But what a fortnight! A triumph of integrity, professionalism and accountability.

Devastated. Heartbroken. When King Charles dabbed away a tear at his mother's funeral, it wasn't because he was moved by the poetic way in which Liz Truss read the lesson. Or even by the solemnity of the occasion. What had upset him so profoundly was the jokey text message from Kwasi Kwarteng, informing him that Gavin Williamson had been left off the guest list by Wendy Morton. Thank God the Queen was no longer alive to witness one of her oldest friends being 'pussed about'.

Few knew how close the Queen and Gav had been. Fewer still knew that they had spoken every day by phone to natter about staffing issues. Who was bullying whom. That kind of thing. The two had met when Gav came to Sandringham to sell the Queen a new fireplace. One from the ever-popular Elizabethan range.

The Queen had been the first to write to congratulate him when he subsequently won Fireplace Salesman of the Year in 2007, and from then on the pair were inseparable. The Queen had even made a point of presenting Gav with the coveted trophy again the following year, the first time any fireplace salesman had won the award back to back. Stick with the winners! Liz had.

After that, the rapport just developed naturally. The Queen couldn't quite see why Gav was sacked as defence minister for leaking details from national security council briefings. Surely he was just being picked on for his easygoing and pleasant manner. Nor could she see why he was also sacked as education secretary, just because he made a complete mess of the exams system. Still, it had been the proudest day of her life when she finally got to knight him. Arise, Sir Gav.

The King thought back to his last conversation with his mother. How she had implored him to intercede with whoever happened to be prime minister that week – even she was struggling to keep up – to get justice for Gav. The least he deserved was another cabinet job. Even if no one, including Gav, really knew what he was meant to be doing. The royal family knew the value of non-jobs better than most.

So when Rishi Sunak became prime minister, Charles had been happy to put a good word in. A last act of duty to the Queen from a devoted son. To the King's surprise, it had been like pushing at an open door. Rish! had been only too happy to insist that Gav's reputation as a total liability, who could be depended on only to be the most untrustworthy and unpleasant person in any room, was entirely undeserved. The fact you couldn't find anyone to admit they had been bullied by Gav proved it was all a plot.

It would be an honour to have someone whom even Boris Johnson had been obliged to sack back in the cabinet. Not out of weakness. Far from it. Everyone knew that Rish! had never needed to make any grubby deals to ensure his coronation as prime minister. No. It was from a position of strength. Gav was clearly the right person for the job. Whatever that job happened to be. He'd work out the details later. For now it was just nice to have Gav back around the place. Minister without portfolio. To convey the right 'don't give a toss' attitude to the cost-of-living crisis. Gav was a man made for *levitas*.

Perhaps in time, Rish! had thought, he would find something for Gav to do. Minister for making everyone feel good about being British. Minister for something to do with national security: that would give him something to leak. Minister for government press officers – or minister for bullying, as it was otherwise known. That would do. Not that Gav was a bully. Just a bit high-spirited and excitable. Someone who couldn't help getting priapic at his proximity to power. Someone whose sense of humour meant he took whipping literally.

So Gav had told the chief whip to fuck off. To stop pussing him about. That was just everyday bantz. And he had told a senior civil servant at the ministry of defence to slit his throat. That had been an act of kindness. He had simply thought the person had been choking on a crisp and was merely suggesting an emergency tracheotomy. He was trying to save a life.

And as for Gav telling someone to jump out of the window, that was just a bit of fun. He had never intended anyone to die. Just to get paralysed from the waist down. People should just learn to chill a bit more. So Rish! wanted everyone to know that Little Gav had his utmost confidence.

Up to the point when more evidence emerged that Gav was yet another Billy-No-Mates Bully with a fragile ego. Then Sunak would pretend he had no idea about Gav's reputation for treating people in an unacceptable manner. And no one had mentioned to him Gav had twice been sacked for disloyalty and incompetence. But if push came to shove, Rish! would sack him in a heartbeat. Anything to protect himself.

And so it proved. As it turned out that virtually everyone who had ever worked with Gav had found him irresistibly hateful – to know him is to loathe him – and that the complaints system was in danger of grinding to a halt under the weight of people coming forward to tell their truth, brave Rish! chose to pull the plug. Third time unlucky. 'It's not me, it's you,' he had said to a tearful Gav. 'One of us has a career to worry about.' Though he might have thought of that sooner. So much for his integrity, professionalism and accountability. In the background, you could hear Suella whoop. She could have sworn she would be the first cabinet minister to be sacked. Two weeks and counting . . .

It was left to Cabinet Office minister Jeremy Quin – Sunak's iteration of the unctuous Michael Ellis, who could be sent to the Commons to defend any irretrievable situation – to try to salvage a shred of decency on behalf of the government. He didn't succeed. Labour's shadow home secretary had used a humble address to try to force the government to reveal all the evidence that had been available to the prime minister before he handed out cabinet jobs to Suella and the Gavster. It wasn't successful, but that was beside the point. What it did was expose the hollow emptiness at the heart of government. The moral vacuum.

All Yvette Cooper wanted to see were papers, scraps, anything that would help the country to understand why Leaky Sue and Gav had been given their jobs, when they both had a track record for both breaking the ministerial code and being generally useless. Didn't we deserve something a bit better than this? Apparently not. The Tory party was clean out of talent. So we just had to suck it up. And the government wouldn't be releasing any documents because . . . . . . Just because.

Many of the same arguments had been used in an earlier opposition day debate, in which Labour tried to get the government to commit to the pensions triple lock. 'Sorry,' said the work and pensions secretary, Mel Stride. He couldn't possibly second-guess what was going to be in next week's autumn budget. Er, right. But it was the Tories who had committed to it in their manifesto. Surely someone ought to be able to confirm whether Sunak was going to do what he had promised? He couldn't.

We were just going to have to wait and see. Live dangerously. Live like Gav.

* * *

Meanwhile, Matt Hancock was finding there was life outside cabinet. Outside parliament. Matt had started to take his sex god image extremely seriously and seemed to think he could act as a role model for the nation. With this in mind, he signed up to appear on I'm a Celebrity . . . Get Me Out of Here! *for a mere £400,000. He promised he would give some of his fee to charity . . . make that about £10,000. Generous to the last. Needless to say, Matt was mercilessly picked on and bullied by both the viewers and the other contestants. But in his own mind, Matt was a winner. Er . . . we'll be the judge of that.*

Nine things we've learned about Matt Hancock on *I'm a Celebrity*

11 NOVEMBER 2022

Matt is still toxic. The first reaction of the comedian Seann Walsh said it all. He saw Matt Hancock and he burst out laughing. As if he'd just come across the last person he'd want to meet. Others weren't so kind. The *Corrie* actor Sue Cleaver reckoned he shouldn't be skiving off when parliament wasn't in recess. The singer Boy George said that if his mum had died of Covid, he would have walked out of the camp. The former rugby player Mike Tindall observed that Matt just talked 'bullshit, bullshit, bullshit'. The radio DJ Chris Moyles looked as if he wanted to throw up. The rest didn't say much. The least hostile response came from the *Hollyoaks* actor Owen Warner. But then he didn't appear to know who Matt was. By day two, some of the camp had relaxed a little, as if they had made a decision to try to get along with him in the interest of harmony. But several clearly dislike him intensely. Imagine.

Matt is just trying to be human. At least, that's what he keeps telling us. He wants us to see the real Matt. The Matt behind the politician's mask. The man behind the podium, as he self-importantly put it. The guy who wanted to understand economics, so he went to work in the Bank of England, before going on to become an adviser to George Osborne. The everyday story of an ordinary bloke who just happened to become a cabinet minister. So what he's doing on *I'm a Celeb* – other than trousering £400K: it's astonishing how no one ever mentions they are in it for the dosh – is something of a mystery. The last place any sane person would expect to be real is on a reality show. But Matt is arrogant and delusional enough to think he can beat the system. Either that or he's never watched the show. *I'm a Celeb* is one of the most sadistic shows on TV, and the only reason Matt has been brought on is to be the hate figure against whom the country can unite. A thought: why would Matt imagine anyone was that interested in his human side? He's actually rather dull.

No one is in any mood to forgive. Matt might want to move on, but the country is not yet ready to do so. Most people are more interested in the inquiry into the government's handling of the Covid pandemic. How people with Covid were discharged into care homes. How contracts for PPE were handed out to mates, with little or no public scrutiny. How people in government repeatedly broke the lockdown laws they had imposed. And yes, that includes you, Matt. At the beginning of the pandemic, Matt insisted it was a police matter when the epidemiologist Neil Ferguson was caught visiting his girlfriend. When Matt was captured on CCTV groping Gina, he insisted it was just 'an act of love'. Two star-crossed lovers. The TV presenter Scarlette Douglas quizzed him on this, but Matt clearly has no regrets.

Matt can't sing. When Seann first met Matt, he asked him to name his favourite band. You could see the panic in Matt's eyes. What was the band that would make the public love the 'human' Matt? Eventually he stumbled on Ed Sheeran. After all, everyone likes Ed Sheeran, don't they? Er . . . To try to prove he did really, really like Sheeran, Matt started singing the words to a song he couldn't name initially. 'Don't sing, Matt,' he said to himself as he carried on singing. Finally the song's title came to him. Perfect.

Matt will do anything to be loved. It shouldn't be any surprise that Matt has been selected for the first three trials. It was what he was paid to come on the show for: so we could watch him suffer. Nor should it be much surprise that Matt has been rather good at them so far. Like many politicians, Matt is a narcissist with a limited sense of danger. So he will rush into situations where more normal people would hesitate. Matt doesn't care if he's forced down a tunnel where shit is tipped on his head. Nor does he mind going *mano a mano* with snakes and crocs. Anything for a bit of attention. Matt's worst nightmare is being totally ignored. The celeb that nobody much cares about.

Matt thinks Rishi is doing a great job. When asked why he thought it was OK to bunk off parliament when he was paid to be an MP, Matt breezily insisted the prime minister was managing just great without him. If by doing great he meant that Rishi was leading the economy into recession, had already had to sack his first cabinet minister, had U-turned on going to COP27 and was useless at PMQs, then yes, Rishi had made the perfect start. Sadly Matt is so delusional, he hasn't yet realised that most people can't sack off their day job – even if everything was going just fine – if they get a better offer.

Matt isn't so keen on telling the world about his dyslexia campaign after all. Before he went into the jungle, Matt was adamant that his motivation was to highlight causes that were dear to him. Maybe he's saving that for later in the show, because up until now he hasn't mentioned dyslexia once. Nor has he talked about his favourite hospice, to which he will be donating £10 of his fee.

Matt doesn't know his career is over. Matt imagines he will be able to slip back into Westminster, his reputation enhanced, and continue as before. He doesn't know that he's washed up. That no one will ever take him seriously again. That the best he can hope for is another payday on another reality show. His adviser knows the game is up, though. He has been busy sending reporters unsolicited WhatsApp messages that highlight any tweets that have been vaguely supportive of Matt. As if the floodgates are about to open and we're all going to fall in love with him and realise he's one of the good guys after all.

We've already had enough Matt. From the fake laugh to the endlessly awkward conversations with the other celebs, Matt is sucking the life out of the show. *I'm a Celeb* is meant to be fun, but Matt has such an uncomfortable aura he is making the experience of watching him a trial in itself. There is no more fun to be had with Matt. Just sending him off for more and more trials has become boring, as well as making us viewers complicit in his narrative. So far the story of the show has all been about Matt. It's time to relegate him to a bit part. Better still, to vote him off the show. Matt's job on *I'm a Celeb* is done.

Psycho Raab's vein goes into throbbing overdrive over bullying claims

16 NOVEMBER 2022

Every cloud and all that. What with the threat of the Third World War, Rishi Sunak probably had better ways of spending his last few minutes at the G20 in Bali than scribbling a brief note to Dominic 'Psycho' Raab, agreeing that an investigation into his deputy's behaviour was the right way to proceed.

If nothing else, it was all very embarrassing. The prime minister had spent much of the previous few days insisting he had never heard a bad word said about Psycho. Not a dickie. He had always found him completely charming to work with. If a little abrupt. And aggressive. But that was all part of his manly charm.

Now it turned out that civil servants in two of the departments Raab had worked in had lodged formal complaints of bullying. The only wonder was that so far no one had come forward from the former Department for Exiting the EU. Give it time. And just wait until the police start identifying some of the unknown bodies fished out of the Thames.

But, for Raab, there was definitely an upside. He had been due to stand in for Rish! at prime minister's questions. And he had feared he would be in for a rough time from Angela Rayner over the numerous bullying allegations being made against him. Just imagine. In anti-bullying week as well. People should have known better than to pick on him at such a sensitive time. But we were where we were. And at least now he would be able to say that he was far too traumatised to give a statement and would wait until the outcome of any investigation.

It was far from a full house on the government benches for Psycho's first outing at PMQs since his reappointment as deputy prime minister. If he has his fans, they had chosen to mark the occasion by staying away. As had most of the cabinet. Jeremy Hunt was there to show his face before Thursday's autumn statement, but he made little effort to conceal the fact that he was there under duress. Perhaps he had been bullied into it. Being seen as close to Raab isn't a great career move these days. Otherwise the forgettable Alister Jack was the closest we got to an A-lister. And he was only there because he couldn't sneak away after Scottish questions.

The session got under way with a non-mea culpa, Raab's standard response to everything. He has never yet found a situation in which his standards of behaviour fell short of expectations. It still hasn't occurred to him that it might be an idea to raise his game. Thinking you must have been a top bloke just because junior staff left the room alive having wiped away their tears doesn't quite cut it.

But Labour's Clive Betts tried to get Psycho to commit to something on the record. Would Raab admit that bullying wasn't quite what Rish! had in mind when he said he would govern with integrity, professionalism and accountability? And would any minister found to have a complaint upheld against them be obliged to resign?

Raab went into legal overdrive. He didn't want to say anything that might prejudice any investigation, but he was sure he would be proven innocent on all counts. Especially if the prime minister did the right thing and appointed an investigator who was house-trained in overlooking bullying complaints. Such a pity the prime minister hadn't yet bothered to appoint an ethics adviser. He went on to say he would comply with any decision. Which wasn't quite the same as saying he would resign. Always best to leave yourself a bit of wriggle room.

For now, though, Psycho was doing his best to look intensely relaxed. As if these kinds of complaints were the sort of thing every cabinet minister routinely had to deal with. Angela Rayner looked curiously unnerved. It was almost as though she had imagined she just had to turn up and Psycho would disintegrate on first contact. Only now the ball game had changed. She had already got the investigation she had been planning to demand. And she had no other line of questioning prepared.

She began well enough by aligning Labour with the government response to Russian aggression in Ukraine. Though Raab would have settled for that all day. Just bring on five more questions with which he could agree.

This was one of the rare occasions when he wasn't actively looking for a fight.

Next, Rayner brought up the forthcoming autumn statement. She used the same 38th out of 38 OECD growth statistic that Rachel Reeves had quoted in Treasury questions the day before. Still no answer. Was Hunt going to do anything to upset Rish!'s wife and various Tory donors by abolishing non-dom status? Psycho was horrified. The Tories were the party of aspiration. And closing tax loopholes would just deter people from working hard to acquire the connections and wealth to avoid paying what they owed.

Then Labour's deputy leader piled into Raab on the bullying claims, and her attack lines rather fizzled out. She had nowhere to go with them. Psycho could just stonewall. There was going to be an investigation. He couldn't believe the people he had bullied had really been bullied, otherwise they wouldn't be coming forward now. The people he really bullied were normally so incapacitated with PTSD that they never left their psychiatric wards. So he was quite certain that anyone covered in flying tomatoes would be able to see the funny side. Just bantz. His way of trying to bring out the best in junior staff was to treat them like shit and submit them to a near-death experience.

Labour's Bambos Charalambous stirred things up by referencing Raab's previous. Was it true that before he became an MP he had forced one member of staff to sign a non-disclosure agreement? No, Raab insisted.

The person had just had to sign a document agreeing not to disclose anything. Which was completely standard practice. Especially when the boss is an aggressive lunatic. By now Psycho's anger vein was beginning to throb. Pulse. Pulse. Pulse. Raab took a breath, willing himself back under control. He could kill someone later. Just because.

Jacob Rees-Mogg tried to come to his rescue. Various Labour MPs had been accused of bullying, so it was hypocritical of the opposition to moan about Raab's excesses. By far the best way forward was just to forget about all bullying complaints. Not that the government wasn't taking them seriously. Raab was already forbidden from meeting junior staff unsupervised. Lee Anderson was just idiotic. No change there then. He thought Labour daring to question Suella Braverman's multiple breaches of the ministerial code was the most wicked act of bullying.

The session ended with Raab on a high. Sunak was going to choose the person to lead the investigation. So it wasn't going to be in the slightest bit independent. Better still, Rish! had made it clear that it was ultimately up to him whether Psycho was guilty or not. Just in case the investigator didn't follow orders. All would be well. That's our Dom. A licence to bully.

* * *

Another day, another scandal. Rishi Sunak had been in office for barely a month and he was already on to his third major scandal. First Suella. Then Gav. Then Raab.

And now there was another bombshell. So much for integrity, professionalism and accountability . . .

Tories run for the hills rather than face Labour over Michelle Mone and PPE

24 NOVEMBER 2022

Spare a thought for Neil O'Brien. A minister so beige, so junior, that not even his colleagues know he is working with them. At home, he merges into the muted pastel paintwork. So much so that his family aren't always aware if he's there or not. So it's a wonder he even became a minister, given that few had ever seen him, let alone heard of him. But when the Tory government ricochets from crisis to crisis as often as it does, then almost everyone eventually gets a go. Only the actual brain-dead remain on the backbenches in the current Conservative Party.

O'Brien first came to anyone's notice when he resigned as a bag carrier at the Department for Levelling Up in the dying days of the Boris Johnson regime. Which came as news to the Convict, who couldn't remember appointing him. But lightning struck twice, and O'Brien was invited back by Rishi Sunak to serve in the most junior role possible in his government, this time in the Department of Health and Social Care. There to be forgotten, as his brief was to do as little as possible.

Which was how things stood on Thursday morning. O'Brien had just been going about his usual daily routine, his weightiest decision whether to have one or two Weetabix for breakfast. Then came the call. Would he report to the Commons at 10.30 to answer an urgent question on the Michelle Mone PPE scandal that had broken the night before in the *Guardian*?

No one at cabinet level could possibly do it as they had all been up late at the *Spectator*'s Parliamentarian of the Year awards the previous evening. Then No. 10 had tried to get someone from the Cabinet Office to do it – the UQ had been directed there, after all – but no joy. No one was answering their phone.

The same had happened in other departments. Until someone happened to remember that O'Brien was still working for the government in some capacity. His schoolboy error had been to answer his phone. He had tried telling Downing Street he didn't have a clue about Mone or Medpro PPE, but that had cut no ice. In fact, he was told his ignorance would be his greatest asset. Less chance of accidentally incriminating the government. 'Take one for the team,' he had been told, before the caller rang off.

So it was a queasy-looking O'Brien who turned up for the UQ. A man who looked as if he had spent the previous couple of hours throwing up rather than trying to prepare some answers. The Speaker, Lindsay Hoyle, got the session under way with a reminder to the house not to mention any cases currently under investigation. Labour's Angela Rayner nodded politely and then went on to more or less ignore him. She wasn't about to let parliamentary procedure spoil her day.

Rayner began by welcoming O'Brien to the dispatch box. Along with everyone else, she had never met him before, and she wished him well. O'Brien gave a dry heave. Rayner was just about the last person he wanted to face on his first time answering a UQ. Someone a little less direct, preferably.

Then she cut to the chase. What due diligence had been done? How come Medpro had been granted a contract via the VIP fast lane? How come tens of millions of pounds of public money had ended up in private offshore accounts? Why wouldn't the government publish its correspondence regarding attempts to reclaim the money? What was going on in the Randox scandal? And why was the government wasting £700,000 a day on storing unusable PPE?

O'Brien did his best not to look clueless, but failed. It was like this. You had to remember the panic that engulfed the world at the start of the pandemic. When governments were buying up every item of PPE. Even the bits they didn't need. And the UK was no exception. So mistakes had been made. But due diligence had been done. About 19,000 companies had submitted bids, and only 2,500 had passed the sniff test. Presumably because all the others had offered one left glove and demanded money with menaces. He didn't say why the Medpro bid was accepted. But he did want everyone to know there was nothing sinister about a VIP lane. It was just a way of making sure that people with access to Tory MPs were given priority treatment. But they were still subject to the same low levels of due diligence as everyone else. There were no special favours. And getting money back was proving quite tricky. There was no VIP service for the government to reclaim money that had been obtained for worthless contracts. The VIP channel was strictly one-way. The government's way of reaching out to business.

It wasn't a convincing performance exactly. And it wasn't helped by the fact that there were only three Tory MPs in the chamber to back O'Brien up. And of them, Christopher 'Upskirting' Chope could be classified as a hostile, attacking the government for wasting money on PPE that was unfit for purpose. Only Peter Bone and James Wild were helpful. Useless PPE was better than no PPE, apparently. And who cared if some people had made a profit selling rubbish.

After that, it was a Labour and SNP pile-on. What was Matt Hancock doing? Apart from going through a mid-life crisis Down Under? Why did there even need to be a VIP lane for Tory mates? When would the government get the money back? Did they remember nurses wearing bin bags? Would there be an inquiry? Come the end,

O'Brien looked on the verge of tears. Desperate to get back to obscurity.

Still, he wasn't the only one having a bad day. Dominic Raab was on the wrong end of yet more bullying complaints – it would be quicker now to find someone who hadn't been bullied by him – and allegations that he broke the ministerial code by using his personal email for government business. The transport secretary, Mark Harper, meanwhile, belatedly woke up to the fact that the government might have some part to play in settling the rail strikes. The same went for the health secretary, Steve Barclay, and the nurses' strike.

We live in a world where the government's first instinct is to do nothing. The hedgehog principle: roll into a ball and wait to be run over. It feels like the end of days.

Sunak has created a cabinet in his own image – one of weakness and invisibility

28 NOVEMBER 2022

Just who is running the country? Your guess is as good as any. In theory, it's meant to be Rishi Sunak. Only he has taken the homeopathic approach to being prime minister. Less is more. He talks a good game about the UK being a global power. How China should go away and shut up. How the good times are just round the corner.

Except it's been a never-ending downwards curve for the past 12 years. No one in their right mind thinks anything is going to improve any time soon. Most of us are hunkering down, expecting the worst. Rish! is the incredible shrinking leader. Only effective when he is doing nothing. Little more than the memory of a prime minister.

On Monday afternoon, the Commons was meant to be debating the levelling-up bill. Only that was called off, when Sunak decided to pull it. Theresa Villiers had become the de facto leader of the country. Just for one day. Anyone who had seen her vacant stare into the void when she was chanting, 'Who do we want? Andrea Leadsom. When do we want her? Sometime in September,' during the 2016 Tory leadership campaign should be terrified.

Villiers had decided that the last thing the country needed was more houses. Despite there being an acute housing shortage. Or, to be strictly accurate, St Theresa, the patron saint of nimbyism, didn't think there should be any more homes built anywhere near her or her friends. Or in places that she might want to visit one day.

Astonishingly, she is not a lone voice. More than 50 other Tory MPs also agreed that if new homes were going to be built, construction should take place well out of their eyesight. At which point Rish! the Brave chose to run for the hills. Rather than stick to his principles and build the houses that need to be built with the backing of Labour votes, he decided to drop it. Just in case he looked weak.

Go figure. Just how weak does he think he looks, caving in to a bunch of his more swivel-eyed backbenchers? Now he had come to think about it, maybe levelling up wasn't such a great idea after all.

Sunak was also struggling with onshore wind. Back in the summer, Rish! had been dead against it. One of the few points of principle in his leadership campaign had been his commitment to not build wind turbines. As far as he was concerned, the only way that wind energy could be developed on land was if every member of a community was totally in favour of it. And that included getting the permission of people who had died at some point within the last 20 years.

All of which was a wee bit mad. Not least because onshore wind is one of the cheapest and greenest forms of energy and almost all of the country is in favour of it. And now we have the weird situation where Simon Clarke, one of the last believers in Trussonomics – that bad – has become a champion of environmentalists by making a stand for onshore wind turbines.

So, faced with some actual opposition, Rish! has now decided that he quite likes the wind thingies. At least, that's what he seems to have instructed Grant Shapps to say – a minister who has never seen a turbine he didn't want to destroy, as he's terrified his private plane might fly into one.

All morning, Grant had been saying Sunak hadn't changed his mind. It was just that everyone had completely misunderstood what the prime minister had said all along. Clarke hadn't been a one-man vigilante squad. He had been a government cheerleader. No wonder some politicians struggle for credibility.

And Sunak has created a cabinet in his own image. One of weakness and invisibility. Starting with Suella Braverman. Immigration is supposed to be the home secretary's number-one priority. At least, that's what she says if you ever happen to find her. She's harder to track down than a red squirrel.

Over the past six weeks, there have been countless statements and urgent questions on the processing of asylum-seekers who had arrived on small boats, and Suella has made a point of giving or answering none of them. She has sworn an *omertà*. Any speaking engagements are left to Robert Jenrick, her junior Home Office minister.

Monday afternoon was no exception, as the government was called upon to explain why one asylum-seeker had died of diphtheria and countless others had been infected by the disease. First, though, Yvette Cooper, the shadow home secretary, wanted to know why Braverman had bunked off yet again. Was it something Cooper had said or done? Was Suella phobic about immigration? Could Labour help her out with some cash for therapy?

Jenrick ignored her. What went on between Braverman and the homeopath would have to remain confidential. Instead, he tried to hard-sell the diphtheria outbreak as a national triumph. At least there were no cases at the Manston processing centre. Mainly because the Home Office had managed to move anyone infected with the disease out into the wider community.

And yes, there were now at least 50 cases, but only one person had died. So no harm had been done really. Look at it this way: it was best to do nothing until things got completely out of hand. That way the government could look as if it was taking more decisive action. Besides, they were only foreigners, so why the fuss?

There was no sign either of the foreign secretary for an earlier urgent question about executions in Saudi Arabia. The Saudi government has been using the World Cup to launch a large advertising campaign promoting the country as a tourist destination. Camels, dune buggies, beaches, food. Though surprisingly no mention of the fact that it's one of the few places where you can catch a public beheading. An odd miss, that.

David Rutley, a junior Foreign Office minister, said he deeply regretted that the Saudis were executing more and more people. And he would like to whisper very loudly that the UK was not happy about this. But on the whole, he didn't want to rock the boat too much. Live and let live. Apart from those being executed. Once again, Britain was a beacon of light and of hope. When someone spots a minister showing leadership, do give us a shout. Right now, they are an endangered species.

It felt very much as if the country were coming apart at the seams. The cost-of-living crisis was getting worse, not better. The NHS was on the brink of collapse. More and more trade unions were electing to go on strike, their members having taken a real-terms pay cut of up to 25% since 2010. Inflation was well into double figures. The UK economy consistently ranked last out of all the G7 countries. The government would always try to pretend this was solely down to Covid and the war in Ukraine. As if other countries hadn't had to deal with these crises. What the Conservatives ignored was their own incompetence and Brexit. Leaving the EU was estimated to have caused a 4% cut in GDP. Though no one was allowed to mention Brexit any more. Even the Labour Party had banned the word.

The government was also failing according to the metrics on which it wanted to be judged. For example, more and more refugees were crossing the Channel in small boats. Amid all this, Rishi Sunak appeared to have gone missing. He was a leader in absentia. *The only time the country got to see him was for a brief half-hour at the weekly session of prime minister's questions. Where was Rishi?*

Sunak is a puzzling PM – the more you see of him, the less there appears to be

20 DECEMBER 2022

Christmas must be a bundle of fun round the Sunaks'. 7 a.m.: 5km run. 8.30 a.m.: breakfast of granola with manuka honey. 9 a.m.: check against delivery to make sure all presents are under the tree. 10.30 a.m.: invite family to open presents. All members are to keep a profit-and-loss spreadsheet to make sure the presents they have received are more valuable than the ones they have given.

12 p.m.: short Xmas lecture on the importance of winning. 12.30 p.m.: all family members are to write a brief lessons-learned dashboard on the lecture. 2 p.m.: lunch of organic turkey crown with no trimmings. 3 p.m.: unfinished homework to be completed. 4–4.45 p.m.: at leisure. No TV, console games or handheld devices. Children may read books if they want. 4.46 p.m.: children and adults to write thank-you letters. 6.30 p.m.: stop Alexa playing 'Ghost Town'.

7.30 p.m.: invite family to complete survey. Tick the option that best describes the day. (A) I was very happy with my Christmas experience. (B) I was quite happy with my Christmas experience. (C) I was neither happy nor unhappy with my Christmas experience. (D) I was quite unhappy with my Christmas experience. (E) I was very unhappy with my Christmas experience. Now list one thing that would have improved your Christmas. 8.30 p.m.: *University Challenge*. 9 p.m.: bed.

Rishi Sunak is a conundrum. Schrödinger's prime minister. The more you see of him, the less there appears to be. A man who doesn't much care about anything. A man so rich he can afford to be seen to not even care about his wealth. His beliefs dictated by a Goldman Sachs training manual. The country just an intellectual playground for him. Its people just problems to be solved. Preferably with a PowerPoint presentation. He is a man without emotional affect. Either dead or empty inside. Or just completely disconnected.

All of which was just perfect for Rish!'s first appearance before the liaison committee – the supergroup select committee made up of the committee chairs that Bernard Jenkin, the liaison chair, allows to attend. And admittedly, this time Jenkin had chosen a predominantly D-list cast of committee chairs – all the really good ones have either been promoted or excluded – so Sunak was not unduly taxed. But even so, he was perfectly robotic in his meaningless management-bollocks replies. His handlers would have been thrilled. He didn't even once make eye contact with anyone in the room.

Alicia Kearns, the new chair of the foreign affairs committee, went first. In a hurry to make a splash. Was the government growing cold on Ukraine? Absolutely not, said Rish!. It was just that he could never appear too excited about anything. Was he going soft on China? No, it was a coincidence that Chinese diplomats had been allowed to leave before they were expelled.

'Are you robust?' Kearns persisted.

'I'm really, really robust,' Sunak replied.

'But are you?'

'I am. I am,' he creaked in a grinding monotone. He was the most robust person in the room. More robust than anyone. When no one was looking, in his spare time he made RPGs for Ukraine.

Jenkin started to hurry the committee chairs up. He didn't want them accidentally asking any pertinent questions. And besides, Rish! had said he could only spare 90 minutes of his time. Most prime ministers gave up two or three hours to the liaison committee. But Sunak had promised not to say anything worthwhile, so why go to the trouble of wasting everyone's time?

OK, said Diana Johnson, the home affairs committee chair, one of the brighter members on view. How big would the backlog of unprocessed refugees be next year? Er . . . We'd clear up most of this year's backlog, apart from the ones we wouldn't count. And then there would be a backlog of all the refugees who would arrive next year. So we'd be back where we started. But Rwanda would help a lot. Refugees would see what an ideal destination it was and try to get there directly. So we'd save ourselves a fortune in air fares. Or something.

We then moved on to the cost of living. Was there anything he regretted about his time as chancellor? Rish! thought for a minute. Not really, he said. He'd done everything pretty much perfectly. As was plain to see. Though if he did have a fault, it was that the UK was not quite ready for his brilliance. Or his modesty.

Inflation was an issue, Sunak admitted. Though he made it sound like an abstract irritant rather than a matter of heating or eating. Certainly not something that lost him any sleep. Nor was he that bothered about food banks. On balance, he would prefer that people didn't use them, but he wasn't going to stop anyone. It was almost as if he had misheard the question. Except he clearly hadn't. Food banks are just too alien a concept to impinge on his blinkered reality.

Nor was Rish! much interested in the first-ever strikes taking place in the NHS. Nurses and ambulance staff ought to be happy with people clapping them. And he was saddened that they wanted more money because he had hoped they wouldn't be so greedy as to want more than a real-terms pay cut. Shame there wasn't someone in the room from the NHS to put him right.

Sunak was equally condescending when it came to Scotland. He would be delivering for Scotland. He couldn't say what he would be delivering or when he would be delivering it, but he expected the Scots to be grateful when he did deliver something. On his delivery dashboard.

Various committee members sneaked off before the end. As well they might. We had learned nothing. Other than that Rish! is a master of complacency. Listening to him speak, you'd think the country had never been in better shape. When the reality is we're all Christmas Sunakered.

Would anyone notice if the government went on strike?

10 JANUARY 2023

Here's a thought. How could you tell if your MP is on strike? Especially if they were a backbencher, under no obligation to do anything very much. Just take a look at the chamber of the House of Commons – Tuesday's statement on industrial action, for example – and it's seldom more than a quarter full. If that. Some may be busy with committee or constituency business, but it's fair to assume a few might just have decided, after the appropriate consultation with themselves, to withdraw their labour. To picket by pursuing an alternative career.

Take Theresa May. Since 2019, she has pocketed the best part of £2.5 million for public speaking. And she hasn't even given me a 15% agent's fee. I made her. Without me, she would be just another washed-up Tory prime minister whom everyone would rather forget. But

I created her Maybot persona, and now people are queue-ing up to hear her give ponderously dull, monochrome speeches. Just for the lols.

Take Boris Johnson. He's raked in the best part of £1 million in less than a month. No wonder he's not sure how seriously to take Nadine Dorries's efforts to reinstate him as prime minister: he's not sure if he can afford such a drop in salary. No wonder he's out on strike: his terms and conditions are at risk of being unilaterally rewritten.

Then there's John Redwood. Someone has paid him an extra £700,000 over the past three years. Why? He's known to be certifiable. Guaranteed to be wrong on almost any topic. Other Tories must be green with envy. You get the picture.

So what about Steve Barclay? He's not officially on strike. Though he might as well be. The excess deaths through the underfunding of the NHS are staggering, even when no staff are taking industrial action. The health secretary has a duty of care to the country that he is clearly not fulfilling. At the next cabinet meeting, Grant Shapps should suggest that Baldrick Barclay gets the sack. It's what the government would have wanted.

Same with the transport secretary. The trains don't operate a recognisable minimum service level, even on non-strike days. The Avanti West Coast line is a joke. Bye-bye, Mark Harper.

Which brings us to Rishi Sunak. It's hard to think of one area of government that is functioning properly. He is the politician's anti-politician. The man who fails at politics 101. Give him a choice, and he's a certainty to pick the wrong one. His efforts fall well below any minimum safety level. He's a liability to himself and the country.

At some level, the government recognises this. No one more so than Shapps. The business secretary has stared into the abyss. Had it been during the Johnson or Truss administrations, he would have been far more gung-ho about introducing new trade union legislation. Grant would have been the first to channel his inner Norman Tebbit with a triumphalist Thatcherite agenda. It's what comes most naturally to him.

Instead, it was a more emollient – almost apologetic – Shapps that gave a statement on the new union proposals. It was as though he understood that taking on the nurses and the ambulance drivers wasn't the wisest of moves, as most of the country supported the NHS staff. So he wanted to say how much he loved the nurses – couldn't manage without them – and he was just hoping to nudge the ambulance drivers into being a bit more organised about service levels on strike days.

Hopefully, this legislation would never need to be called upon. It was just a fail-safe. It wasn't about curbing union powers. Heaven forbid. He couldn't understand why opposition MPs were saying it was. All he wanted to do was bring the UK into line with other Western countries, such as France, Spain and Germany. How could anyone possibly object?

Let Labour's deputy leader, Angela Rayner, enlighten him. For one thing, if the government really wanted to make sure the health service was running safely, it should be going the extra mile to resolve the industrial disputes. Had it not occurred to Shapps or Rish! that one of the main reasons the NHS was at breaking point was because there were so many staff vacancies? And the NHS couldn't recruit because people didn't want to work burn-out shifts and still have to rely on food banks to get by. It was also disingenuous to blame everything on Covid and the war in Ukraine. Other countries were coping far better than we were. And what about the government's own efforts to turbo-boost inflation and crash the economy with the seven-week Trussterfuck roller coaster? And another thing: the ambulance workers had agreed a minimum safety level on a region-by-region basis. And another thing: European Union legislation was far more liberal than ours already. So what was the problem?

A few Tories stood up to give Shapps support. They'd waited months for some decent union-bashing and weren't going to miss out. Even if they weren't entirely sure what the problem really was. Richard Drax just wondered why we couldn't bring in the army to deal with everything. There's always one.

In any case, they were drowned out by the opposition benches. Andy McDonald pointed out that the government's own impact assessment of the proposed legislation was that it would be unworkable and would lead to even more strikes. Rachael Maskell observed that there were more excess deaths on working days than strike days, and the solution was to fix the NHS. The SNP's Chris Stephens noted that all unions had emergency cover on strike days.

Inevitably, it all petered out, with Shapps insisting he knew best. And if people didn't agree with him, he would go on strike. Not that anyone would notice.

* * *

New year, new you. Hardly. Rishi Sunak had tried to wipe the slate clean in the first week back after the Christmas recess with a speech about . . . the nation's need to get better at maths. The prime minister may have had a point – who hasn't wished they were better with numbers? – but he could have started closer to home with his own government. All of the UK's statistical data was heading in the wrong direction. Inflation up, and no sign of any of the long-running strikes coming to an end. After 13 years of real-terms wage cuts under successive Tory governments, people had decided enough was enough; they didn't want to accept yet another below-inflation pay offer that would mean they were effectively worse off than the year before. And the year before that.

On top of all that, Sunak was having to deal with the fact that the carousel of Tory sleaze showed no signs of stopping. What goes around, comes around.

Clunk click: Rishi buckles up on the greasy ethics pole

23 JANUARY 2023

Integrity. Professionalism. Accountability. Remember them? The three pillars on which Rishi Sunak promised to build his government. On the off chance he could differentiate his administration from those of his predecessors. Some hope. That holy trinity has long since checked out.

Now it's just got a whole lot worse. Starting with Sunak himself. Rish! the Recidivist. Having picked up one fixed-penalty notice for a lockdown birthday party with Boris Johnson, he's gone on to pick up another for not wearing a seatbelt. Hardly the biggest crime, certainly. But definitely one of the dimmest. After all, he was caught only because he happened to film himself breaking the law. Call that professional? He's never going to make it as a career criminal. Not sure that not knowing or ignoring the law counts as integrity. Which leaves us with accountability. And I guess that pleading guilty and paying the £100 fine does just about qualify. Though whether we want a serial offender as prime minister is another matter.

Still, Sunak is undeniably a step up the greasy ethics pole from Boris Johnson, aka the Convict. The man who continues to take the Tory party into the sewer even from the backbenches. You can tell he knows he's busted. Where was he at the weekend? Visiting President Zelenskiy in Ukraine. Where he always goes when he's bang to rights. It's his subconscious crying out for absolution. His way of acting out his guilt. His crime this time? Same as it ever was. Sleaze and incontinence. A basic refusal to engage with the normal rules of behaviour.

When most people are hard up, they cut back on their lifestyle. Johnson, not so much. He is the exception. The man to whom the usual rules don't apply. His needs must be satisfied. So a Tory donor, Richard Sharp, put the cabinet secretary in touch with a long-lost relative of Johnson who happened to be offering an £800,000 credit facility. For wallpaper, alimony, fun and excess? Not for accommodation – Boris had already found someone else to stump up for that. In the meantime, Sharp was appointed as chair of the BBC. Because obviously there was no question that Dicky Sharp was the right man for the job.

Only it turned out that a loose regard for potential conflicts of interest was contagious. Because when Sharp was chosen by Johnson to head up the BBC, it never once occurred to him to mention the loan at any of his pre-appointment hearings before the Digital, Culture, Media and Sport select committee. And there we all were. Being told by the Conservatives that the BBC was staffed by a bunch of left-wingers who were hell-bent on bringing down the government. But now we know better.

Then we come to the man of the moment, Nadhim 'He Pays What He Wants' Zahawi. Or rather, the man for whom hubris has kicked in after a long career in business with Jeffrey Archer, not to mention him claiming parliamentary expenses for the heating of his stables – and who hasn't done that? Now he finds he has to pay what HMRC wants. Somewhere along the line, HMRC appears to have hit Zahawi with a penalty, as well as a demand for the unpaid tax. Even so, Nadhim doth protest too much, saying the mistake was the result of carelessness. Here's the weird thing, though: when millionaires say they have been careless in the tax department, they have never carelessly paid too much. We don't get to see them weeping with joy as they get an unexpected rebate. The accounting errors are always in their favour.

And what of Rish!'s involvement in all this? Did he not wonder if there might have been a conflict of interest in Zahawi – or the chancellor, as he was then – negotiating his own deal with HMRC? Of course he didn't. This was the sort of thing that could literally happen to anyone. Too trivial to mention. Because that's the kind of liberal attitude to paying tax Sunak wanted to encourage among Tory donors. Zahawi: the perfect welcoming committee. Up until Monday morning, he had Sunak's full support. Now Sunak has kicked things into the long grass by handing things over to his newly appointed ethics adviser. Somewhat late in the day.

But even if Rish! was happy enough with the integrity, professionalism and accountability in his party – a view not shared by many of his MPs – Labour can spot sleaze when it sees it. So it was no surprise that its deputy leader, Angela Rayner, secured an urgent question on the quality of vetting procedures in the government. This was just a general question, insisted the speaker, Lindsay Hoyle. It wasn't about anyone in particular. Yeah, right. The paymaster general, Jeremy Quin, reluctantly got to his feet. Pain and suffering were etched onto his face. Lying doesn't come as easy to Quin as it does to some of his colleagues. The rules were whatever the rules were, he said. He had no reason to assume they had not been followed, as he had gone out of his way not to find out.

Rayner stormed in. How could the government not see that there was a clear conflict of interest? When everyone else in the country could? How could we trust a word Zahawi said? How come Zahawi was banned from getting a knighthood but not from serving in the cabinet? Were there lesser standards required for being in government? And how come No. 10 had changed its story about what it knew and what it didn't? Did Zahawi have some kind of hold over the prime minister?

Three Tory MPs stood up to make a lacklustre defence of the government. Could we just forget about the whole thing until the ethics adviser reported back sometime in 2030? But most sat in a glum silence. It felt like the end of days. A moral decay. The SNP's John Nicolson raised the Sharp case. Was this transparency? Or merely Tory transparency – an opaque transparency? Quin tried fobbing opposition MPs off but finally remembered he had his own integrity to consider. So he said he 'genuinely' couldn't say whether Zahawi had been telling the truth about his tax situation before he got busted. Zahawi had been cut loose. Sort of.

In a TV clip, Sunak went on to say that 'integrity' really mattered to him. But it doesn't. Integrity is an action. If Sunak really cared, he'd have fired Zahawi and made sure Sharp stood down from the BBC. Don't hold your breath.

Spirits of Downing Street present and past submit to TalkTV's finest inquisitors

2 FEBRUARY 2023

Rishi Sunak and Boris Johnson have both given interviews to TalkTV. The Guardian *got to see the out-takes.*

Piers Morgan: Good to see you, Prime Minister. It must be an honour for you to come on my show.

Rishi Sunak: It's a pleasure to be on a programme whose ratings are lower than my own.

Morgan: Let's start with the biggest issue. Meghan Markle. She's a right piece of work.

Sunak: I'm not sure I've got anything to say . . .

Morgan: How about Prince Harry then? What a woke wuss the man is. He shouldn't be invited to the coronation, should he? He's a disgrace . . .

Sunak: Er . . .

Morgan: I'll take that as a yes. On to you, Prime Minister. Today marks your 100th day in office. How do you think it's going?

Sunak: Thank you. Far better than expected. At one point I wasn't sure I was going to last 100 days. My priorities are the country's priorities.

Morgan: Then your priorities are to get a Labour government elected.

Sunak: Precisely. And we are totally on track.

Morgan: Let's go first to some breaking news. Shell has just announced record profits. Are you having second thoughts about putting a more effective windfall tax in place?

Sunak: We are the party of low taxation . . .

Morgan: You could have fooled me. Taxes are at record levels . . .

Sunak: As a Conservative, my instincts are not to raise taxes. It is wrong to punish companies for being in the right place at the right time. That's why Infosys is still operating in Russia. If a business can't get rich on the back of an illegal war, then when can it?

Morgan: Do you think everyone should pay their taxes?

Sunak: Of course not. I'm a Conservative. The rich should pay as little as they can get away with. And there should be breaks for oligarchs donating to the party.

Morgan: I blame Meghan . . .

Sunak: What for?

Morgan: Everything. The Bank of England has just raised interest rates to 4%. Do you worry that many people will default on their mortgages?

Sunak: What's a mortgage?

Morgan: It's when people borrow from the bank to buy a house.

Sunak: Why would they want to do that? Why don't they just buy a house with their own money? It doesn't make sense. People should live within their means.

Morgan: Do you worry that all the opinion polls suggest you are out of touch?

Sunak: No. Why?

Morgan: You've promised to halve inflation . . .

Sunak: Yes. That's my number-one goal.

Morgan: But it's forecast to fall anyway. Regardless of what you do.

Sunak: I know. That's exactly why I've promised to do it. It's important that people can be confident the government will do what it says.

Morgan: Let's move on to the strikes. We all know you are going to have to do a deal with the unions. When are you going to start negotiating?

Sunak: Sorry?

Morgan: Negotiate. As in talk . . .

Sunak: Oh. I hadn't thought of that. Aren't the nurses all militant lefties who are in the pocket of union barons? That's what Grant Shapps says. Sometimes the right thing is to do nothing and to let things get worse. And as a strong leader I will not hesitate to do nothing.

Morgan: Let's take you back to your first day in Downing Street, Prime Minister. You said you would govern with integrity, professionalism and accountability. How do you think that's going?

Sunak: Pretty well. I mean, I've got to be an improvement on Boris Johnson and Liz Truss, haven't I? At least under me there's a sense of managed failure.

Morgan: Gavin Williamson . . .

Sunak: Who?

Morgan: Nadhim Zahawi . . .

Sunak: Look, I've gone on the record on this before. I made a huge effort not to know anything about anything before I appointed my cabinet. It seemed only fair to give a lot of deadbeats an even break. Myself included. No one could have been more surprised than me that Honest Nadhim turned out to be a liar and a tax avoider. But it was only £5 million, including the penalty. That's just a rounding-up error on my tax return.

Morgan: Dominic Raab . . .

Sunak: A lovely guy. Total sweetheart. A real joker. Only yesterday he popped into Downing Street to say that if I dared say a word against him, he'd slit my dog's throat and stuff the body under my daughter's pillow! How we laughed.

Morgan: Suella Braverman . . .

Sunak: When I said there would be zero tolerance for breaking the ministerial code, what I meant was there wouldn't be.

Morgan: I've got to press you. Meghan. She totally fancies me, doesn't she?

Sunak: Gosh. Er . . .

Morgan: Thank you, Prime Minister.

Sunak: I hope no one was watching . . .

Morgan: You've no worries on that score.

A muffled banging comes from the fridge.

Boris Johnson: Is it safe to come out now? Has Piers gone?

Nadine Dorries: It's OK, my darling Bozzy Bear. The nasty man has gone. Let me just ask you some really tricky questions. Is it true that the Conservative Party treated you appallingly and that you would make a far better prime minister than that halfwit Sunak?

Johnson: Um . . . er . . . Yes, and cripes, I suppose you are right.

Dorries: You're so handsome. I bet all the ladies say that to you . . . Now what about those suggestions that you tried to cover up your involvement in the Downing Street lockdown parties?

Johnson: Of course I didn't. That's for the birds.

Dorries: You're so right. It would be so out of character

for you to lie. Now whisper me some Brexit bonus sweet nothings . . .

Johnson: Thanks to Brexit the pandemic was not nearly so bad in the UK because we had closed our borders and the virus couldn't get in . . .

Dorries: YES!

Johnson: Thanks to Brexit we were able to supply arms to Ukraine like other EU countries . . .

Dorries: YES! YES!

Johnson: Must go. I've got a couple of mill to make giving rubbish speeches in the US. Can you just check that the idiot Bamford is covering my expenses as per usual?

Dorries: Bon voyage, my darling Bozza. I love you so much.

* * *

Cometh the hour, cometh the man. With the economic outlook still dire and the Tory government unable to shake off its various scandals, Rishi Sunak chose to break the mould by appointing Lee Anderson as deputy chairman of the party. Yes, that would be 30p Lee. The knee-jerk right-winger from the 2019 red-wall intake who had claimed the reason people were using food banks was because they were too lazy and stupid to cook properly for themselves. Lee reckoned he could eat for as little as 30p per meal. And have change left over.

What's that sound? It's Rishi scraping the barrel with this desperate plea to populist Conservative roots. Anderson would prove there was no bar too low for him. Especially the dimness bar. In 2022, he had said that all MPs should be barred from having £100,000 per year second jobs. So what did he do in 2023? He took a £100,000 per year second job as a presenter on GB News.

Bring back hanging and real men: making the Tories great again, by Lee Anderson

9 FEBRUARY 2023

The Guardian *has been given exclusive access to the 10-point plan put forward by the Conservative Party's new deputy chair.*

Make England Great Again, or MEGA: And I mean England. For far too long we've wasted far too much time on trying to keep the rest of the United Kingdom happy. But think of it this way: name me one thing that Scotland, Wales or Northern Ireland has done to make an Englishman proud. Precisely. Nothing. All we've had is one long moan. 'It's not fair.' 'We want more.' Well, I say enough is enough. Time for England to put England first. The sooner the rest of the UK understands that what's good for England is good for them, the better.

Capital punishment: There is currently an epidemic of violent crime in the country. Even the police, God bless them, are at it. People think they can get away with murder these days. But it's got to stop. So now is the time to bring back hanging. Have you ever heard of a person who has been executed going on to reoffend? No. So it clearly works as a deterrent. And who cares if you occasionally kill the wrong person? Even if they hadn't done that crime, they would probably have gone on to commit another one. So no harm done. In any case, you can get too hung up on innocence and due process of the law. In any clampdown on serious crime there will be some collateral damage. People are far too squeamish. We could even reintroduce public executions. I'm sure people would want to pay to see them. Tory party members could have priority booking.

Food banks: The country has gone soft. Everyone knows you can eat like a king on 30p a day, so if you're struggling to make ends meet, then you just don't know how to budget. So it's time to get rid of all food banks. They merely encourage people to overeat and not take responsibility for their own lives. If people want to eat, they should learn to get a job and not waste their money on trying to heat their homes. They should realise their place in life and just put on a coat.

English football: There's a reason the England men's team haven't won the World Cup since 1966. Back then, the players were real men. You wouldn't have caught

Bobby Moore, Jack Charlton and all the other heroes taking the knee for Black Lives Matter. What a load of woke nonsense. So come on, England. Give us a team of which we can be proud.

Discipline: Kids these days think they can do what they like. Give them a clip round the ear when you catch them littering at a bus stop, and they start yelling about being violated and threaten to take you to the European Court of Human Rights in Strasbourg. If Brexit means anything, then we should all have the right to Taser oiks in the street. And schools should bring back corporal punishment. Six strokes of the birch and children would think twice about talking back to a teacher. Respect. That's what we need.

The BBC: We've had more than enough of the so-called British Broadcasting Corporation. It may have once served a purpose, but now all it does is talk England down with its relentlessly woke, multicultural agenda. I don't know what part of England it thinks it represents, but I don't see my life reflected on any of its programmes. It's reached the point where you can't even install a Tory donor as chair through the establishment back door without half the country being up in arms. What we want is GB News to become our national broadcaster. Someone who understands English values and English news. Bring on Laurence Fox. And while we're about it we can also get rid of that pinko rag, the *Guardian*.

Small boats: You won't find any true patriot who doesn't think the country has been overrun by immigrants. So some employers can't fill their vacancies? Well, I say far better to run the economy into the ground than have the wrong kind of workers. First and foremost, though, we've got to stop the small boats crossing the Channel. Right now, we're as good as saying 'Please do come' as we put them up in five-star hotels and don't even deport them to Rwanda. It's time for more drastic action. Either we need to send gunboats and shoot them out of the water or we need to mine the Kent beaches. As soon as the Albanians see TV pictures of their compatriots getting blown to pieces they'll stop making the crossing.

The NHS: We can all see the health system is over-stretched. So we need to make some tough choices. For a start, we can get rid of the interpretation service. We are an English health service, so all appointments should be in English. If a patient wants to see a doctor who speaks Urdu, they should go to Pakistan. It's also time to stop treating people for conditions that result from their own lifestyle choices. Offering surgery for cancers and heart disease brought on by obesity only encourages people to overeat. People need to learn there are real consequences for their actions. Fat people should just be allowed to die. The one exemption is for smoking. Cigarettes are part of what helped England win the war.

School curriculum: Yet another part of English life that has fallen victim to the wokerati. You can't move without some new book being banned or issued with a trigger warning. Back in my day, we cheered when the albatross got it in the neck when we read the *Ancient Mariner*. The bird had it coming. Now kids break down in tears, sobbing, when it croaks. Worst of all is the history syllabus. Since when did England have to get all apologetic for having an empire? Far from saying sorry, we should be glorifying our past. We should also concentrate a lot more on the people that matter. The kings and queens. Though maybe not Prince Harry.

Identity: Aren't you sick of not being able to tell if someone is a man or a woman? I know I am. So all men should be made to have short hair, while women's hair must come down to at least below their ears. Then we'll know. And pronouns should be as they were. 'Him' for a man, 'her' for a woman. Just to keep it simple. People who are confused about their gender should just make up their minds. We should also get rid of the title Ms. Women can go back to Miss and Mrs. That way we will all know exactly where we are.

* * *

Politics in Westminster had settled into a steady pattern. No great theatrics, just a prolonged period of more or less managed decline. Rishi Sunak had avoided the chaos of his predecessors, merely to replace it with a feeling of grinding inevitability that things could only get worse. Everything was going to fall apart; it was just a matter of when. Even Tory backbenchers could see no sign of hope, and over the weeks fewer and fewer bothered to attend prime minister's questions. Presumably, they were all eyeing up other job opportunities.

Not even Jeremy Hunt's spring budget could break the sense of inevitability. There again, few people know less about economics than Hunt. When he was appointed chancellor, the first thing he did was to buy himself a copy of Quantitative Easing for Dummies. It's a scary prospect when the chancellor knows less than you do, but we were where we were . . .

Starmer grabs the limelight and shows practice almost makes perfect

23 FEBRUARY 2023

When is a pledge not a pledge? When it's a mission.

Keir Starmer's speech on Thursday had all the feel of a manifesto launch during a general election. The atrium setting of the Co-op building in central Manchester. Hundreds of people watching from the balconies above. Party activists bussed in to create a vibe. Several people stuck in the revolving doors. Most of the shadow cabinet squeezed into the front row, eyes rapt with wonder and hands bruised from the applause.

Only there's no election. At least, not for another 18 months. At the earliest. Possibly longer. The Tories are

25 percentage points and counting behind in the polls. There's no way Rishi Sunak is going to call an election unless he actually has to. 'I'm sorry that everything is a lot worse than it was 13 years ago, but trust me to sort out the mess my party has created' doesn't quite cut it as an election slogan.

So what was Starmer doing in Manchester? You'd have thought he might have been happy just to sit back and let the Conservatives carry on making mistakes. After all, it's worked well enough so far. But with Sunak currently doing his best to remain invisible, maybe the Labour leader thinks it can't do any harm to grab the limelight. To let people see that there is an alternative. That he has some ideas. And he gets to look like the real prime minister.

Then again, Starmer does quite enjoy making speeches. Depending on how you are counting, this Thursday was his 11th or 12th major relaunch since he became party leader three years ago. Sometimes whole policies have been junked. Sometimes they have just been fine-tuned. And the speeches seem to have been coming with ever-increasing frequency. It feels as if we have had at least four since December last year. Come the autumn, we could be up to two or three a week.

But practice does make . . . if not perfect, then something not far off. When he first became leader, Starmer had a well-deserved reputation for being a wooden performer. Someone who wasn't entirely sure he believed in what he was saying, having been forced out of his natural habitat into a public arena. He looked sweaty. Nervous. As if he had something to hide. Now, though, Starmer seems to relish the TV cameras. Comes alive on the big occasions. He's grown into the job. He's seen off Boris Johnson and Liz Truss. And Sunak has given him no reason to believe he can't see him off as well.

Not that Keir will ever be a total natural as an orator. He will never have the evangelical power of a Gordon Brown. But he's found the self-belief and the confidence. He's more than good enough as he is. The country doesn't want a snake-oil salesman offering shares in a promised land. We've given up on the all-too-fallible Tory messiahs. Our sights are lowered. We now want someone decent and competent. Someone who looks as if he knows what he's doing and can be more or less trusted. And Starmer knows he can deliver that.

Keir stripped off his jacket and raced to the podium in the centre of the atrium. He wasn't here to make any pledges. Pledges were so last year. Instead, he was on a mission to deliver his five missions. There are always five. It's not a credible election offer unless there are five. Good growth. An NHS fit for the future. Safe streets. Equality of opportunity. Clean energy. Nothing to frighten the horses. Nothing to which anyone could possibly object. No one would have been that surprised if the Tories had come up with something similar.

At this stage, most of the missions were kept a bit vague. Though Starmer repeatedly insisted there was nothing vague about his missions. They would all have measurable targets one day. Most importantly, they weren't just the mindless Sunak promises to try to fix the stuff he had broken. But they were all fully costed and would be achievable inside 10 years. He hadn't even won his first election yet and he was already making a pitch for a second term.

The one mission where Keir did offer detail was growth. The UK would have the highest sustained growth of any country in the G7. This certainly wasn't an easy target. Only once, in the 1990s, has the UK ever grown faster than Germany. And Germany hasn't made the schoolboy error of leaving the EU. Starmer never did quite explain how we were going to make up the 4% Brexit hit to GDP and overtake the US and Germany. Brexit was not up for grabs. It was a fait accompli. Though he would manage to negotiate us a better deal. Good luck with that.

The missions might have been tough, but the overall message wasn't. The UK needed to stop the short-termism. Sticking-plaster solutions for the NHS. Never stopping to wonder why the same problems hit the health service every winter. Now was the time for a radical overhaul. To prevent the problems occurring. At times, it all sounded too good to be true, but Starmer always had the perfect comeback. After 13 years of Tory government, name one thing that works better now than it did in 2010. There's no comeback to that.

After a prolonged standing ovation – no minister wanted to be seen to be the first to stop clapping – Starmer took questions. Few took issue with the missions. More were interested in the number of promises/pledges/ missions – delete as necessary – that had been junked along the way. What had happened to the halfway-house Corbynista promises on which he had been elected? How could anyone trust him again?

Starmer didn't miss a beat. A year or so ago he might have got flustered. Tried to ignore the questions. Now he went in with a smile. Almost a laugh. He's no longer ashamed of who he is. Those promises were then. This was now. People change their minds. His goal was a Labour government, not some kind of ideological purity. A promise that could never be met because you were in permanent opposition was completely worthless. Besides, Sunak U-turned on everything. So why shouldn't he? And if the Tories were so worried about Starmer's trust-worthiness, they knew what to do. They could call an election. And then we could see who the country trusted. Over to you, Rishi.

Is Brexit finally done, or is everyone just done with Brexit?

27 FEBRUARY 2023

Getting Brexit done. Again. We've been here before. Theresa May thought she had a solution to Northern

Ireland with the Chequers agreement. That lasted only a few days. Boris Johnson had the lie of the 'oven-ready' protocol. That was enough to win him a general election – mainly because the Tories were so desperate they were prepared to sign up to any old fantasy – but it fell apart soon afterwards, when people bothered to look at the detail.

Now we have Rishi Sunak's Windsor Framework. To fix the Boris nonsense. The likeliest contender yet. Not least because everyone is so fed up with Brexit – no one wants reminding of what a disaster it has been – that even the hardest of hardliners can't be bothered to oppose it.

Jacob Rees-Mogg and David Frost broke the habit of a lifetime by not publicly rubbishing the deal. The Democratic Unionist Party said it would need time to read the detail. Boris could feel his support ebbing away. Only Nadine Dorries was prepared to openly voice her outright opposition. So sweet. She will do anything for her Bozza Bear.

Shortly after 2.30 p.m. on Monday, the government announced that a deal had been done. Which was odd, as we all knew that a deal had actually been done a couple of weeks ago, only for everything to be put on hold as No. 10 worked out the best way to choreograph events in a manner that would stop the shit-baggers from trashing the deal immediately. If it could survive unscathed till Tuesday morning, it would be a result. By then the headlines would be in and the deal alive, with everyone wanting to move on. To Anything But Brexit. If the DUP and the European Research Group of Tory Brexiters chose to trash it thereafter, then they would be on their own. Wreckers out to spoil everyone's fun. Or if not fun, then absence of pain. As close to fun as Brexit gets.

An hour later, Sunak and the European Commission president, Ursula von der Leyen, appeared at a press conference in the Windsor Guildhall. Rish! tried to look surprised. It was a real coincidence that they were in a wood-panelled room, decked out with portraits of various kings and queens. Symbolism with which to batter the DUP.

Rish! got things under way, struggling to make himself visible behind the lectern. A box might have helped. His deal was hereafter to be known as the Windsor Framework. The Framework was to be a new way forward. Well, not that new, as much of what he had to say had been leaked weeks before. There would be a green lane for goods coming from the UK mainland to Northern Ireland. And a red lane for goods destined for the Republic.

'The same foods will be on sale on supermarket shelves in Northern Ireland as in the rest of the UK,' Rish! declared triumphantly. Er. That would be nothing, then. Most supermarket shelves in the UK happen to be empty at the moment. Our very own Brexit dividend. Much more of this and even the DUP might think about rejoining the single market. At least that way no one in Northern Ireland would go hungry. Just a thought.

What was new was the Stormont Brake. This would allow Northern Ireland to veto any EU laws it didn't like. Except that would probably never happen. Here was the brilliance! First of all, the DUP would have to reconstitute the Stormont assembly for the Stormont Brake to be viable. Then they would have to find another five assembly members from other parties who were as mad as they were. That might be tricky. And even if this were to happen, it would still need the prime minister to sign off the Brake. Guess what? Rish! had promised Ursula he would never do it. Guess what, again? When he was gone in a year or so, Keir Starmer would never apply the Brake, either. So it was all an illusion. Schrödinger's Brexit, yet again. Fantasy heaped on fantasy. It was also just about the only sensible piece of politicking the government had done in the last eight years.

Next up was von der Leyen. She didn't want to piss on Sunak's parade by going on about EU law still applying in some areas – she was far too excited about meeting the King. That wound would open soon enough. So she restricted her remarks to a few pleasantries. She loved Windsor. It was so historic. And, by the way, the only reason she had been willing to make a deal with the UK was because she was no longer having to work with that untrustworthy scumbag. Boris could do one, as far she was concerned. Rish! nodded involuntarily.

After just a few questions, Sunak and VDL parted company. Job done. The Commission's president could get on with her awayday break, and Rish! could see how his deal landed during his statement to the house. He needn't have worried. Tory MPs from all sides of the party cheered and waved their order papers as he entered the chamber. Consensus had broken out. It had all been the fault of the Convict that the Windsor Framework had needed to be negotiated. They couldn't believe they had allowed themselves to be duped by such an obvious fraudster. It was time for Year Zero. This was a new start. The past was another country.

Even the DUP weren't going to trash the Framework. Not yet, anyway. Rather, Jeffrey Donaldson said he would think things over. He recognised he had been backed into a corner. All of the alternatives were spectacularly worse. Maybe it was time to finally say yes. As for Boris, he was nowhere to be seen. There was to be no comeback. His NI Protocol Bill was dead in the water. His days were over. Just another Brexit deadbeat.

The Tories are doing the same thing yet again, and nobody expects results

7 MARCH 2023

If insanity is doing the same thing over and over again and expecting a different result, Rishi Sunak and the Conservative government must need 24-hour psychiatric supervision. There have been dozens of initiatives and six new bills aimed at stopping people entering the UK since 2015. The most recent one, the Nationality and Borders Bill, promised to end small-boat crossings once and for all. That went well. Last year saw a record 45,000 arrivals.

But Rish! is nothing if not pig-headed. So he's now made stopping the small boats an election promise. And to make good on it, he has now introduced yet another bill that to all intents and purposes looks hopelessly flawed and completely pointless. The chances of it achieving its objectives are nil. It's performative Dadaist politics. Something designed to con his dimmer backbenchers and a small minority of the country. And if all else fails, Sunak could go begging to voters. 'I know I've failed. But at least I tried.' Good luck with that.

Still, there are a surprising number of Tory MPs willing to be duped. They will get fooled again. Nobody ever lost money by underestimating the stupidity of the current Conservative mob. They know that every previous immigration bill has been a crock of shit. They know the current one is almost identical. And yet they are desperate to believe in miracles.

So about a hundred or so of the lumpenconservatariat were crowded in at the far end of the Commons as Suella Braverman prepared to share her dreams about barring foreigners. The other end was more sparsely populated. Those Tories with more synaptic engagement and human sensibilities had chosen to stay away. These days, sticking up for refugees in public can get you into an awful lot of trouble in government circles.

Shortly after 12.30 p.m., Braverman, flanked by a nervously grinning Rish! – he's more and more becoming an absence rather than a presence – got up to deliver her statement on the Illegal Migration Bill. Aptly named, because most of it is illegal. 'Yesterday's laws are not fit for purpose,' she began. Er, that's not what the last home secretary said. Or indeed you, when you gave the French more money to police their coast. But hey, whatever. Let's just close our eyes and roll with the nonsense. Because this time it really is going to work. I can feel it in my bones.

It was like this. If we continued to do nothing – she wasn't shy about slagging off both herself and her predecessors – then 100 million asylum-seekers would be turning up on our shores next week. Yup, you heard that right. Probably an underestimate. Why not include China? Nothing odd about so many people coming to the UK. Two and a half million small boats with 40 people on each would turn up on Dover beach at the same time. It would be by far the biggest flotilla in history. The UK's population would almost treble in a day. Suella looked completely serious as she said this. A worry. Perhaps she really is that stupid.

Anyway, to stop the 100 million coming here, she was going to introduce a new law. One that was almost identical to the previous ones. Here was the plan. We'd round up everyone who arrived at Dover and bang them in a detention camp that we hadn't yet built. Regardless of whether they had a legal right to asylum. The modern slavery law could also do one. Far too woke. We would then fly them all to Rwanda. Only we hadn't yet dumped anyone in Rwanda. And in any case, Rwanda had said it would only take 200. Perhaps we'll just throw them in the sea. None of them would ever be allowed near the UK again.

But the net result was she had no idea if the bill was compatible with the European Convention on Human Rights, and no one would be deported for years as most cases would get held up in the justice system for years. So the chances of Rish! stopping the boats before the election were zero. Genius! All this would save the British taxpayer billions by costing billions more. Amazingly, she wasn't even embarrassed.

Labour's Yvette Cooper tried to point out some of the logical inconsistencies, but Braverman wasn't listening. She was rushing on her run. Anyone who tried to talk her down was just out of touch with the British public. She wasn't a racist, nor were any Brits – really? There are some who look that way on your own benches – but enough was enough. You give these foreigners an inch, and they take a mile. It was time to get tough and kick ass. There would be blood.

The Tories lapped it all up. None seemed to be aware they had just been sold a bridge. A while ago, Tim

Loughton had a brief incarnation as a liberal when he realised he was going to lose his seat to the Lib Dems, but now he appears to be resigned to being unemployed. He just wanted asylum-seekers to suffer as much as he was. Not even a pretence at morality. Others were all for detention centres, just as long as they weren't built in their constituencies. They had more than enough foreigners already. No vacancies.

Predictably, Braverman hadn't gone far enough for some Tories. Iain Duncan Smith, Simon Clarke, Bill Cash and Mark Francois all begged the home secretary that Britain should leave the ECHR. If international law was going to be tricky, then just ignore it. We could go it alone. What was wrong with turning the UK into a pariah state? Suella didn't disagree. She didn't say the ECHR was a legal necessity. She didn't say the ECHR underpinned Brexit and the Good Friday Agreement. She just muttered non-committally. Here was the Tory manifesto for the next election.

Meanwhile, Rish! hightailed it to Dover. Looking for a refugee who had just arrived. 'Haha. You've blown it. It's the detention centre for you. And then you're off to somewhere!' Maybe to find a boat he could slash with a knife. All the while telling the world how much he valued foreigners. How welcome the one Afghan who had reached the UK via a safe route in the last year was.

Hours later, he was back at No. 10 to give a press conference from a podium branded 'Stop the boats'. In which he said nothing, while trying to sound like a billionaire man of the people. The bill would work because it would work. 'I promise what I deliver, and I deliver what I promise.' He and the country were just all compassioned out. Refugees were so last year. He didn't really sound as if he believed a word of it. Just pure cynical politics. His parents would be ashamed.

Quite the day in Westminster. Hard to know what had won. Stupidity? Nastiness? Hypocrisy?

Sunak spells it out for Suella and gets *très sérieux* with Emmanuel

9 MARCH 2023

Rishi Sunak: Good work this week, Suella.

Suella Braverman: Thank you, Prime Minister. I really think we have got illegal immigrants on the run now.

Sunak: What makes you say that? All our other bills have failed. Why should this one be any different?

Braverman: Then what was the point of it?

Sunak: Sorry. I forgot that you're not very bright. Let me spell it out for you. Obviously, we have no centres to detain anyone. Nor do we have any deportation agreements with third countries. Apart from Rwanda, which will take 200. Though we haven't deported anyone there yet. And obviously the lefty lawyers will try to make us obey the law in order to stop us. But we'll get great headlines from the *Mail* and the *Telegraph* for looking as if we're trying.

Braverman: Oh. I see.

Sunak: Really?

Braverman: Not entirely. Let me just check. We do still hate immigrants, don't we?

Sunak: Of course. Very much so.

Braverman: Well, that's all right then.

Sunak: Just keep on doing what you're doing. Don't get hung up on what I said about integrity, professionalism and accountability. That was just a Downing Street soundbite. Hell, I'd never have appointed you as home secretary if I'd meant anyone to take it seriously. After all, you had only been caught breaking the ministerial code – again – just six days earlier. Your job is just to be a lightning rod for halfwits like Jacob Rees-Mogg and Lee Anderson.

Braverman: Phew!

Sunak: Talking of which, how are you getting on with the ghastly woke Blob?

Braverman: You mean my civil servants?

Sunak: Absolutely.

Braverman: But I never sent that email.

Sunak: Of course you didn't. It was one of our morons in CCHQ. But that doesn't matter. What counts is everyone knows that's what you really think. And being at war with civil servants is a great look for us. Dog-whistle populism goes down a storm with Tory voters.

Braverman: I have sent out another email saying how much I love the Blob.

Sunak: Any replies?

Braverman: A couple of anonymous ones telling me to fuck off.

Sunak: Excellent. As long as no one is talking about the cost of living or hospital waiting lists reaching their highest levels, then we're still in the game.

The phone rings.

Sunak: Sorry. It's the chairman of the BBC. I've got to take this.

Richard Sharp: My dear Rishi. How are you, old boy? So good of you to spare the time to speak to me.

Sunak: Not at all.

Sharp: I can't tell you how sorry I am that Gary Lineker has spoken out of turn about your superb immigration bill. The BBC must be impartial at all times.

Sunak: Don't give it a second thought.

Sharp: No, no, really. I can't apologise enough, darling Rishi. It was unforgivable.

Sunak: You misunderstand me, Dicky. I was delighted Mr Likener, or whatever his name is, compared the bill to Nazi Germany. Please keep it coming. Because when snowflakes like him speak out, it helps to create the impression that we really are going to do something about the small boats after all.

Sharp: I catch your drift. Good thinking. I will encourage him to go on Twittering.

Sunak: Excellent. And may I thank you for your impartial donations to the Tory party in the past. And we'd be delighted if you felt able to give to the party again in the future. I can send you the direct debit form, if that helps.

Sharp: Splendid. Let's do lunch sometime soon.

Sunak: Take care. I'm just off to Paris to see Macron.

24 heures plus tard.

Sunak: *Bonjour, Monsieur le President.*

Macron: *Bonjour.* Can I see your passport?

Sunak: Why?

Macron: Just to make sure you have the right visa stamp. Since Brexit, there are formalities to be observed . . . Not that one. That's your US green card.

Sunak: We need to talk about *les petits bateaux.* They must be arrested.

Macron: What do you suggest?

Sunak: We will pay you a few euros for more *gendarmes sur les plages.*

Macron: You've tried that before, and the number of crossings has increased.

Sunak: That's because your police have been pushing the boats towards the UK.

Macron: Not that nonsense spouted by the demi-wit Natalie Elphicke.

Sunak: It's *très sérieux.* We have reason to believe there are at least 100 million migrants on the northern French coast at the moment. Possibly billions. Everyone *veut venir a Angleterre.* It won't be long before the whole world is in Dover. So we want you to agree *droit main-tenant* to take back everyone who crosses the Channel.

Macron: *Vous avez perdu* the plot. So what's your plan regarding the European Convention on Human Rights?

Sunak: *C'est comme ça.* We're not going to *quitter* the ECHR. We're just going to carry on breaking international law by detaining migrants in non-existent centres and threatening to send them back to countries with whom we have not signed a returns treaty.

Macron: You're having *un rire*! This is the most fun summit I've ever attended! I can't wait to go back to the EU and tell them all about it. You make me look sane. No wonder every far-right group in Europe loves you. Talking of which, can you tell Boris Johnson he can't have a Légion d'honneur?

Sunak: Sorry?

Macron: He emailed to ask for one in his resignation honours list. But do give my respects to Monsieur Lineker. I love *Allumette du Jour*.

* * *

With things feeling stagnant, there was a familiar face mucking things up and railing from the sidelines against the privileges committee inquiry into whether he had lied to parliament.

Impervious to advice or rules, Johnson held up the shield of stupidity

22 MARCH 2023

It wasn't quite the Old Bailey. But it wasn't far off. A former prime minister on trial for what was left of his reputation. A guilty verdict from the privileges committee and a suspension from parliament could effectively end Boris Johnson's political career. Even if it didn't take the nuclear option of a 10-day sentence that would trigger a recall petition. His legs would be cut off. No need then to shoot him as well.

He would leave the stage unmourned. The prime minister who blew an 80-seat majority and an almost guaranteed three terms in office now sent to roam the world as a washed-up end-of-the-pier entertainer, giving the same over-priced speech to people he doesn't care about and will never see again. A pointless existence for a narcissist hooked on constant attention.

Johnson had come prepared, flanked by Lord Pannick, one of the UK's most expensive barristers, and three of his gofers. But they could only sit and watch as their defendant crashed and burned. You can coach the Convict to within an inch of his life, but you can't get him to perform to order. This was Boris at his worst. Angry, fidgety, arrogant. His contempt for the committee evident in almost every sentence. Then it was probably always going to be this way. Johnson seldom looks good under pressure.

This was a trial about honesty. Never Boris's strong point. For a while the public indulged his lies. They were so brazen, so shameless, that they made people laugh. No one really thought he had a simple deal that would Get Brexit Done, but they chose to collude with the lie because it was simpler. They were sick to death of politicians fighting over the EU like rats in a sack while the country burned. They needed to believe.

But during Covid, Johnson crossed a line. While the rest of us obeyed the rules and guidelines, he felt free to interpret them more loosely. And then lie about it. Always the lies. Though it wasn't the lies alone that did for him. It was the hypocrisy also. People died on their own while he and the rest of No. 10 partied. Always the lies, though. So it was no surprise that Boris doubled down. A committee session about lying to parliament was dominated by Boris again lying to parliament. At times, it felt almost meta. Lying about lying about lying.

The committee chair, Harriet Harman, got proceedings under way by talking about the parameters of the session. This wasn't about whether the parties had actually taken place or not. That had long since been established. What was at stake was whether Johnson had deliberately or recklessly misled parliament about them. Boris fiddled with his papers and appeared bored. This was all about him, not Harman. It should be him setting the agenda. His legal team looked on helplessly, banking the money. Not the best of starts.

Then Johnson took the oath on the King James Bible. Amazingly, the bible survived contact with Boris's hand. I guess it must have come across many liars in its time. That done, Johnson went off on a rant, only to be interrupted by a division bell reminding him to vote against Rishi Sunak's Windsor Framework. On his return, he mounted the first outline of his defence. He was too stupid to lie. If he had a fault, it was that he was too honest. There again, he might also be too stupid to stop himself lying. After all, if everyone knows you're lying, then no one is being misled.

Boris warmed to his stupidity theme. He genuinely believed that no rules had been broken, because no one had told him any rules were being broken. He wasn't responsible for his own actions. Besides which, he had no idea what the rules and guidance were because he hadn't yet worked out who had been prime minister at the time.

He still wasn't finished. You couldn't trust the Sue Gray report as it was clearly biased. Harman gently pointed out that the committee wouldn't be relying on Sue Gray. Johnson looked unconvinced and started slagging off the committee for being a kangaroo court. How to make friends. The ever-diminishing group of Tory MPs, including Jacob Rees-Mogg, Michael Fabricant and Scott Benton, who remain loyal to the Boris flame and were sitting near the back nodded in agreement. It was disgraceful that Johnson should be tried by a committee that had decided on its verdict already. Especially when he was clearly innocent.

Then Harman handed over to the rest of the committee: Bernard Jenkin, Yvonne Fovargue, Allan Dorans, Andy Carter, Alberto Costa and Charles Walker. They talked Johnson gently through some of the parties that he had attended. Though not, for some reason, the Abba party that took place in his own flat.

Now things became positively surreal. Because it turned out that when Boris had imposed the Covid rules and guidelines, he had never intended anyone to obey them fully. Least of all his own staff. They had done their best, but everyone needed a break sometimes. Though obviously not anyone working in the NHS. But Downing Street was a special case. Johnson now introduced the concept of 'personal drift'. You started off meaning to socially distance but somehow mysteriously ended up vomiting into bins, falling into flowerbeds or having sex with random strangers. This was all apparently totally normal.

Nor did it ever occur to Boris that any of the parties that weren't parties might have been against the rules, because whenever he attended them, he was afflicted by sudden-onset deafness. And blindness. He literally did not see anything that caused him the slightest of misgivings. What was wrong with inviting 200 people to a party? Or having them crammed indoors? This was just a normal work event in Downing Street. And people had been offered hand sanitiser. The caring, sharing Bozza.

OK, said the committee. So why didn't you correct the record when you realised the rules had been broken to the tune of 126 fixed penalty notices? Now Boris lost it. Because, he said angrily, no rules had been broken. Because none of his advisers had told him the rules had been broken and because he was too stupid to come to that conclusion on his own. He forgot to mention that his advisers had been hand-picked by him to accommodate his untruths. But by now he was rambling incoherently.

Eventually, Harman brought the session to a close. She hoped Johnson would think he'd had a fair trial. Some chance. He would do if they found him innocent, Johnson replied. Pannick rolled his eyes. A sure give-away. He had known for a while which way this one was going. It had always been a long shot. Always is with sociopaths. But hey, one of the upsides of being a top defence lawyer is that you're never short of mugs praying for a miracle.

* * *

And north of the border, change was afoot . . .

And it's goodbye from her: an emotional Nicola Sturgeon quits the stage

23 MARCH 2023

Some rage against the dying of the light. Boris Johnson is howling into the wind. Crying out for meaning, begging for attention. Anything but to be forgotten. But his time is up. All that remains for him is life as another old curiosity on the after-dinner speaking circuit. A job he hates almost as much as he hates himself for doing it. He despises the people – the little people – to whom he is obliged to talk. Most of whom listen with only one ear open at best. He is the *amuse-bouche* entertainer who has backed himself into a narcissistic cul-de-sac.

Others, though, leave the political stage at a time of their own choosing. On their own terms. Just over a month ago, Nicola Sturgeon surprised even her closest allies by announcing she was standing down as leader of the SNP. Some bits of her resignation statement didn't quite make sense. She claimed her party was in good health and had never been nearer to achieving independence. In which case, why walk away now? But the other, more personal stuff felt real. She had had enough. Her entire adult life devoted to frontline politics. She just wasn't feeling it so much any more. She wanted more Nicola time.

That time has almost come. On Thursday, Sturgeon took her 286th and final first minister's questions in the Scottish parliament. Of her three possible successors, only the heir apparent, Humza Yousaf, was in attendance. He kept a low profile: this was Nicola's day. Kate Forbes is still on maternity leave. Ash Regan was nowhere to be seen. There again, she always has been an outlier in the leadership race. Disliked almost as much inside the SNP as she is outside it.

Sturgeon looked as if she was struggling to contain her emotions. This was quite a moment. A tectonic shift in Scottish politics. Nicola might not be regarded quite so highly inside Scotland as she often is outside. The Scots are less tolerant of the SNP's shortcomings in government. South of the border, she appears somehow more significant. Especially when compared with the likes of David Cameron, Theresa May, Boris Johnson and Liz Truss. And even her opponents have to admit that hers is a rare political career that isn't ending in abject failure. Most leaders would kill to win eight elections on the bounce.

The Tory leader, Douglas Ross, appeared hell-bent on living down to the occasion. Not even an acknowledgement of an adversary who had achieved far more than he ever would. No memento mori. Just a straight attack on Sturgeon and the SNP for lying about losing 30,000 members and then trying to cover it up. Repeating the claims that Forbes and Regan had been making at the leadership hustings. That the SNP leadership had become mediocre and incompetent. Maybe they should have thought that one through a bit before serving up some easy attack lines to the opposition. He ended by quoting a Scottish government report on a ferry contract which criticised Sturgeon for costing the country millions. Just what Nicola needed on her last day.

Sturgeon looked a bit peeved that Ross hadn't done more to mark her last FMQs and went on the attack herself. How many members did the Scottish Tories have? Could you fit them all into a small room? And how many elections had he won? And which annoying little Dougie were we seeing today? The one who had backed Sunak? The one who had backed Truss? The one who had backed Johnson? Or the one who had flip-flopped between the three? Such a man of principle.

Labour's Anas Sarwar was altogether more gracious. Able to separate the personal from the politics and appreciate the hard work and effort Sturgeon had put into running the country. Even if he hadn't agreed with everything she had done. Then he rather went through the motions – politics by numbers – and sat down. Now was not a time for point-scoring. More a time of truce. The real work could resume again in a week's time, when the new leader was in place.

Come the end of FMQs, there was a 30-minute slot for valedictory speeches. Sturgeon used hers to praise Scotland's efforts during the Covid crisis, say it was the honour of her life to have been first minister – nothing in the future would ever come close – and to thank family, friends and her fellow Scots. She didn't mention her husband, Peter Murrell, by name. Best not. He was implicated in the membership cover-up. At times, she looked close to tears.

Ross merely went low again. Damning Sturgeon with faint praise. She had always governed in her party's interests rather than the country's. A cheek, considering the Tories had crashed the UK's economy as part of a vanity project. It was crass. Shabby. But no more than anyone expected from him. Dougie is just another Tory leader who will soon be heading for the exit. Though at least he will have £100 to take with him: he had a bet with Sturgeon on who would be first to quit.

Only a few Tories applauded Ross's speech. It was too much even for them. The SNP's MSPs just sat stony-faced as attention switched to other speakers. Once they were finished, Sturgeon picked up her files, concentrated on keeping her emotions in check and headed for the exit. She's going to be a tough act to follow.

SNP's arrested development gives Humza Yousaf a new headache

18 APRIL 2023

You couldn't make this stuff up. Within weeks of Nicola Sturgeon announcing her decision to step down as party leader – she was just burned out, she said – the Scottish National Party has gone into total meltdown. Less the ruling party in Scotland, more the Keystone Cops. Only it's not entirely clear whether we're in the middle of a farce or criminal proceedings. Perhaps both.

It began with the arrest of Sturgeon's husband, Peter Murrell, the chief executive of the SNP, at his home in Glasgow, allegedly in connection with £600,000 of donations that may or may not have been used for day-to-day party expenses. Within hours, his front and back gardens had forensic tents erected in them, and the police were reportedly digging up the patio. Everyone was tight-lipped about what the search was for. Money? Accounts? Laptops? Bodies? Anything was possible. All we needed was Emilia Fox and the *Silent Witness* TV crew.

Then we heard that a £100,000 motorhome had been seized from the home of Murrell's 90-year-old mother. By now, we were well through the looking glass. Almost into *Breaking Bad* territory. Finally, on Tuesday, the SNP's treasurer and MSP Colin Beattie was arrested as part of the investigation into the party's finances. He was released without charge later that day.

In the midst of all this we have Humza Yousaf, the man who was narrowly elected as leader to replace Sturgeon. At the beginning of his leadership campaign, he had acted as the chosen one, Nicola's anointed successor. The man who could be trusted to protect her dreams and visions. Within a short time, it looked more and more as if Yousaf was the fall guy. Sturgeon is adamant it is just a coincidence that the SNP has been caught fiddling the party membership numbers and that her husband has been investigated. In which case Yousaf is the unluckiest fall guy in Scotland.

Certainly, Humza does himself no favours. Not least because he has the unerring knack of making a bad situation worse. Too much more of this and some MSPs will be asking themselves if there's a way of rerunning the leadership election to make sure Kate Forbes wins this time. Back to the Future. Shortly before giving his state-of-the-nation address in Holyrood, Yousaf gave a brief 90-second press conference. Safe to say that every word was a car crash.

'I can't comment on a live police investigation,' he began. 'It's a very serious matter.' Though he made it sound as if we were dealing with an armed robbery or a serial shooter. Maybe that's just how it feels to him, being constantly on the wrong end of questions he doesn't know how to answer. 'I'm always surprised when a colleague is arrested.' He really ought not to be. It's getting to be a habit.

Had he suspended Beattie from the party? Yousaf looked nervously from side to side. Sweaty. On edge. Beattie was innocent until proved guilty, he grudgingly replied. He didn't seem to realise that suspension was a neutral act. One that implied neither guilt nor innocence. Just a convenient way of getting someone out of the way when they have become a distraction.

Who said anything about a distraction? Colin was a lovely man. Wouldn't hurt a fly. All this was in the eyes. Would he be taking Beattie off the public audit committee? 'Colin Beattie is still in the police station being questioned,' Yousaf added unnecessarily. Just in case we thought he might have been released after a few hours. 'I'll need to have a conversation with him. But not about the investigation.' Quite. That was so far above Yousaf's pay grade. No point in him risking getting whacked by the SNP cartel. Why ask him about the one thing anyone would want to know?

'I'm surprised this has happened,' he said. Like a man staring at the debris on the road after a multiple-car wreck. But he was certain this wouldn't derail his vision for the future. He would move on from this in no time. Why would a trail of arrests, some allegedly unexplained financial transactions and a brand-new motorhome create a problem for his party? Weren't all political parties regularly under investigation for similar offences?

A generous person might say that Yousaf had more or less held it together. Up till now. A long way from convincing, but just about passable. Not for long. The killer question came when he was asked if the party had been operating in a criminal way while he was leader. 'I don't believe it is at all,' he said, not altogether convincingly. Because these were the unknown unknowns. He had no idea of how the SNP had been run either before or after he took over the leadership. It was a mystery. He'd just taken Nicola at her word.

The brief press maul had clearly unsettled Yousaf, as he plodded his way through his state-of-the-nation address a few minutes later. There was no excitement. No verve. Little in the way of new direction. Just that a bottle-deposit scheme would be postponed. His MSPs applauded politely, but you could tell they had their doubts. Both the Tories and Labour piled in, saying the SNP was out of ideas and had become mired in sleaze and criminal investigations. Humza tried to fight back, pointing out that the Tories had their own problems in those areas. Somehow that made it worse.

Meanwhile, down in Westminster, nothing stirred. It's as if Rishi Sunak is on a mission to do as little as possible. Less to go wrong that way. Today, he was reannouncing the announcement on zombie-style knives for the fifth time. The biggest distraction to be found was Nadine Dorries's new column for the *Daily Mail*. Though even that was dull. The *Mail* will be hoping to get more for their £100,000 than this. But then, perhaps she's saving up her all-out assault on the MSM in the MSM for next week. Nadine and Paul Dacre can't wait for their peerages for ever.

* * *

Many Tories were beginning to nervously eye up the local elections that were to take place at the beginning of May. Mainly, they were trying to work out how to put a positive spin on results that – based on current polling – looked set to be disastrous. The same local council elections that saw the Tories suffering losses running into the thousands four years previously, so further substantial losses would be a reminder to them of just how tough the 2024 general election would be. Some right-wing papers tried to prepare the ground. Expectation management. Losses of 600 or so would be just about manageable. The Conservatives would be able to survive that. Hmm. In your dreams.

Meanwhile, yet another Tory sleaze scandal was approaching resolution. Justice secretary and deputy prime minister Dominic Raab had been accused of bullying by just about everyone who had ever worked with him. The report into his behaviour was about to land.

Psycho goes down raging: the liberal wokerati finally get to Raab

21 APRIL 2023

Dominic Raab hadn't had the best of nights. His sleep had been broken by repeated nightmares. Him being nice to people. In one he had even dreamed that he had befriended an asylum-seeker. It was disturbing to find the liberal wokerati had forced their way into his subconscious. This just wouldn't do. Much more of this and he'd become a paid-up member of the Blob.

Time to start acting like a real man again. He tossed the duvet to one side and got out of bed. He stared in the mirror lovingly as he oiled his biceps. Hard. So hard. They could take a man down with a single blow. Or a woman. Psycho wasn't misogynistic. He'd hit anyone. His fists were equal opportunities employers.

Next, on with his favourite budgie smugglers. His sequined posing pouch. No winky shrinkage for him. God, he really was a great catch. His family and friends didn't know how lucky they were. Finally, the morning fix of steroids. His life. His wife. He reached for the syringe and tenderly pushed the needle into his thigh. He pressed down the plunger and was overwhelmed by that familiar comforting sensation. That feeling of power that came with infinite rage. No one could reach him here. Dom's safe space.

Just then Psycho's phone rang. It was the prime minister.

'Um, yo, Dom,' stammered Rish! Sunak. 'How are you doing, man?'

'Never better,' the Raabster spat back. 'Just get on with it. What's the score?'

'Er, well . . . you see . . . It's like this. I've been rereading Adam Tolley's report overnight . . . and it would be really helpful if you could, er . . . resign?'

'You're fucking kidding me, you fucking fuck. You're really taking that piece of shit report at face value? You and I both know it's a total fucking establishment stitch-up.'

'Er . . . I thought we were the establishment . . .' Rish! observed.

'Don't be so blind,' screamed Psycho. 'Our whole English way of life is under threat if someone in a senior position isn't allowed to bully someone junior. And if you can't see that, then I'll have to come round to Downing Street to flush your head down the toilet again.'

'But the thing is, Dom, I sort of did promise to govern with integrity. And though I obviously never meant that to apply to you, it would be more embarrassing not to sack you than to sack you. I've done my best for me. I mean you. I phoned Tolley to see if he would consider changing "The minister was intimidating and persistently aggressive" to "The minister was not intimidating or persistently aggressive", but he was adamant he wouldn't change a word. So I'm a bit stuck. The thing is, no one really likes you. They think you're a twat.'

'So that's it?'

'I'm afraid so.'

'You're going to regret this big time. Your dog won't last the day.'

Psycho hung up. Time to take the initiative by writing his own letter of resignation. He'd make sure to go down as gracelessly as possible. Fighting all the way to the bottom. Staying on brand at least.

'Dear Prime Minister.' He could barely write that 'Dear'. On to the substance. Yes, he knew that he'd once said he would resign if the bullying allegations were upheld, but he'd never imagined that a KC from the liberal elite would conclude that publicly humiliating civil servants counts as bullying. What was the world coming to? Next, someone would say that using junior members of staff as a punchbag was out of order. Or killing someone, for instance. Would no one allow for accidents in the workplace any more? Health and safety gone mad. God knows, Psycho had killed a few people in his time. And there might well be a few more before the day was out.

Then there was the fact that only two of the bullying complaints had been upheld. That meant he had got away with at least six. And shouldn't a minister be allowed a free pass on his first two charges? Especially as civil servants these days couldn't take any criticism that involved bodily harm. Woketards, the lot of them. And weren't all complaints meant to be registered within three months? That would have been ideal. Because when the Raabster bullied someone, they stayed bullied. Most ended up in a psychiatric hospital, unable to speak thanks to PTSD for at least a year.

Yeah, that was sticking it to the prime minister. To think he'd once been Rish!'s cheerleader-in-chief during his leadership campaign. His deputy prime minister. Sunak had turned out to be a softy like all the others. Cuthbert Cringeworthy. A sack of shit. Just another feeble apologist. Would no one stick up for GBH? God, stand up for bastards.

Psycho was on a roll. The *Daily Telegraph* wanted more of his resignation nonsense, and he was thrilled to oblige. No, he wasn't sorry for anything. He had done nothing wrong. It had all been a left-wing media plot to remove the most talented politician of his generation. The only man standing who still believed in Ultra-Violence. Just a normal guy who believed in the right to bully anyone. It was the thin end of the wedge. First, they had come for him. Next, they would come for Michael Gove's crack den on his department's roof.

Back in No. 10, Sunak had had the security detail doubled. Just in case Psycho reappeared. When he felt the coast was clear, he put out a statement of his own. He had done the right thing. The brave thing. By sacking the Raabster. Who was a moral man. Of course he was. But he had narrowly crossed the line by bullying everyone he had ever worked with.

Rish! then announced Alex Chalk as the new justice minister and Oliver Dowden as deputy prime minister. Ideal fits. Chalk was hopeless and as wet as they come, so he'd do no damage. And he couldn't do any worse than Dom, who'd driven the department into the ground. As for Dowden, the thinking man's Chris Philp, he had his head so far up everyone's arse he hadn't seen daylight for weeks.

Psycho reached again for the comfort of the syringe, before applying camo paint to his face and donning a balaclava. He was off to Dover to see if he could stop a few asylum-seekers arriving in small boats. Permanently. He would have to take his pleasures where he could find them from now on.

Coffey muddies the waters as Tories wash their hands of sewage scandal

25 APRIL 2023

Who needs to go for a walk by a canal or river? Why bother to go to the beach? All you need to do is take a dump at home. Where to have an open cesspit is the latest status symbol. The estate agent's dream. Your very own swimming pool. What more could anyone want?

To be fair, Thérèse Coffey has done more to level up the country than any of her cabinet colleagues. Though, technically speaking, one should call it levelling down. For on the environment secretary's watch there isn't a river in England that isn't hopelessly polluted and subject to sewage overflow many times a day.

Windermere now has a five-mile stretch of shoreline that's turned bright green. William Wordsworth would have been able to write quite the poem about that. Earth has not anything to show more fair . . . And you take your life into your own hands taking a dip in the sea. Hepatitis? That will do nicely.

But every cloud and all that. Water may be a national health hazard, but it's an easy win for a Labour opposition day debate. And just over a week out from the local elections, any opportunity to stick it to the Tories is too good to pass up. Because whether the Conservatives like it or not, they have no one to blame but themselves. Sewage and God knows what else – a few limbs from Dominic Raab's victims maybe – have been spilling out by the tonne on their watch.

That's if anyone has been actually watching. Because the environment secretary has never appeared really bothered about it. Or anything else much on her patch. She is the minister for whom everything is too much trouble. Apart from racking up the air miles on jaunts around the world. On her watch Coffey has managed to fall out with just about everyone. From the farmers to conservationists to ordinary people who would quite like to go outdoors without needing to wear a hazmat suit.

The shadow environment secretary, Jim McMahon, opened the debate with a long catalogue of Tory failures. He looked as if he was enjoying himself. The proverbial pig in shit. Time and again he barked out the phrase 'Tory sewage scandal', and time and again the 30 or so Conservative MPs who had showed their faces recoiled in faux outrage. It wasn't exactly clear who they had imagined had been in government for the past 13 years. Selective memories and all that.

There would be 70 more sewage dumps just in the course of this three-hour debate, McMahon went on. And it was all down to Coffey. Because in her previous incarnation as a junior minister, she had written to all the water companies to say they could pretty much do as they liked. Under Labour, the water quality had been unsurpassed. Apparently. So pure it could have been bottled. He dared Tory MPs to shout him down, while refusing to take many interventions. He didn't say exactly how he was going to fix the situation. That was something for another day. When Labour were in power.

Next up was Coffey herself. Keen to make it clear that she would happily go knee-deep in sewage on any beach. Because that was what being British was all about. It was time for people to stop moaning and embrace the filth. After all, it never killed anyone. Well, not many. And it was all just as bad as it was under Labour. Back in 2010,

317

we didn't know how bad things were. Now we do. So that must be an improvement, mustn't it? At least we could now take ownership of our own shit.

'We've got a grown-up plan,' said Coffey. It was unfortunate, then, that she couldn't remember exactly what it was, as she had no idea how she was going to punish the water companies for the spills. Though she didn't think automatic fines were the right way forward, as the spills might turn out to be worse than we thought. So best to fine the water companies next to nothing.

If we were to nationalise the water companies and stump up the £56 billion needed, then we'd have to stop funding our hospitals. She seemed to have forgotten that the government had been underfunding the NHS for years. Then she said she was looking forward to winning the next election. So we can put her down as a little confused.

Thereafter things rather fell apart. As debates go, file this one as unenlightening. Labour MPs said the sewage was symbolic of the Tory administration as a whole. 'You're poo.' 'No, you're poo.' The kind of insults eight-year-olds hurl at one another. Lee Anderson said he didn't want to get into divisive party politics, but Labour were just a pile of shite. Irony rather escapes our Lee.

Other Tories leaped up to say you couldn't blame the Tories for England but you could blame Labour for Wales. Bob Seely said that under Labour, the UK had been fined by the EU over water quality. He had forgotten that now we couldn't be fined as we had left the EU. There was a Brexit bonus no one had told us about. The right to pump crap into our own rivers without the EU checking up on us.

It was all a bit tawdry. But for the opposition it was job done. The Tories might have thrown in a wrecking amendment to render the whole thing meaningless, but Labour could still claim that Tory MPs had voted to make it easier to pump shit into our water.

* * *

With only a few days to go before the local elections, Labour had one goal: to not make any unnecessary mistakes. The public were sick to death of the ongoing moral failures of the Conservatives, and Rishi Sunak was struggling and failing to reduce inflation and stop the number of small-boat crossings. The early gloss with which the right-wing media had portrayed the prime minister – competent and decent – had begun to wear off. Sunak was no more able to govern effectively than any of his predecessors. And his fundamental decency had been called into question by his decision to appoint Suella Braverman as his home secretary. These were Rishi's calls, and he was found wanting. Inside the tech-bro image was a man who, at the very least, was far-right curious. Not such a nice guy after all. Rather, someone more interested in inane soundbites and doing whatever it took to remain in power for a little while longer.

All looked good for Labour, though that didn't stop them trying to screw up their chances.

Starmer goes quantum with Schrödinger's tuition fees

2 MAY 2023

When you're 15 points ahead in the polls, with the local elections just two days away, some might argue that it is best to keep quiet. Especially if you haven't really got much new to say. Why rock the boat when you've got a comfortable lead? No need to go for another goal when you're five–nil up, with only added time to play. Just keep it safe, bank the win and save your resources for the more important games to come. Don't give the Tory party chair, Greg Hands, an excuse to fire off another desperate tweet about Labour having spent all the money.

Keir Starmer saw it rather differently. He had chosen to do a morning tour of the BBC's studios. A last-chance power drive to remind everyone of what was at stake this week. Only he didn't really appear to have given it much thought, as his only consistent message was that every-one was more broke than they had ever been. Almost as though he had imagined that just saying the same thing over and over again would get him through any 15-minute interview.

But sometimes the truth is not enough. You need an argument. A direction. Passion. And by the time Starmer had got to the *Today* programme, he appeared somewhat lost. As if he'd forgotten what he was doing and why he was on the radio. He would start sentences without having any clear idea how they would end. Somehow or other he managed to talk more about the things he wasn't going to do, without giving a look-in to anything he would be doing.

It was far from a car crash. But it did feel like a misstep. With the Tory government seemingly out of ideas for dealing with the cost-of-living crisis – or much else for that matter – the door is open for opposition parties to stake a claim on the country's imagination. The situation cried out for Starmer to take control, to make voters believe there was an alternative to the managed decline of Tory miserabilism. But the Labour leader was nervy. Diffident. Defensive. His affect curiously downbeat. Almost as if his replies had been written by a terminally depressed AI chatbot.

In the absence of any clear direction from Starmer, the BBC's Justin Webb chose to bend the interview to his own will by focusing on stories in the morning papers. It had been reported that Labour was now planning to go back on its promise to abolish university tuition fees. Was this yet another promise that had bitten the dust?

Starmer sounded startled. As if he hadn't expected to be asked about a news story in which he featured. It was like this: tuition fees were obviously unfair, but he would now be looking for a way of funding students that was more fair but which didn't involve abolishing tuition fees. Was that clear? Er, yeah but no but yeah but no. The economy had moved on, so he would be moving on to something that he couldn't yet talk about as it was all top secret and he basically hadn't had time to give it a moment's thought. He couldn't say fairer or unfairer than that. Tuition fees would be both going and staying. Politics in a quantum universe. Schrödinger's students. Maybe they too would be both here and not here.

Webb was understandably confused. So he pressed on. How about the promise to tax the top 5% of earners more? And to increase the capital gains rate? Did they still stand? Yes and no. Or rather, they had both fallen into a black hole in deep space. Of course those with the broadest shoulders should pay more, Starmer mumbled. It was just that the top 5% no longer had broad shoulders. Most of them were near broke. So it would no longer be right to tax them more. It was time for the country to think of the destitution in which Rishi Sunak now lived. The high-tax, low-growth economic model was broken. Though he wouldn't necessarily be reducing any taxes. Just not putting them up. So it wasn't clear just how broken the system was.

Um . . . my mother was a nurse and my father was a toolmaker, Starmer reminded himself – the rest of us need no reminding – before adding that the family's phone was once cut off. Could we talk about that and the cost of living? the Labour leader asked. We couldn't. Webb was having way too much fun. He wanted to pin down Keir on tax. Did he really think the very rich could not afford to pay more? After all, some appeared to have done very well for themselves over the past 13 years, with asset prices rising.

Starmer again started mumbling. Borderline incoherent. He was going to grow the economy. How? By growing it. Top secret. If he told us how, he'd have to kill us. Hmm. If it was that straightforward, it's a mystery why no one's thought of it before. And yes, but could we stop talking about the pledges he wasn't going to keep but focus on the ones he was? Besides, he had only made those promises to get elected as Labour leader. Now that he was hoping to become prime minister, he had to jettison anything that might scare off floating voters. In any case, how come he got a hard time for breaking promises when Rish! did it the whole time and no one batted an eyelid?

What Starmer longed to say was that people expected the Tories to lie to them, while pundits went mad if Labour did the same. Just give him a break. If he needed to be more Tony Blair than Tony Blair to get elected, then that's what he'd do. Judge him on what he did in power. Not what he said in opposition. But those words died on his lips.

Hell, people had short memories. The Conservatives had even forgotten that Sue Gray didn't think the Abba party was worth mentioning. Despite the sex, lies, video-tapes and puke, her report had been almost a cover-up. So much for her being a Labour stooge.

Devil of a local election result for Tories makes work for idle Hands

5 MAY 2023

First, manage your expectations.

When the Tory party chair, Greg Hands, announced last week that he expected the Conservatives to lose 1,000 seats in the local elections, he was being characteristically disingenuous. What he really meant was that the Tories would lose between 500 and 600 seats, and he would be able to take to the airwaves and crow about his party having done far better than anyone imagined. The plucky Conservatives yet again seizing triumph from a potential disaster. And it would all be down to him and his idiotic tweets of a 13-year-old Liam Byrne gag. At least we won't be seeing them again.

It didn't really work out that way. Even though only about a quarter of the councils had been declared by 7 a.m. – the rest had delayed their count until later in the day – a clear pattern had emerged. Labour, the Lib Dems and the Greens had all performed at the top end of their projections, while the Tory share of the vote had been, in the words of many councillors – make that ex-councillors – decimated.

Losing 1,000 seats was looking realistic. Hopeful, even. The real damage could be worse still. And don't forget that these seats are the same as those fought in 2019, when the Tories also lost 1,000 of them. So this was a wipeout piled on a wipeout. Back in 2019, Theresa May had had to apologise to her party for the election disaster and was removed from office just months later. That same result now would be regarded as an electoral triumph. But no one was about to start apologising for anything.

'We always knew it was going to be tough,' Hands said, sounding shell-shocked during his media round. Only he clearly hadn't ever imagined it would be this tough. Much of his earlier campaigning had had an air of complacency. A man who expected everything to be all right on the night just because it always had been for the last 13 years. A man who had learned not to try too hard. By the middle of the afternoon, he had been reduced to sending an email to Tory supporters begging for more money. Most would have been deleted unread. Timing is everything. The coronation was turning into a Tory funeral.

There had been no inkling of what lay in store when the election-night broadcasts had fired up late on Thursday. Most pundits were hedging their bets. Another Labour false dawn seemed to be in the back of many people's minds. But then the results started coming in. Stoke, where Tory MP Jonathan Gullis was for once reduced to silence. He should try it more often. It suits him better. Medway. Plymouth. Local MP and government minister Johnny Mercer looked as if he had been mainlining ketamine. 'It's terrible,' he muttered over and over again, his eyes dead, his eyeballs pinpricks. Windsor and Maidenhead, Theresa May's backyard, where the Lib Dems had romped home.

Tory MPs had started openly arguing with one another. Kelly Tolhurst was certain it was unrealistic housing targets that had done for the Conservatives. Charles Walker thought the Tories hadn't built enough. John Redwood insisted the losses were all because of the party not being nasty enough to foreigners and abandoning the Liz Truss economic model. Really. Rehman Chishti – remember him, the leadership contender with just one supporter? – thought voters had been put off by the knee-jerk dog-whistle politics of Suella Braverman.

Shortly after 8 a.m., Rishi Sunak appeared outside Tory party headquarters. Things weren't as bad as everyone was making out, he insisted. People loved the core Tory message. Just that they had forgotten to vote for it. And there had been a stunning success in Bassetlaw, where the Tories had picked up about four seats on a Labour-dominated council. Really. The one disappointment was that efforts to stop the wrong people voting under the new photo ID rules had not made as big an impact as he had hoped. Maybe next time.

Not long after, Keir Starmer, looking every inch the modern football manager in a crisp black shirt, arrived in Chatham for a photo op. He looked chuffed. As well he might. Medway had been a target council, and an area that had voted heavily in favour of Brexit. Those divisions look to have healed. Labour was in sight of the sort of swing it would need for an outright majority in a general election. 'This is about the cost of living,' he said. 'And the Tories have had nothing to say about it.' Which was true. They haven't. They've sat back and done next to nothing as people chose between eating and heating.

By midday, more results had started to trickle in, and the pattern was the same. Over on *Politics Live*, Andrea Leadsom was giving her most spellbinding performance since her never-to-be-forgotten leadership bid in 2016. For the most part, she stared stubbornly ahead, looking for all the world like a woman about to embark on a psychotic killing spree. Then, when she spoke, she wouldn't stop. Talking over everyone. Even herself. Her incoherence was startling. First, she insisted the losses were all down to local issues, such as potholes and planning regulations. When she was contradicted by every Tory councillor who had lost their seat, she went on to say that voters had been sending the government the message that they were unhappy with the cost of living. Remarkably, she went on to infer that losing 1,000 seats was a sign voters wanted more of Sunak's policies and that the prime minister should take some comfort from the results. Presumably, if the Tories had lost 2,000 seats, Rish! would be ruling in perpetuity.

The bad news kept rolling in for the Tories. Blackpool. Hopefully, local MP Scott Benton would have had a sponsored bet on the chances of him keeping his seat. He'll need the money. Swindon, where the Conservative former leader of the council moaned about the performance of the government. He could always vote to replace it at the next election.

By now, Leadsom had been removed in a straitjacket and replaced on the panel by the equally deranged Liam Fox. He too spoke in tongues. It was all very disappointing, he said, but also strangely encouraging. Because what it showed was that Sunak was doing all the right things, though if he just did them all completely differently, then that would be better. Low tax, high growth, he mumbled. Bring back Truss! He had also detected a cunning plan dreamed up by Tory voters. They had decided to stay away to lure Labour into a false sense of security. And they would all come back to vote for a Tory landslide in a general election.

But even the Magnificent Mr Fox was forced to shut up when the BBC published its projected national share of the vote, which had Labour 13 points ahead. More even than in 1997. Labour's Jonathan Reynolds tried and failed not to look smug. He could be forgiven. Labour have waited a long time for a day like this.

The Tories hadn't just taken a beating in the local elections. They had been annihilated. They had lost more than 1,000 council seats, on top of the 1,000 they had lost four years earlier. If this had been Labour, pundits would have been gleefully predicting the end of days for the party. As it was, there was more of a tactful silence around the defeat. A silence in which the Conservatives could only hope and pray for a miracle at the next election.

In the meantime, there was always the coronation of the new king. A chance to forget. To move on. For a day or so, at least . . .

Strong bladders required for interminable faffing of King Charles's coronation

6 MAY 2023

It rained. Of course it did. It wouldn't have been a proper coronation if it hadn't. Brits wouldn't have had it any other way. We were born to suffer. Keep calm and carry on.

The first guests had started arriving at Westminster Abbey from early in the morning, among them the lucky MPs who had received an invitation. Though many Tories had been complaining it was all a stitch-up by No. 10. That Rishi Sunak had hand-picked favourites and those he wanted to get on side. Whatever. Let's hope they had strong bladders. It was going to be a long morning.

As the cameras panned round the congregation, the BBC's Huw Edwards tried desperately to pick out a few people he recognised. There was Ant and Dec. He didn't know which was which, but few do. Nick Cave. You can't miss the jet-black hair. Stephen Fry behind a pillar somewhere. Jill Biden and her granddaughter near the back (the US president never attends these kinds of dos). President Macron wandering in, totally at home. He's almost an honorary royal these days. In his own mind, at any rate.

Others started arriving. The Lord Speaker processing behind what looked like a large Toblerone. The seven former prime ministers. Boris Johnson and Liz Truss bringing up the rear. Johnson looking a right state, as ever. There was no way he was going to make an effort, even for this. Truss with the widest smile. She can't believe her luck. Just 49 days, during which she wrecked the country, and she's guaranteed a spot on every guest list for life. Living the dream. Near the end, Prince Andrew and Harry. Andy was allowed a cape from the dressing-up box, Harry was in civvies. The message was clear: you can be accused of being a sexual predator, but don't dare marry a black woman and spill the beans in your autobiography. Huw could barely bring himself to mention either of them.

Out in the Mall, Clare Balding was watching a horse walk sideways while the royal coach carrying King

Charles and Camilla made its way to the Abbey. Balding pointed out all the flags of the Commonwealth countries, forgetting that many of them wanted to have their own heads of state. Then the cameras also forgot to broadcast the procession going through Trafalgar Square, where republican protesters were gathered. Nor did we get to hear Andrew being booed. This was too much *lèse-majesté* for the occasion. Huw wouldn't have stood for that.

Once the King and Camilla reached the Abbey, a new procession made its way to the altar. Led by Sebastian Coe. What on earth was he doing here? He gets everywhere you don't want him to be, and even the royals haven't found a way of keeping him out. Prince William, Kate and their children all looked as if they were extras from a remake of *Cinderella*. Then so did a lot of people. Brits like to think no other country does these occasions quite as well. Other countries may have a bit more self-worth. Still, the music was wonderful.

We'd been told that the King had wanted this to be a celebration of all faiths, but in reality this was a full-on Protestant extravaganza. Other faiths were restricted to either a one-line cameo or just a walk-on part. This was a sacred ritual in all but name, honouring Charles as the one true king and the Church of England as the one true religion.

And in truth, everything quickly began to drag a little. Justin Welby's sermon was borderline unintelligible.

Meaningless to most people. The two-hour service could have done with editing down to 75 minutes. Still, at least it was an hour shorter than the late Queen's in 1953. Prince Louis went missing for large chunks. Lucky him. Perhaps he couldn't be separated from his PlayStation.

'I am here to serve. Not to be served,' said Charles. Really? It didn't look that way. The whole thing was being done for his benefit, after all. Though he did look strangely detached throughout. As if he didn't really want to be there. As if it was all a bit much for him. He could take the trinkets, but the obligations of kingship were too heavy a burden. Luckily, for once the pen with which he had to sign his name worked perfectly. Otherwise he might have snapped. The only time he looked vaguely cheerful was when the gospel choir sang.

Then we got to the real ceremony. First, the anointing with holy oil, which took place behind a screen because it was too sacred to be broadcast. A ritual that we were told went back to the time of Solomon. Hmm. But 'Zadok the Priest' always adds a touch of class. Then the Orb of Excellence, the Mace of Magnificence, the Spurs of the Surreal, the Gauntlet of Devotion, the Goblet of Fire. Or something.

Still, Penny Mordaunt was the breakout star with the Sword of Sincerity. Thank God Truss got ousted. Otherwise we might have had Jacob Rees-Mogg doing it. The archbishop struggled to get the crown on, but eventually the King was crowned. Prince William swore allegiance and kissed his father. The one tender, personal moment of the entire ceremony. Even so, it was hard to escape a sense of the absurd. A modern 21st-century democracy reliving a medieval fantasy. It was like royalty as scripted by Disney. Hard to take seriously. Maybe it would have made more sense in black and white.

At least Camilla looked as if she was enjoying herself. She smiled and struggled not to burst out into giggles as she was asked to hold a sceptre. She clearly thought the whole thing was ridiculous. Meanwhile, the King carried on suffering in this piece of Dadaist performance theatre. After more interminable faffing, he and the Queen nipped round the back of the altar. Presumably, Camilla needed a cigarette and a quick laugh to release the tension. Most of the rest of us were by now bored. Couldn't wait for the thing to be over. Enough was enough.

Eventually, they reappeared and headed for the exit, while the audience sang 'God Save the King'. Charles stopped to thank the ministers from other faiths for being ignored throughout the service. Then into the golden carriage. Princess Anne, looking like Napoleon, leaped on to a horse. 'She's now the Gold Stick in Waiting,' Balding said excitedly. Only in Britain.

Timid Rish! goes missing in action in the face of Boris Johnson's lies

19 JUNE 2023

Cometh the hour, disappeareth the man. You'd have thought that wild horses wouldn't have kept Rishi Sunak away from the Commons for the debate on the privileges committee's report on Boris Johnson. After all, when he took office in October last year, Sunak had promised that he would govern with integrity, professionalism and accountability. And since then we've all been waiting for a sign. The smallest nod that he had meant what he said.

And here was the perfect opportunity. The most binary choice imaginable. Johnson had been definitively found to have lied and lied and lied again. To parliament. To the country. To just about everyone he had ever met. Lying is what he does. What he always has done. Quite why it took so many MPs so long to realise what had been blindingly obvious to some of us for years and years is another question. But hey! They got there in the end. Just rejoice at that.

So Rish! had the simplest of tasks to establish his moral credibility. Just turn up to parliament and vote to accept the report's findings. Compiled by a committee, elected by parliament, with a Conservative majority. He didn't even have to speak. How difficult was that? This could have been integrity in action. A physical recognition that a proven liar was a proven liar. The sort of thing that barely requires the memory of a conscience. And Rish! is an honourable man. Hell, he's told us so often enough.

Only come the big day, there was no sign of Sunak. Yet again, when push comes to shove, he had gone missing in action. The first sign of his impending cowardice came when he phoned Volodymyr Zelenskiy on Monday morning to assure him that nothing had changed since last week and that the UK was still fully behind Ukraine. A sure sign the prime minister was desperate to look busy. He always calls Zelenskiy when he's feeling guilty.

Next, we were told Rish! just had to meet the Swedish prime minister in the afternoon. Even though he couldn't remember who the Swedish prime minister was or why he had to see him. Maybe he could invent an imaginary trade deal that no one was going to agree to. Just as long as the meeting took place sometime late in the afternoon.

Then there was the evening speech to a charity. That had taken some arranging. A global email to all organisations to see if anyone wanted a prime minister to talk to them that evening. And he wasn't even going to charge for it. The deal of the century. There had been only the one taker. But one was all he needed. His diary was officially full. It had taken some ingenuity. That just left a bit of time to have a pedicure and take the dog to the groomer's. Essential government business.

And that was the last we saw of integrity, professionalism and accountability. Sunak had failed at the lowest possible hurdle. There would have been some virtue if he had been able to tell the truth. That he was doing everything possible to stay away because he was too timid to risk upsetting Johnson and his supporters. But they are too few on the ground for Johnson to risk mobilising as people might notice his sinking popularity. Just Jacob Rees-Mogg, Nadine Dorries and a few other losers. But Rish! couldn't even manage that. In his desperation to remain invisible, he had been seen by everyone for what he was. A fraud. A man too weak to stand up for himself against Johnson.

Rish! wasn't the only one to go missing in action. Michael Gove had retreated to his department's roof, trying to square his lack of backbone with his imagined virtue. Something only drugs can achieve. Jeremy Hunt was nowhere to be seen. He never is these days. Not even Suella Braverman could be bothered to hang around, and she had just given a ministerial statement in the previous business. So the government front bench consisted of just Penny Mordaunt. Someone had to do it, but she did it with style. She accepted the committee, she accepted the report and would vote for it. She also took a swipe at Johnson's dishonourable honours list.

Much of the rest of the debate quickly fell into a pattern. Opposition MPs – including Harriet Harman, the privileges committee chair – forensically went through

Johnson's history of lying. The contempt for parliament. Worse still, the contempt for the country. People had obeyed the rules. Relatives had died alone. Johnson, not so much. It would be hard to think of a worse prime minister in living memory. Or at all.

The Tory benches were sparsely populated. It wasn't just Rish! who was running scared. Not even Andy Carter, Bernard Jenkin and Alberto Costa – three of the Conservative members of the committee – could be bothered to show their faces. But some, like Theresa May, were vocal in their support for its findings. Not so long ago she was a deadbeat prime minister. Now she sounds like a parliamentary colossus. We live in desperate times.

Johnson wasn't totally bereft of support. Rees-Mogg attacked Harman's bias – something she convincingly refuted – while Lia Nici was positively deranged. She said that she had been a parliamentary private secretary to Boris, which made her a neutral in the game. And she was adamant there hadn't been any parties, because Johnson had assured her of this.

But at least there was an honesty to Rees-Mogg and Nici. They were wrong, but they were prepared to defend their man in their speeches, even if they didn't follow through by voting against the report. Not so all those other Tories who were going to abstain. They knew Johnson was lying but couldn't bring themselves to act on it or speak out on his behalf. Labour was determined to flush them out. To force a vote. Come the next election, their shame should not be forgotten.

Don't worry about inflation, folks — Rish! is 100% not on it

22 JUNE 2023

If it walks like a duck and quacks like a duck, the chances are it's probably a duck. Ever since Rishi Sunak became prime minister, he and his team have been trying to sell him to the country as a different kind of politician. The type of leader who gets things done. Who makes promises and keeps them. Is straightforward with people about the challenges ahead. The Goldman Sachs tech bro who is effortlessly competent. The safest of safe pairs of hands.

It's almost as if Rish! is on a mission to stop us thinking for ourselves. Because the longer it goes on, the clearer it becomes he is trying to gaslight us. There's only so much cognitive dissonance anyone can take. Trying to persuade yourself that someone who is demonstrably a bit hopeless is some kind of new-age statesman eventually becomes an impossibility. You have to accept the evidence of your own eyes.

And the evidence is that Sunak is failing. Not waving but drowning. He knows that. His MPs know that. Most have already given up on the next election and are busy trying to secure alternative employment. Life as an opposition backbencher isn't that attractive. Crucially, almost all voters know the game is up. That Sunak will be little more than a footnote in the UK's political history. An unhappy interregnum between the chaos of Boris Johnson and Liz Truss's regimes and a new Labour government.

Even by his own piss-poor benchmarks, Rish! is beyond help. Inflation remains high, interest rates are going up, hospital waiting lists are not falling, government debt is increasing, the cost-of-living crisis shows no sign of ending . . . You get the picture. Just about everything that could go wrong is going wrong. And nothing Sunak is doing is making any noticeable difference. More and more he looks like some latter-day Canute trying to turn back the tide.

Faced with all this, Rish! could have been forgiven for running for the hills. Instead, he ran – no publicly funded helicopter this time – to Dartford in Kent. In the background, we had the Ikea warehouse. In the foreground, we had an impossible-to-assemble piece of talking flat-pack furniture: Sunak himself. It's hard to convey how uncomfortable and awkward he seems when faced with real people. Members of the public. He normally sees them only as numbers. Objects to be moved around a spreadsheet. Best kept at a distance.

Weirdly, No. 10 seems to think that these 'PM Connect' events – aka 'PM Disconnect' – showcase the prime minister at his best. That he genuinely engages with people, rather than shows how out of touch he is. Which goes to show that there must be people in Downing Street who are desperate to see the end of Sunak. Whether they are Labour supporters or just keen to put him out of his misery is anyone's guess.

Sunak bounced around uneasily. Trying to do his man-of-the-people impression. After an attempted meatball gag that drew no laughs, he got into his rhythm. 'Hi, guys,' he said. 'You might have one or two concerns about inflation.' No shit. Most people's mortgages had just gone up substantially. 'But don't be. Because I'm 100% on it. We're going to get through this.' Oh, really? You and your many millions, and the rest of us with bills not all of us can pay.

On and on he went, sounding more and more like a dodgy boyfriend. Desperate to reassure us that everything was going to be OK, even though his body language suggested otherwise. Not someone to be trusted even to book a restaurant for dinner. 'Oh, I just thought we'd do Burger King tonight.' Thanks for nothing, Rish! 'But hey, just chill out and feel the vibes. Those inflation blues will soon be over.'

It was like this. He had said he had a plan to halve infla-tion. Only it wasn't really a plan. More like a hope that the Bank of England could deal with inflation by increas-ing interest rates, which would tip us into recession. And who didn't love a recession? And if that worked, then he would take the credit for it. If it didn't, then he would blame the bank. Brilliant.

'Why do I feel confident?' he asked. God knows. Because he is delusional? Or maybe because his sense of entitlement is so ingrained that he has never yet been disappointed in life. Just wait a little longer, Rish!. But there was also a cunning second part to his plan. And that was for him to do nothing. Not spend anything on public sector pay or hospitals, because that would stop inflation. Never mind that everyone would be getting more and more broke. Just remember, he was the man. And we were all in this together.

Sunak ran through his five priorities like some superannuated 1980s AI, before wrapping up with more of his greatest hits. 'We're on this. We are good together, aren't we? We are going to get through this.' Moments before saying he was actually going to dump us. It wasn't us, it was him. Commitment problems. It was intended to reassure. It had the opposite effect. Panic. Bye-bye, the economy.

For a brief period during the Q&A, Rish! was in his Goldman Sachs mode as Ikea workers asked him about leadership values and the importance of strategy and logistics in the furniture business. Sunak was happy to bullshit with the best. He too thought that being a good communicator and honest were important. Which was odd, as he is neither. His words merely fill space like aural Valium. And honesty . . . well, not so much. He was still unable to say whether he would have voted to endorse the privileges committee's report had he not organised countless subsequent engagements. No one believes or trusts him on this. Everyone knows his integrity is shot. Sooner or later he will have to call Johnson out. The longer he leaves it, the worse he looks. For a politician, Sunak isn't even very good at politics.

'I'm 100% on it. We're going to get through this,' he said, as he made for the exit. Of course we are. 'I've never pretended this was going to be easy.' Er, yes, you have. That's precisely what you did. And why you chose to halve inflation as your main priority. Only now it's all gone wrong. And even if inflation does fall, we'll all still be broke. Happy Brexit anniversary on Friday, everyone.